The Ohio Valley

THE OHIO RIVER

N

W E **INDIANA**

S

ILLINOIS

DEARBORN
Lawrenceburg
Rising Sun OHIO
SWITZERLAND Vevay
JEFFERSON
Madison
CARROLL
Carrollton
CLARK Bedford TRIMBLE
Jeffersonville La Grange
New Albany
FLOYD OLDHAM
English Corydon JEFFERSON
CRAWFORD HARRISON Louisville
SPENCER PERRY MEADE HARDIN
WARRICK Cannelton Brandenburg
Rockport Elizabethtown
VANDERBURGH BOONVILLE BRECKINRIDGE
Evansville Hawesville Hardinsburg
Mt. Vernon POSEY Owensboro HANCOCK
GALLATIN Henderson DAVIESS
Shawneetown HENDERSON
Elizabethtown UNION Morganfield
HARDIN
Golconda CRITTENDEN
POPE LIVINGSTON Marion
Metropolis Smithland
MASSAC Paducah
PULASKI McCRACKEN
Mound City BALLARD
ALEXANDER Wickliff
Cairo
MO.

In its 981 miles from Pittsburgh to Cairo, the Ohio River touches 72 counties
in the Heartland of America. This map shows the location of each county
and county seat, with county names in capital letters.

PENN.

OHIO

Lisbon
COLUMBIANA

JEFFERSON
Steubenville

St.Clairsville
BELMONT

Woodsfield
MONROE

WASHINGTON

Marietta
ATHENS
Athens

Athens
MEIGS

Pomeroy

Gallipolis
GALLIA

HAMILTON
CLERMONT
Batavia
Georgetown
BROWN
West Union
ADAMS
Portsmouth
SCIOTO
LAWRENCE
Ironton

Greenup
GREENLIP
Vanceburg
Catlettsburg
BOYD
LEWIS
Maysville
MASON
Brooksville
BRACKEN
Falmouth PENDLETON
Alexandria CAMPBELL
KENTON
ington BOONE

Huntington
Wayne
WAYNE
CABELL

Point Pleasant
MASON

BEAVER
Beaver

New
Cumberland
HANCOCK
BROOKE
Wellsburg

Wheeling
OHIO
Moundsville
MARSHALL

New Martinsville
WETZEL

Middlebourne
TYLER
St.Marys
PLEASANTS
Parkersburg
WOOD

JACKSON
Ripley

WEST

VIRGINIA

ALLEGHENY
Pittsburgh

KENTUCKY

MILES
0   100
0   100
KM

palacios

The Ohio Valley

YOUR GUIDE TO AMERICA'S HEARTLAND

By George Laycock and Ellen Laycock

DOLPHIN BOOKS
DOUBLEDAY & COMPANY, INC.
GARDEN CITY, NEW YORK
1983

Library of Congress Cataloging in Publication Data

Laycock, George.
  The Ohio Valley, your guide to America's heartland.

  Includes index.
  1.   Ohio River Valley—Description and travel—1981–
—Guidebooks. I. Laycock, Ellen. II. Title.
F520.L39   917.69′0443
ISBN 0-385-17591-4
AACR2
Library of Congress Catalog Card Number 81–43579

Contents

PART III   THE NORTH SHORE

Ohio

Preface

When we speak of the beauty of the Ohio Valley, the fun of exploring its back country, and the appeal of its cities, we admit to a certain prejudice, for this is our valley. Because we are native to it, we thought we knew it well. Then we set out to gather the latest information for this book and found scenic ridgetop roads and river vistas we hadn't seen before, explored river cities and quiet villages new to us, and along the way talked with people in factories, offices, and on farms and riverboats about our valley.

For the purposes of this book, we explored the Ohio River and all the counties in six states that touch its shores. On occasion, we went beyond these riverside counties to visit attractions of special interest, and these became our "Up the Road" trips.

The Ohio, from its point of origin in Pittsburgh to the end of its journey at Cairo where it joins the Mississippi, is 981 miles long, and it flows through the heartland of our country. We found that there are endless adventures and discoveries waiting for those who explore the Ohio Valley. So we say: Break out of the mold, do something you've not done before, marvel at the glassblower's art, get lost on a country road, square dance at a festival, read the historic markers, see the moon rise from a riverboat, rediscover this valley—and enjoy!

Part I

Origins

Pittsburgh

A River Is Born

From the moment of its birth the Ohio is a full-grown river. It is born of streams with other names, rivers in themselves large by most standards. One of these flows down from the green hills of Pennsylvania and western New York gathering water from a thousand creeks and rivulets to become the Allegheny, 325 miles long.

Meanwhile, to the south, in the mountains of West Virginia, other streams flow out of the mountain hollows collecting the waters that form the Tygart River and the West Fork and when these streams join they form the Monongahela, sometimes called "The Mon."

These rivers, the Allegheny and Monongahela, move toward each other, sometimes turning in one direction, sometimes another, but in the end drawing closer and closer until the land separating them is a point where the rivers join.

Now, there is a new stream—the mighty Ohio which from its birthplace, flows on for 981 miles through one of America's busiest and most beautiful valleys.

The point of land where the Ohio begins is a fitting place to start any tour of this valley. The Point is a 36-acre state park at the apex of the Golden Triangle in the heart of Pittsburgh, a gleaming, modern metropolis.

From the first, white men who came to this point sensed its importance. George Washington, a twenty-one-year-old surveyor, first saw it in 1753 and returned to Richmond urging Governor

The mighty Ohio River is born in the heart of downtown Pittsburgh at the confluence of the Allegheny and Monongahela rivers. (Photo by George Laycock)

Dinwiddie to erect a fort at the Point. That small fortress was named Fort Prince George. The French, who had already claimed the Ohio Valley, retaliated by sending a force that overwhelmed tiny Fort Prince George, then replaced it with a large fort of their own. They called the new fort, Duquesne, in honor of the commander of French forces in North America.

During the summer of 1755, Indian messengers brought word that a large British force was advancing from the east. General Braddock led the advancing forces of hundreds of English and

Colonial soldiers plus Indians friendly to them. In Fort Duquesne surrender was considered because the enemy was vastly superior in numbers, but the French decided instead to surprise the British and meet them along the trail. Eight miles east of the Point the

This fountain, a Pittsburgh landmark, is in Point State Park where the Ohio River begins. (Photo by George Laycock)

famous battle began. The sudden surprise attack by the French completely defeated the British, and Braddock died of his wounds.

Three years later General John Forbes led a new British army of several thousand soldiers over the mountains. They marched out of the forest, however, into a strange and silent scene. Where Fort Duquesne had stood there were now ashes and piles of smoking half-burned logs. This time the French had withdrawn their forces and abandoned the Point without a fight.

Among the officers on General Forbes' staff was Colonel George Washington leading the Virginia colonials. Washington wrote to a friend, "I have the pleasure to inform you that Fort Duquesne, or rather the ground on which it stood, was possessed by his majesty's troops on the 25th and the British flag flies over the bastion."

A new British fort rose on the Point and this was the strongest one on the frontier. It had five sides and was large enough to house a regiment. Completed in 1760, the fort was named Fort Pitt for William Pitt, the British Prime Minister. Traders soon established themselves in the shadow of Fort Pitt, and as settlers crossed the mountains they added their cabins to the settlement. Pittsburgh was starting to grow.

The best place to trace the early history of Pittsburgh is in the Fort Pitt Museum in Point State Park on the land the fort once occupied. In the main gallery we discovered a display of striking paintings that capture the early scenes as European people struggled for supremacy at the Point. In the center of the hall is a large model of Fort Pitt, and in the galleries are models of other scenes plus collections of historic tools and weapons. We strongly recommend that this museum be part of your visit to Pittsburgh.

Outside the museum stands one of the original redoubts, or fortifications, now open to visitors and furnished with historic exhibits.

When the city celebrated its two-hundredth anniversary, Rose Demorest of the Carnegie Library wrote of it, "The past creeps in to remind us, this is the land of historic memories. Here . . . men and women of vision changed a wilderness area into the city of Pittsburgh."

As Pittsburgh grew, diverse people came here from more than

The Fort Pitt Museum in Point State Park in Pittsburgh's Golden Triangle brings to life the role of this city in America's history. (Photo by George Laycock)

forty countries. Pittsburgh was once the world's leading center for the manufacture of glass, and also at one time the leading producer of petroleum products. Giant steel plants rose on the banks of the Allegheny and Monongahela. The mills and the coke ovens added their odors to the air and so did homes, coal-burning trains, and industries of many kinds until Pittsburgh was choking on its own smoke and soot. It fully earned its reputation as a dirty city.

Layers of smoke hung over the city perpetually. One writer, standing on Mount Washington a century ago, looked down on the flaming furnaces and clouds of black smoke issuing from them and likened Pittsburgh to "hell with the lid taken off." The famous architect Frank Lloyd Wright once said, "As for cleaning up Pittsburgh, it would be cheaper to abandon it." The city had become so dirty that street lights burned at midday, and buildings everywhere were covered with layers of soot.

Some cities faced with the staggering task of rescuing themselves, lack the energy, vision, or resources needed for the task. Pittsburgh people, however, had these qualities, plus a bulldoglike confidence in their ability to set their town right.

Toward the end of World War II, Pittsburgh's business and political leaders tackled the problem of rejuvenating their city. In 1943 they formed the Allegheny Conference on Community Development to unify planning and marshal leadership. Industry, organizations, and private citizens rallied to this call, and in the two decades that followed, Pittsburgh underwent a renaissance that is difficult to believe.

Smoke was brought under control, and in the downtown area gleaming new buildings replaced the slums and run-down business structures. New hotels and shopping facilities were created, and downtown Pittsburgh became a pleasant place to visit. Today, Pittsburgh is perhaps the country's outstanding example of how a city can pick itself up by its bootstraps. It is a bustling, clean city where neighborhoods are proud of their ethnic origins, parks are green, and cultural events so varied that there is not time for people to sample all the things they like to do even if they live here.

One of the early improvements was the Civic Arena, highly visible to visitors in downtown Pittsburgh. The huge structure with its giant dome, provided the city with a place to stage athletic events, conventions, and presentations of many kinds. The arena seats 18,000 people and cost over $20 million. Its stainless-steel dome roof can be drawn back in two minutes and twenty-five seconds by the flick of a switch, opening the giant arena to the sky on fair evenings. The area, surrounded by new thoroughfares and giant modern buildings, stands where there were slums within memory of local citizens.

Heinz Hall

Pittsburgh takes its culture seriously. This is evident in the concerts, plays, operas, ballets, and special programs staged in the city. And it is seen in the splendor of the settings provided for

Heinz Hall for the Performing Arts is among Pittsburgh's most famous buildings. (Courtesy Heinz Hall)

these programs, particularly in Heinz Hall for the Performing Arts.

Heinz Hall is the old Penn Theater after a $10 million renovation converted it into a concert hall that has gained an international reputation for its beauty.

It is located at Sixth Street and Penn Avenue, among the new

*Heinz Chapel, on the campus of the University of Pittsburgh, is a
famous landmark open to all faiths.* (Photo by George Laycock)

buildings of Pittsburgh's renovated downtown. This is the home
of the Pittsburgh Symphony Orchestra, Pittsburgh Opera Society,
Pittsburgh Dance Council, Civic Light Opera, and the Pittsburgh
Youth Symphony, as well as the scene for productions of the
Pittsburgh Ballet Theatre and numerous other groups, including

hit musicals and stage productions from Broadway. More than half a million people come here each year to attend some three hundred productions. Others come just to see what Heinz Hall is like with its marble columns, rich carpeting, and 368 crystal lights and glittering chandeliers.

The owner of Heinz Hall is the Pittsburgh Symphony Society whose orchestra, under the leadership of André Previn, ranks among the finest orchestras anywhere.

For twenty-four weeks a year the Pittsburgh Symphony Orchestra performs in Heinz Hall. It may then go on tour, both in this country and abroad, make television appearances, or work in the recording studios. Its music spans the age groups with concerts for the youngest listeners, and programs include Pop concerts as well as free concerts in the outdoors. This is a busy orchestra, a popular one, and in its travels has been a major goodwill agent for the city at the birthplace of the Ohio.

American Wind Symphony

River barges are no strangers to us. We've seen these long, low working craft on the Ohio and its tributaries since childhood, and always they look alike. The exception, however, was a barge we found tied up at Point State Park one bright summer morning.

This barge bears only slight resemblance to any other watercraft—anywhere. Like any barge it is long and low, but there similarity ends.

This barge was painted a sparkling silver and carried a strange superstructure. Painted on the sides in bold letters were the words "American Wind Symphony," and this led to our investigation of the musical career of Robert Austin Boudreau, who sometimes thinks of himself as the last of the river showboat captains.

As a boy, growing up on a chicken farm in Massachusetts, Boudreau played the trumpet. Seriously. He studied at Boston University, the Juilliard School of Music, and the Paris Conservatory.

He came to Pittsburgh as a teacher and began creating a special orchestra composed of brass, woodwind, and percussion instru-

The American Wind Symphony is the unique orchestra that travels on its river-barge home to give concerts up and down the Ohio River and beyond. (Courtesy American Wind Symphony Orchestra)

ments. He also created a repertoire for the wind orchestra by commissioning composers to write the music.

There followed another fresh idea: Given the proper vehicle, he could bring the music of his American Wind Symphony to audiences up and down the Ohio Valley. The rivers were there. All he needed was the boat. The players would be young professionals and serious, advanced students signing on for a summer tour. At first they used an old coal barge and hitched rides with passing tows.

The American Wind Symphony during a concert on its floating stage, at Point State Park. (Courtesy American Wind Symphony Orchestra)

Then Boudreau found contributors to help build his double-hulled steel boat. He likes to call the boat, which is named the *Point Counterpoint II,* "a center for the arts." Below decks is a traveling exhibit of paintings and a small stage for dramatic productions.

Each new summer season for the American Wind Symphony may be different from those that went before. Typically, Boudreau will direct the orchestra in a series of free concerts at Point State Park, then cast off and follow a carefully arranged schedule, bringing music to cities and hamlets along America's waterways. At each stop the musical group from Pittsburgh offers free symphonies, and in addition, small groups of its musicians accept invitations to play at clubs for senior citizens, in back yards, or in city parks.

This brand of showboating has taken the *Point Counterpoint II* and her musicians to cities and villages the length of the Ohio as well as the Mississippi, the Great Lakes, and the Intra-coastal Waterway. Boudreau has even taken his boat to the Caribbean for a six-month-long tour.

When Boudreau had trouble finding a qualified engineer to pilot his floating stage, he did the obvious thing and took over the job himself. He is pilot and captain, as well as musical director.

While the *Point Counterpoint II* slides down the river at 8 miles an hour, the 65 musicians are traveling overland in vans to meet her at the next destination. Aboard the boat are Boudreau, his wife, and three of his six children, plus four or five other crew members.

Watch for the *Point Counterpoint II*. The boat and its famous

Pittsburgh is shaped by its rivers and hills. Mount Washington is in the background. (Photo by George Laycock)

orchestra may be seen on the Ohio River—or just about any other water that appeals to her captain the maestro.

The rivers that flow through the heart of Pittsburgh have been avenues of commerce since the Point was first settled. But the people use the rivers for fun as well. Visitors crossing the bridges or viewing Pittsburgh from the heights of Mount Washington will see party boats and tour boats belonging to the Gateway Clipper Fleet.

Largest of the fleet is *The Spirit of Pittsburgh* with two enclosed decks for dining and dancing. There are sightseeing cruises, day or night, dinner cruises, dance cruises, and other affairs afloat. There are even special cruises featuring the music and food of Pittsburgh's ethnic groups. Call for the schedule of these cruises. The polka parties are a Pittsburgh favorite.

Other specials arranged by Gateway Clipper Fleet include a fall foliage cruise, a river cruise combined with a tour of Old Economy, the Harmony Society settlement at Ambridge, or a country river jamboree. There's a "Good Ship Lollipop" Cruise for children.

The fleet is docked at Station Square and the telephone number is (412) 355-7979.

Finding Your Way

Travelers should accept the fact that Pittsburgh is a difficult place in which to find one's way. Local residents giving directions to visitors commonly end with "good luck." The best advice, short of hiring a guide, is to obtain the best city map you can find and mark the main streets and highway routes leading to the destinations you hope to reach. As in any city, the major streets soon become familiar. In Pittsburgh you will still get lost, but don't let this dismay you. It happens to the natives too.

Before you have driven long in Pittsburgh, you will notice color-coded signs designating "belts." The belt idea was developed to help Pittsburgh drivers find their way around their hometown. We are assured by people who live here that the belt signs help.

There are five belt routes, each of them following crooked but roughly concentric circular routes around all or part of the city. The Blue Belt is the innermost, and in some 40 miles it leads drivers over a route that circles the city. Beyond it lies the Green Belt, a semicircle around the north side; then the Yellow Belt, a complete 80-mile circle that leads to the county's North and South parks; followed by the Orange Belt, which leads to the airport. Then the Red Belt forms a line across the northernmost part of the county from Ambridge to Tarentum. Given these belt routes, superimposed on a map that shows the named neighborhoods, the traveler should get lost less frequently.

Mount Washington

One of the adventures awaiting us at the crest of Mount Washington was a ride on the inclines in what may be the strangest antique vehicles operating anywhere. Of the 17 inclines that once scaled the hills of Pittsburgh, 2 still operate. The one we chose was "Old Mon," the Monongahela Incline, which has been going up and down the hill since 1870. And we don't care if half a million passengers a year do ride Old Mon without incident or accident, we defy a first timer to take the trip without at least a passing thought about the possibility that the whole machine might break free and go crashing down.

The idea of the inclined plane is to outfit a triangular-shaped platform with wheels that fit a set of tracks. The top of the platform is level and on this is mounted the car, which then carries passengers uphill or downhill while keeping them on the level.

Old Mon is a little on the shabby side. She is operated by the Port Authority and is not so brightly painted as her sister incline, the Duquesne Incline, which also travels up and down Mount Washington. We bought round-trip tickets and settled ourselves on the hard benches inside the cagelike car. The door slides shut and the car rumbles under you. Then the cable car is out of the shed and moving down the 38° slope at 6 miles an hour to complete the run in a respectable 1 minute and 45 seconds.

The inclines of Pittsburgh had their start with the German set-

There were once seventeen incline railroads transporting Pittsburgh people to the hilltops. The remaining two are important tourist attractions. (Photo by George Laycock)

tlers who reached home after a long work session in the steel
mills down by the river by climbing the hill. There was no road
up the mountain prior to the arrival of motor cars.

Old Mon was completed and ready for her maiden voyage up
Mount Washington on May 28, 1870. That day 900 bold souls
made the trip. None of the dire predictions of catastrophe came
true, and the following day there were 4,000 riders, marveling at
the convenience. The incline, as well as those that followed, was
a big success, and they continued working until automobile roads
rendered them of less value.

The Duquesne Incline attracts more tourist traffic than Old
Mon does. It provides a splendid view of the Golden Triangle,
the rivers, and the skyline of Pittsburgh. It is also an excellent
vantage point from which to take pictures. There are few places
anymore where these strange rail cars can be found still working.

This incline was threatened with abandonment and rescued by
a citizens group formed for the purpose, The Society for the Preservation of the Duquesne Heights Incline, whose members are
proud as punch of their traveling museum piece, which sends its
little red cars rumbling up and down the unbelievable slope from
Mount Washington to the river's edge.

Station Square

Pittsburgh's outstanding example of turning a white elephant
into a major tourist attraction and convention center is found
along the foot of Mount Washington on the south side of the
Monongahela River. Here the buildings of the P&LE Railroad
fell into disrepair and created a shabby complex across from
downtown Pittsburgh. The answer was to set about renovating the
railroad buildings and planning new ones to add to the complex.
Nor did the plan stop there.

The old railroad freight house was converted to a mall with
dozens of small specialty shops and restaurants. Office buildings
and a new Sheraton Motor Inn with 300 rooms are also part of
the complex. The Grand Concourse has been converted into one
of Pittsburgh's finer restaurants—and one of its largest—with a

stained-glass ceiling 45 feet overhead. And at the Gandy Dancer Saloon next door there are clams, oysters, and shrimp served either steaming hot or on ice, however you like them.

Outside there is a collection of antique railway cars and engines, while nearby stands the very last of the Bessemer Converters honoring the industry that helped make Pittsburgh wealthy. Station Square is an adventure. It is reached from downtown by crossing the Smithfield Bridge.

North Side

With a local guide from Creative Convention Services, Inc., we went one day to Pittsburgh's North Side across the Allegheny. The lady, a lifelong resident of the city and enthusiastic about its features, drove us through several streets in the Mexican War section, designated a National Historic Landmark, where some old homes are already renovated and others are still in the process. The land here lies level and the row houses and streets are well maintained and clean.

The first prominent feature of this section is Three Rivers Stadium, an overwhelming structure, the home of the Pirates and the Steelers, Pittsburgh's professional baseball and football teams.

For people interested in seeing the working side of a major sports arena, Three Rivers Stadium conducts regular tours. These trips through the Stadium usually take one hour for a walking tour of the facilities. The two-in-one tour includes a second hour in the Hall of Fame, which is part of the Stadium. Reservations are required. There is a charge for the tours, and the number to call is (412) 323-5000.

Baseball and Pittsburgh

Baseball fans in Pittsburgh make no apologies for the fact that they sometimes go slightly berserk, especially when their team is enjoying a winning streak, as it often is. This is baseball country.

Three Rivers Stadium is the home of the Pittsburgh Pirates and Steelers. In the foreground is the Duquesne Incline's antique cable cars that transport passengers to Mount Washington. (Photo by George Laycock)

Big league player John Milner watches a long ball head for the stands in Three Rivers Stadium. (Courtesy Pittsburgh Pirates)

The earliest professional baseball team in Pittsburgh, the Pittsburgh Alleghenies, played their first game at Union Park in 1876. In 1887 Pittsburgh began playing in the National League. The Pittsburgh baseball team has been known as the Pirates since 1890 when it earned the name by allegedly pirating a valued player from Philadelphia during a series of stormy salary disputes. The Pirates moved to Exposition Park north of the Allegheny River in 1891, and played there until Forbes Field opened in 1909. Then, in 1970 the team moved to the new Three Rivers Stadium.

The Pirates roster through the years is dominated by names of players who are remembered wherever baseball is played. Baseball Hall of Famers from Pittsburgh include Honus Wagner, Fred Clarke, Pie Traynor, Paul Waner, Max Carey, Bill McKechnie, Lloyd Waner, Branch Rickey, "Kiki" Cuyler, Ralph Kiner, and Roberto Clemente.

The Steelers

In Pittsburgh and far out into the surrounding countryside, football is a serious subject. Many fans can recite off the tops of their heads the high points of the Steelers' seasons, especially during the 1970s. In their early years the Pittsburgh team went a long time without rising to the top. Then in 1942 the Steelers had their first winning season.

In 1974 they won their first NFL crown, then repeated the performance the following year, becoming only the third team to win the Super Bowl two years in a row. Then in 1978 they became the first team to win it four times, as well as the first team to win two back-to-back Super Bowls. Almost every year in the 1970s they had made the play-offs, and in that golden decade enjoyed greater success than any other professional football team.

The team had its beginning in 1933 when it was founded by Art Rooney, whose family brought him to Pittsburgh as an infant. Rooney grew up where Three Rivers Stadium now stands, and in later years continued to live within easy walking distance of the Stadium. Rooney, an outstanding athlete, represented the United

States on the 1920 Olympic boxing team. One of the most famous football players Rooney brought to the Steelers was a powerful All-American from Colorado. He was paid a bigger salary than anyone before had ever been offered for playing football—$15,800. They called him "Whizzer," but in later years he became known as Justice Byron White of the United States Supreme Court.

Bird Country

The Conservatory-Aviary is also on the North Side, at Ridge Ave. and Archer St. We have come to expect a city's displays of live wild animals to be concentrated in the zoo, but the Aviary is some miles from the zoo.

The Aviary began with a trip to Europe by one of the city fathers some years ago. There he saw impressive collections of birds in well-maintained aviaries and the more he thought about it, the more enthusiastic he became. If in Europe, why not Pittsburgh? Given the basic idea, plus funds, which Pittsburgh seems to have for civic projects, the plan was set in motion. The Aviary first opened in 1958 and has been recently enlarged.

The director of the Aviary is Dr. Lindsay Clack who began keeping birds at the age of six in his home in Australia. He eventually found his way to West Virginia and was teaching at the university in Morgantown, when the Pittsburgh Department of Parks and Recreation began searching for a new director for the Conservatory-Aviary. Dr. Clack, after some months on the job, has already increased the number of birds on display. "We have 140 species now," he said, "and about 600 individuals." His main interest lies in encouraging more of his birds to nest and raise young, especially species considered rare and endangered.

In one room of free-flying birds we encountered the hornbills, which are show stoppers. Their oversized bills are out of all proportion to their size. In their native range in Africa and southeastern Asia the grotesque hornbills live in the forests and are believed to mate for life. At nesting time the female hornbill goes into a tree cavity, and her mate begins to seal her in with mud.

In the Conservatory-Aviary visitors walk among hundreds of birds from around the world. (Photo by George Laycock)

There she must stay, entombed in her cramped quarters, from six weeks to three months while she incubates the eggs and raises her young. Her faithful mate feeds her fruit through a small opening in the center of the mud seal. And heaven help the raiding monkey or serpent that tries to invade the nest guarded by her swordlike bill. When the time arrives for the mother and young to leave their chamber, both parents chip away at the hardened clay to remove the seal.

The most popular bird in the Aviary is the jaunty talking mynah bird that told us, "I'm from Pittsburgh!"

Dr. Clack answers frequent requests for advice on how to keep parakeets and budgies happy and healthy. He is also expected to welcome assorted wild birds brought to the Aviary by people who believe the birds to be in trouble. "One person," he says, "brought us an albino robin, all white with pink eyes. We call him 'Whitey,' and he's a favorite with visitors."

Each year the Aviary hosts 125,000 visitors. The bird-loving city father must have had a good idea.

Buhl Planetarium and Institute of Popular Science

Next, our guide drove us to the Buhl Planetarium, another favorite Pittsburgh attraction. This green-domed structure is the center not only for dramatic and realistic shows of the night skies, but also numerous other aspects of science. Its galleries are filled with displays and educational shows, ranging from a man-made lightning machine to a transparent lady. From November through February, visitors come to see the miniature railroad and village displays covering 1,440 square feet. Learning is fun in this lively place; fun for people of all ages. The Planetarium is part of the renovated neighborhood that now includes Allegheny Square, the History and Landmarks Museum in the Old Post Office, the Pittsburgh Public Theater, restaurants, and shopping plazas. The North Side is worth a visit.

The Carnegie Institute

No visit to Pittsburgh is complete without a visit to the Carnegie Institute, a massive stone building at 4400 Forbes Ave. near the University of Pittsburgh and the Carnegie-Mellon University. Under one roof there is a natural history museum, art museum, library, and music hall. The Institute is in Oakland, which can be reached by automobile in fifteen minutes or so from the Point.

When Andrew Carnegie came to America at the age of thirteen, his first job was as a bobbin boy in a damask-weaving plant

at $1.20 a week. Later he taught himself how to operate a tele-
graph and began earning $25 a week. Then, he became a railroad
clerk and next a dispatcher, and in this position began making investments with his limited income. The railroad appointed him division manager of its important Pittsburgh Division when he was
only twenty-four. Carnegie moved into other fields, including
steel production, and in 1873 built his first steel mill.

Carnegie once wrote that the wealthy hold their riches in trust
to benefit the less fortunate. At the time of his death in 1919, he
had given away $350 million, including $1 million to the Carnegie Institute of Technology at Pittsburgh and $60 million to
build free public libraries in hundreds of communities.

The Carnegie Institute is there because in 1890 Andrew Carnegie gave the city a million dollars for a cultural center. Five
years later the building opened. The structure was, and is, an imposing and monumental complex that has grown even larger than
Andrew Carnegie envisioned it. From the beginning, the Institute
housed two complete museums. Visitors to the complex can
spend days studying the exhibits, and nobody should expect to really see the Institute's treasures by sandwiching the visit into a
spare hour.

This is the home of Pittsburgh's famous Museum of Natural
History where we wanted especially to see one of the museum's
most popular exhibits, the Hall of Dinosaurs. Here, surrounded
by complete skeletons of the largest creatures ever to walk the
earth, one wonders what life was like when these giants made the
boglands tremble beneath their ponderous clawed feet. Sixty million years ago, and more, in the quiet of the Mesozoic era, they
ruled the primitive earth, long before there was anything remotely
resembling man. Brontosaurus, 80 feet long and 50 tons heavy,
and numerous smaller dinosaurs consumed tropical plants. Standing in the Hall of Dinosaurs also, is the king of the carnivorous
dinosaurs—*Tyrannosaurus rex,* standing 20 feet high, measuring
50 feet long from head to tail, and carrying a 4-foot-long head
whose mouth is lined with rows of 8-inch-long ivory daggers. The
Hall of Dinosaurs alone is worth the visit to the Carnegie Institute.

Literally breathtaking is the display of dazzling gems to be
found in the adjoining rooms. The Hillman Hall of Minerals and

Gems is among the finest exhibits of its kind anywhere. Even visitors normally unmoved by mineral displays will enjoy this colorful adventure into the world of rocks. There are 2,500 mineral specimens collected from around the world. Special spotlights in mirrored halls bring out their rare colors and sparkling forms. The exhibit includes a display of Pennsylvania mineralogy as well as displays showing the art of the lapidary and a look into the hidden world of the microminerals. There are natural wonders by the hundreds. Forget your schedule and take time to study this one.

Without going outside, move on to the Art Museum and the Sarah Mellon Scaife Gallery, a 1974 addition, given in memory of Sarah Scaife to house the permanent collection of paintings and sculpture.

From the second floor of the Scaife Gallery you can cross to the Heinz Gallery opened in 1975 to house changing exhibits. The following year the Ailsa Mellon Bruce Galleries opened. This gallery houses the collection of antique furniture and tapestries. The Hall of Decorative Arts holds sculptures, porcelains, and fabrics.

The Carnegie Library of Pittsburgh, the city's main public library, is also housed here. Included in the complex is a music hall where there have been Sunday afternoon organ recitals since 1895, and a cafeteria as well as a cafe overlooking the fountain. Admission is charged to the museums, except on Saturday. Parking is on the east side of the Institute.

In this area of the city you will find the University of Pittsburgh which traces its ancestry to a log cabin built in 1787 as the first school of higher learning west of the Allegheny Mountains. Today the university has 35,000 students and 52 buildings, the most impressive of which is the famous Cathedral of Learning, the tallest school building in the country. The Cathedral of Learning towers 42 stories into the sky above the university community.

When construction began on the tower the university administrators realized that there was not enough money to complete the entire 42 floors. Instead of lopping off the top 4 stories, they chose to leave the first 4 unfinished, convinced that the people of

Pittsburgh would rally to the challenge. People from throughout the city, including thousands of schoolchildren, helped raise the money to complete the structure.

Eighteen of the classrooms on the ground floor of the tower are dedicated to the cultures of various nationalities represented in Pittsburgh. Each of these rooms is decorated and furnished in the style of the country it represents, with furniture and works of art sent directly from the foreign countries for the purpose.

These nationality rooms, which are used for a variety of classes, can be seen by the public on tour, or you can simply go into the building and visit the ethnic classrooms on your own when they are not in use. However, a far better plan is to arrange in advance for a student guide. Phone: (412) 624-6000. The names of the nations represented are on the doors and if one country, whether Germany, Poland, Italy, China, Sweden, or whatever, is of special interest, you can search it out. Or you can go from room to room for a visit to various lands around the world. In December each of these rooms is decorated by local ethnic groups in traditional fashion for Christmas.

Facing the Cathedral of Learning across the green open campus is Heinz Chapel where as many as six weddings are performed on a single Saturday. This French Gothic structure was built as a church for all faiths, a gift in memory of Henry J. Heinz and his mother, Marguerita Heinz. The glass cutter labored for ten years to complete stained-glass windows that stand 68 feet high without support.

Also in this section of Pittsburgh is Chatham, fourth oldest of the country's women's colleges. The campus is parklike, with narrow streets winding through rolling green lawns where the one-time homes of famous and wealthy Pittsburgh citizens serve today as college buildings. Andrew Mellon's home is here, and there are now bulletin boards with student announcements in the marble halls where millionaires once resided.

Phipps Conservatory with two and a half acres of gardens under glass, is in Schenley Park. Here among the growing orchids, water lilies, and roses is another favorite setting for Pittsburgh weddings. There are special flower shows in spring and fall.

The Parks of Pittsburgh

In and around Pittsburgh, beautiful and popular parks are numerous. Both the city and Allegheny County operate parks. Those, owned by the county, lie farther out in the country in a ring around the metropolitan area. Activities found in these parks include: swimming, golf, tennis, hiking, roller skating, bicycling, boating, picnicking, fishing, skiing, nature study, musical and dramatic programs, plus a long list of other programs every year.

The especially popular county parks include North Park with its network of trails for hiking, skiing, horseback riding, bicycle riding, and jogging. On the eastern edge of Allegheny County, 15 miles east of the Triangle, is Boyce Park with ski slopes, skating, ball fields, and trails. South Park, reached south of the city by Hwy. 88, offers golfing, tennis, swimming, ice skating, playgrounds and ball fields. South Park, Boyce Park, and Settlers Cabin Park have Olympic-sized wave pools and rentable rafts for riding the white-capped artificial ocean-style breakers. "Great fun," say the wave-pool fans.

The City Parks

Few of the people who have had statues erected in their honor were around to see their stone likenesses at the time they were erected. One exception, however, was Edward M. Bigelow. While he still lived, the city of Pittsburgh erected his statue at the entrance to Schenley Park and engraved on its base the words, "Father of the City's Parks." The title was well-earned. Bigelow, who became city engineer in 1880, spent three decades wheeling and dealing in his relentless efforts to patch together the lands that today are within Pittsburgh's parks.

There are many parks maintained by the city, some of them less than an acre in size. But there are 4 big ones that everyone discovers when exploring the city. Two of these, Schenley and Highland, owe their existence to Bigelow. The first of them,

Schenley, opened in 1889. This is the favorite of many people. It has an 18-hole golf course, ice-skating rink, swimming pool, tennis courts, fishing lake, nature museum, and the Conservatory. It lies 4 miles east of the Triangle and can be reached by the Boulevard of the Allies.

The largest of Pittsburgh's city parks, however, is Frick Park, which was established after Bigelow died. This park covers 476 acres on the edge of Wilkinsburg and is a favorite among people who like their parks quiet and natural.

Riverview Park, 251 acres, has a swimming pool, nature center, bridle paths, and volleyball courts. This park lies along Hwy. 19 on the outer north side. It has tennis courts and picnic areas as well as the Allegheny Observatory where, on clear nights, visitors in groups of 10 or more can, by advance notice, look at the skies through the University of Pittsburgh's big telescope.

Highland Park, in the northeast corner of the city, is reached from downtown by following Hwy. 380 (Bigelow Blvd.), turning left on Negley, and following the signs. There is a swimming pool, fishing lake, playgrounds, and ice skating. It is also the location of the zoo.

The Zoo

In almost any section of Greater Pittsburgh the traveler will spot signs pointing to the zoo in Highland Park. The signs direct you to the parking lot, the only flat area in the zoo's 75 acres. (A writer once pointed out in *Pittsburgh* magazine that any flat area not taken for a ball field serves its highest and best purpose as a parking lot.)

From the parking lot everything at the zoo is up. First it is up an escalator said to be the longest in the world. Before the escalator was installed, the hillside was ascended by an equally long set of stairs. The exhibits are set into the hillside or located on the hilltop.

A favorite section is the Aqua Zoo containing the lemon shark, said to be the oldest lemon shark in an inland aquarium. His neighbors, most of them in separate tanks, include fish and reptiles of a wide variety. Mounted on the wall in the enclosure housing the shark is a giant tuna noteworthy primarily for the family of house sparrows nesting in its open mouth.

The children's zoo is a favorite place, a "hands on" experience for youngsters who pet the goats, rabbits, and other animals, and find out, perhaps for the first time, that some animals, at least in confinement, have a distinctive odor.

Another exhibit area popular with Pittsburgh zoo visitors is the cool, darkened Twilight Zoo, a 300-foot tunnel for night creatures.

Pittsburgh also has the usual large zoo animals—tigers, lions, elephants, giraffes, hippos, and bears; a total of 500 species and 2,500 animals.

The zoo has been undergoing a major renovation, designed to provide its occupants with better living conditions and add to the zoo's appeal to visitors. The $13 million rebuilding program, funded from both public and private sources, moves the zoo animals out of their cramped cages into roomy, moated, outdoor areas.

Kennywood

Eight miles south of the Golden Triangle is the major amusement park in the Pittsburgh area, Kennywood, which has been entertaining visitors for more than eighty years. This traditional amusement park, where the whole family comes for rides, food, and live shows, was originally created to boost passenger business on the streetcar lines.

Kennywood calls itself, immodestly, "the roller coaster capital of the world," and backs up this claim with descriptions of its five roller coasters. Biggest of the lot is the "Thunderbolt." There is also a water coaster, that ends with a 49-foot slide into a pool. Another is the steel looping coaster, the "Laser Loop" that comes to a stop at the near vertical, leaving riders just time enough to scream "Oh, my gawd," before they slip back into a dashing fall that carries them into an upside-down loop.

There are live shows all day long. Food is served both in a cafeteria and a traditional sit-down restaurant.

The million or so visitors who find their way to Kennywood an-

The most daring visitors to Kennywood Amusement Park ride the Laser Loop. (Courtesy Kennywood Amusement Park)

nually come from a hundred miles around. Many of them drive in from northern West Virginia as well as Pennsylvania and parts of Maryland.

To reach Kennywood drive south out of Pittsburgh along the Monongahela River on Hwy. 837.

Folk Festival

As we have said, Pittsburgh is a city of strong ethnic groups, perhaps as many nationalities as live together in any city. Furthermore, the city and its ethnic groups keep alive the cultures from which they came and take pride in their backgrounds. In a land of freedom one can afford to be different. This pride has its strongest expression in the annual Pittsburgh Folk Festival, sponsored by Robert Morris College and held on a May weekend in the Civic Arena.

The idea began in 1955 and grew as its planners visited clubs, churches, and nationality halls around Allegheny County. The first festival was held in 1956. As many as twenty-five ethnic groups have participated in this annual effort to perpetuate their folklore.

Each group erects two booths, and its members, dressed in native costumes, tend the booths during festival weekend. One booth is for food, prepared from old treasured family recipes brought from foreign lands. Festival goers eat their way around the world. The other booth is for crafts and folk art.

Thirty-five hundred Pittsburgh people particpate in this festival, and thousands more come to see again the native costumes, and the dances and dramas of the people who built this city where the Ohio River begins.

Summer Arts Festival

Another popular annual event in Pittsburgh is the Shadyside Summer Arts Festival held in midsummer on Walnut Street in

Pittsburgh's East End. More than 200,000 visitors flock to the free festival to see the work of over 170 artists selected from applicants from around the country. Among the exhibitors are painters, potters, jewelers, candlemakers, photographers, printmakers, and leatherworkers, selling their work.

There are jazz workshops and performances, dramas, and children's shows. Shadyside blocks off the traffic, leaving the streets to the thousands of festival goers who come for the fun.

Three Rivers Arts Festival

There is dancing in the streets when June brings the annual Three Rivers Arts Festival sponsored by the Carnegie Institute. For 10 days the riverfront, the streets, and the hills reverberate to music ranging from bluegrass to classical with special emphasis on jazz. The dancing goes from country clogging to experimental and ballet. This festival was begun by the Carnegie Art Museum and is nationally known for its excellence in the visual and graphic arts with exhibits by many noted artists.

The festivities are at Gateway Center, Point State Park, and various other locations. There are more than two hundred performances during the festival, and the variety ranges from experimental poetry readings to visits by nationally famous bands. Festival week is fun time in River City.

Three Rivers Regatta

For a week in August, Pittsburgh turns its attention to the waterfront and the annual Three Rivers Regatta. This regatta is more carnival than race. The action centers at Point State Park and includes everything from swimming races across the Allegheny to concerts by visiting jazz bands. The mid-America sternwheeler race is staged during the regatta and so is a towboat shoving contest. Add balloon races, water-ski shows, sailboat races, canoe races, hang gliders, sky divers, and a Rosebowl

Parade-like procession of decorated pleasure boats and you have at least part of what festival goers can expect during regatta week in Pittsburgh.

Three Rivers Shakespeare Festival

In midsummer Pittsburgh watches Shakespearean plays at the Stephen Foster Memorial Theatre at Forbes and Bigelow in Oakland. Tickets are free. Phone: (412) 624-4101. Why Stephen Foster? Foster was a Pittsburgh native and most of his songs were written here. He knew the Allegheny well but never once saw Suwannee River.

Special Tours

Some of Pittsburgh's most interesting industrial and cultural centers conduct regular tours for visitors. Here is a sampling of the ones we think are of special interest, particularly to families. Inquire about current charges and double-check arrangements in advance by telephone. All are area code (412).

Braun Baking Company. A tour of the bakery plant. 1700 Island Ave. Phone: 231-2000.

Graphic Arts Technical Foundation. 4615 Forbes Ave. Technical arts used in printing process. Reservations. Phone: 621-6941.

Greater Pittsburgh International Airport. See operation of various departments in a major airport. Need reservations. Phone: 771-2500.

Hartwood Acres. Hay rides and sleigh rides in season. Reservations one week in advance. 215 Saxonburg Blvd. Fox Chapel. Phone: 767-9200.

Heinz Hall for the Performing Arts. 600 Penn Ave. Groups of 10 or more. Reservations needed. Admission charged. Phone: 281-5000.

Pittsburgh Brewing Co., 3340 Liberty Ave. Slide show, plant tour, and samples. Phone: 682-7400.

Pittsburgh *Press*. How newspapers are created and produced. 34 Blvd. of the Allies. Phone: 263-1173.

Round Hill. An exhibit farm. Need reservations two weeks in advance. Elizabeth. Phone: 384-4701.

St. Paul's Cathedral. 108 N. Dithridge St. Reservations. Phone: 621-4951.

Tour-Ed Mine. Memorial Day to Labor Day. R.D. #2, Tarentum. Phone: 224-4720.

Dining Out in Pittsburgh

One Pittsburgh native shook her head when we asked her to recommend a restaurant. "Eight or nine years ago it would have been easy," she said. "There were only one or two. Now there are so many."

Pittsburgh magazine polling its readers for their opinions asked, "If you could have only one more restaurant meal in Pittsburgh, where would you go?" One reader responded, "If dying, La Normande; if moving away, The Common Plea."

Indeed, the native mentioned above did list The Common Plea first. This restaurant is at 308 Ross St., downtown between Third and Fourth avenues. You'll see lawyers and judges from the courthouse eating lunch here. No credit cards. No reservations.

The de Foro Restaurant is in the Lawyer's Building, 428 Forbes Ave. French cuisine and expensive. Impeccable service. Closed Sun.

Frenchy's, 136 Sixth St., is a family-style restaurant where we enjoyed lunch at moderate prices.

Another downtown spot is Klein's, 330 Fourth Ave. This one has the largest seafood menu in Pittsburgh. Garlic puffs, a Klein specialty, are served with all meals. Closed Sun.

Les Nuages, 105 Sixth St., in the Fulton Building, is recommended. French.

Old Allegheny Lounge is a downtown favorite at Sixth St. and Penn Ave., across from Heinz Hall. Dinner and late supper. Moderate prices.

Top of the Triangle, at 600 Grant St., on the 62nd floor of the

U. S. Steel Building. Offers a panoramic view of the city. Moderate to expensive.

Across the Smithfield Bridge, oldest in the city, is Station Square. The grandest restaurant here is the Grand Concourse in the P&LE Terminal. Enter from Smithfield St. and descend the marble staircase. Note the baroque styling and the beautiful stained-glass ceilings. Children's menu. Seafood is featured.

The Gandy Dancer Saloon is in the former baggage room off the Grand Concourse. You'll find a lighter seafood menu here and lower prices.

Houlighan's Old Place is across the street in the Freighthouse Shops. Convivial and friendly. Variety of foods from burgers and omelets to roast duck or steak. Mexican or Italian too.

Mount Washington Dining

Mount Washington may be reached by ascending the Duquesne Incline (the lower station is at 1197 W. Carson St.) or the Monongahela Inclined Plane (starts from W. Carson St. near Station Sq.). If you're driving, take the McArdle Roadway to Grandview Ave. If you are approaching from the south, take highways 51 and 19 (Saw Mill Run) southeast from Hwy. 279, turn left at Woodruff, and follow the signs toward McArdle Roadway, where another left turn brings you out on the very crest of Mount Washington.

Two posh restaurants on Grandview Ave. are LeMont and Christopher's. Both have beautiful views looking down on the Point. Expensive. We found LeMont disappointing in both food and service. Friends recommend The Tin Angel at 1204 Grandview Ave. for a romantic dinner or late night drink.

East of Downtown Dining

Several memorable restaurants have flourished around the university and museum areas of Oakland and Shadyside. The most highly recommended is La Normande, 5030 Centre Ave. in Shadyside. Real French cuisine and expensive, but worth it! Country French atmosphere and friendly service. Also nouvelle cuisine. Menu changes daily. Unusual appetizers and sinful desserts. Patio lunches in summer only. (The 15 percent gratuity is added to your bill.)

Duranti's, 128 N. Craig St., is in the Park Plaza near the Carnegie Institute.

Nino's, 214 N. Craig St., in Oakland, is another favorite place for lunch.

Park Schenley, 3955 Bigclow Blvd. in Oakland. Fine food. Expensive.

Ritter's Diner, 5221 Baum Blvd. in Bloomfield, is an informal, family-style restaurant. Inexpensive.

South of Downtown Dining

The Colony is south at the intersection of Greentree (Hwy. 121) and Cochran roads. This restaurant is famous for its steaks. Also known for excellent fish and liver. Expensive.

West of Downtown Dining

The Hyeholde Restaurant, 190 Hyeholde Dr. off Parkway West in Coraopolis, calls itself one of the last of the great country inns. It is in an old home, surrounded by extensive grounds. Expensive. Excellent food.

Up the Road

Frank Lloyd Wright's Fallingwater

From downtown Pittsburgh, travelers can drive to Fallingwater, one of the best known architectural works of the late Frank Lloyd Wright, in an hour and fifteen minutes, and once there tour the home and grounds—as a million people already have. This is a favorite side trip both for tour buses and vacationers traveling by automobile.

The house, once the property of Pittsburgh department store owner Edgar J. Kaufmann, was designed as a mountain vacation home in the Bear Run Valley. Wright saw in the location an opportunity to create a most unusual house, surrounded by a mature forest, massive sandstone boulders, and mountain wild flowers. There was a waterfall, and this feature held special appeal for Wright. The Kaufmanns wanted their new home situated to give a view of the falling water. Instead Wright suggested that the house be built over the waterfall, cantilevered above it, and fitted into the scene.

The home was completed in 1939 of sandstone quarried on the property and laid up by local stonemasons. In 1963 Edgar J. Kaufmann, Jr., gave the property to the Western Pennsylvania Conservancy, a private nonprofit conservation organization that specializes in saving natural areas. The Conservancy maintains the home and grounds, as well as a new visitors' center, as a memorial to Edgar J. Kaufmann and his wife, Liliane.

Visitors from more than a hundred countries around the world and from every state in the Union have come to see this architectural masterpiece. Open daily except Monday from April to mid-November. In addition to touring the home, visitors may walk the grounds and stop in the visitors' center where there are exhibits, a shop, bookstore, and a child-care center. Admission charged. Phone: (412) 329-8501.

Local guides suggest taking the Pennsylvania Turnpike to Exit 9, at Donegal. Turn left on Hwy. 31, and drive east to Hwy. 381. Fallingwater is on Hwy. 381 halfway between Millpond and Ohiopyle.

Beaver County: The Ohio River Leaves Pennsylvania

The Ohio River flowing out of Pittsburgh swings northward in a great arc that guides it through Beaver County where 200,000 citizens have found happiness surrounded by heavy industry.

Old Economy Village at Ambridge, Pennsylvania, is the scene of an early experiment in communal living.

Away from the river, which is lined with long drab mills and factories, Beaver County becomes a region of pleasant green hills and appealing towns interspersed with parks and farmlands, and visitors are welcomed.

Many of Beaver County's visitors come to Old Economy to see what George Rapp and the Harmony Society were all about. Rapp, born in 1757 in southern Germany, had his own ideas of what a religion should do for a person, and vice versa. Because his beliefs varied considerably from those of the state church, Rapp and his followers decided to immigrate to America. Rapp arrived in Baltimore in 1803; he was now forty-six, and he spent the next two years wandering through Pennsylvania, Ohio, and Virginia searching for just the right place for his settlement. His first settlement was in Butler County, Pennsylvania. By 1806

Rapp's followers included seven hundred pious souls, all of them willing to deed their property to the Society, and accept "Father" Rapp's guidelines for his followers, including the practice of celibacy.

They were self-sufficient at farming and later added weaving and manufacturing to their enterprises. Rapp, seeking better marketing possibilities, moved his group to New Harmony, Indiana, in 1815, but ten years later returned to Pennsylvania and founded Economy, where the settlement stands today as a museum in the town of Ambridge.

The community met considerable success in the business world under Father Rapp's stern eye and guidance. The first setback occurred in 1832 when a visitor started converting Rapp's followers to his own version of communal living, which, significantly, did not demand celibacy. Economy lost one third of its members.

Another blow came in 1847 when Rapp died. Gradually membership and money dwindled until the Society was dissolved in 1905.

The cultural and business center of the community still stands solidly on its original site and thousands of visitors from around the world come each year to see the museum, and take guided tours through the dwellings and shops and to walk through the gardens. Old Economy Village is open the year around, all day on weekdays and on Sunday afternoons.

Father Rapp might not have approved, but there are special events scheduled at Old Economy every year and people come for the fun. One of these is the Kunstfest, or craft festival, the second weekend in June. Another popular one is the nineteenth-century Christmas program conducted the third weekend in December.

Also in Ambridge, on Merchant St. not far from Old Economy, is the Mad Anthony Bier Stube in a building dating to 1830. The Mad Anthony is decorated to give diners and drinkers a feeling for taverns as they were a long time ago. We stopped in for a late lunch when the only patrons were half a dozen local men sitting at the bar. Louie, the venerable bartender, in the middle of one of his stories, adroitly shifted gears in mid-sentence to boom out, "Welcome! Come on in. Make yourselves at home." We settled at a table and looked around.

The late Sheriff John Hineman of Beaver County, Pennsylvania, competes in the annual snow-shovel races.

The woodwork is dark, the floor oiled, the windows stained glass, the walls decorated with old pictures, stag antlers, and a boar's head, while above the bar and the row of dark kegs with spigots hangs a collection of drinking mugs. The place is straight out of Bavaria at the turn of the century and the food is excellent. Treat yourself to the Black Forest layer cake or the fresh apple strudel which our waitress described as "five minutes out of the oven."

One day in Beaver, the county seat, we stopped to talk with Len Szafaryn, a big, friendly man who is the Beaver County Tourist Promotion Agency. Szafaryn, some years ago, faced the challenge of enticing people to the county's recently · opened Economy Park. "Nobody even knew where it was," he said.

Then one winter day he came home to find his son sliding down the slope in the front yard on a snow shovel. Inspiration!

"When I started talking about shovel races, everyone said, 'You're nuts.' " But a determined person, truly inspired is not easily dissuaded. If you visit Economy County Park on the third weekend after the first of January, you will find crowds of visitors gathered on the slope, cheering the 140 contestants as they zoom downhill on snow shovels and compete for trophies.

The official course for the World Shovel-Riding Contest measures 151 feet, and the usual time for the more skilled riders, is in the vicinity of seven seconds. There are special classes for children and adults and for "modified" shovels which sometimes are equipped with special runners or short sections of skis. "Snow has to be right," says Szafaryn, "but if they wear all the snow off the slope, 140 contestants each carrying a shovelful of snow back up the hill can put the track in good condition in a few minutes." One year the races had to be called off. The snow was too deep.

As far as Szafaryn knows this is the biggest shovel-riding contest anywhere. "The beauty of it is," says Szafaryn, "it's cheap to put on and it's not dangerous. How far can you fall off a shovel?" Didn't anyone ever get hurt? "Well, yes, once. One of the judges. He was leaning on a shovel and it slipped. He hit his head on the handle on the way down." Szafaryn assures us that now everybody knows where Old Economy Park is.

Beaver County also has a noted polo team in a most unlikely place. The team's home grounds is a beaten down pasture near the village of Darlington, population 120. Here the community polo team races back and forth with a skill that has drawn top challengers from distant cities. To the village of Darlington have come polo teams from Cleveland, Cincinnati, Detroit, and many major cities. Around Darlington folks like to recall the visit of the Montreal team. Out of that giant Canadian municipal area came the team of skilled and dashing polo players in fancy clothes, accompanied by attendants and twenty-five of the finest polo ponies anywhere. Say the Darlington people with pride, "We beat 'em ten to eight."

When the playing field becomes so dusty that it is difficult to see the white wooden ball, out rumbles the Darlington fire engine to sprinkle the field and settle the dust. This worked out well except one day when the fire alarm went off right in the middle of the sprinkling, and the fire engine had to rush away, siren wailing, in its own cloud of dust. The Darlington team also had to face the problem of where to play the second game of its home meets. The first game comes on Friday evening but the second customarily falls on Sunday—except in Darlington where Sunday games are taboo. No problem. Sunday games are held across the border in Unity, Ohio.

Beaver County has a large state park and three county parks. Raccoon Creek State Park in the southwestern corner, covers nearly 7,000 acres, has a 101-acre lake stocked with trout, family campgrounds, swimming, boating, sledding, skating, hiking, equestrian trail, and hunting in season.

The major county park is Brady's Run, noted for its annual Maple Syrup Festival the last weekend in February or the first in March. There is family camping in this park, plus swimming, boating, and fishing. It's located on Hwy. 51, two miles north of Beaver. Other county parks are Brush Creek on Hwy. 588, and Old Economy, northeast of Ambridge. Both have picnic areas.

There are several museums that attract visitors in this corner of Western Pennsylvania. In New Brighton we found the Merrick Free Art Gallery established in an old railroad station in the 1880s by an industrialist who, at the age of fifty-three, decided he would become a painter and collector of paintings. He put together a fine collection. Admission is free.

In the Carnegie Free Library in Beaver Falls is the Beaver Falls Historical Society Museum. The speciality here is local history, and admission is free.

Another free museum that tells a local story is the Frankfort Mineral Springs Museum in Raccoon State Park.

The Wooden Angel, a restaurant on West Bridgewater St., in Beaver, was recommended highly to us. It's known for delicious food and for an outstanding wine cellar, featuring primarily domestic wines.

The Ohio: A String of Lakes

Those who travel along the Ohio River frequently pass tow-boats for this is one of the busiest rivers anywhere. Coal, petroleum, chemicals, grain, and fertilizers are pushed along the Ohio in huge steel barges locked together in tows sometimes numbering a dozen or more. More than 150 million tons of freight are moved on the Ohio each year, and this is possible because the river has been adapted to large boats. Before there were any structures in the river, sizable boats could navigate it only when the water was high. The installation of dams with navigation locks gave the river a channel of guaranteed depth. This construction began in 1875, and the system was completed the length of the Ohio in 1929, with ceremonies on a hilltop in Cincinnati now marked with a monument.

Almost at once, plans were underway to replace the dams and locks with even larger structures and reduce the number of dams on the Ohio to its present 20, making the impoundments between the dams longer and deeper. Today the Ohio is a series of stair-stepped lakes through which water flows very slowly when the river is in pool stage.

Along the Ohio, especially on holidays and weekends, the tow-boats are joined by sailboats, houseboats, fishing boats, and motorboats pulling water skiers. There are launching ramps along the river, on either shore, and marinas where traveling boaters can refuel and take on supplies. Those wanting to travel into the next pool can lock through the dams no matter how small their boat.

In addition, the locks and dams themselves attract much attention, and the U. S. Army Corps of Engineers provides visitors' centers, parking lots, and overlooks where people can see the system in operation and watch boats pass through the locks.

Typical of these installations is the Markland Locks and Dam at mile 532 between Cincinnati and Louisville. This giant dam replaced five smaller dams and created a pool 95 miles long, extending upstream past Cincinnati. Locks allowing boats to pass this dam are located on the Kentucky side of the river—the left bank when facing the direction the river flows.

Markland Dam is 1,395 feet long and water behind it is controlled by 12 gates, each measuring 100 feet wide and 42 feet high. There are two sets of locks, one 600 feet long, the other 1,200 feet in length. The longer locks made it possible to pass long tows through without having to break them up into smaller units and reassemble them again in the next pool.

Captains of pleasure craft on the river should remember the basic rules for keeping their boats and passengers out of danger. Stay away from passing tows—well away. The towboat captain may not be able to stop his boat in less than a mile, and there is little he can do by way of maneuvering to avoid small craft. Also stay well back from dams and locks unless locking through. The Commander, Second Coast Guard District, 1430 Olive St., St. Louis, MO 63136, publishes a list of navigational aids on the river. The Commandant, U. S. Coast Guard, Washington, D.C. 20590 or the Coast Guard offices in Paducah, KY; Cincinnati, OH; Huntington, WV; Louisville, KY; and Pittsburgh, PA make available free copies of *Rules of the Road, Western Rivers*.

The Ohio River Division, U. S. Army Corps of Engineers, 10th Floor, Federal Office Building, P. O. Box 1159, Cincinnati, OH 45201, issues a publication: *Maps and Charts, Ohio River Division*, which describes available navigation maps and charts for the pools of the Ohio River and gives the cost of each.

When traveling in the valley those who wish to visit the locks and dams will find them at the following locations:

OHIO RIVER LOCKS AND DAMS

Lock	River Mile & Bank (facing downstream)	City	Phone
Emsworth	6R	Emsworth, PA	(412) 766-6213
Dashields	13L	Glenwillard, PA	(412) 457-8430
Montgomery	32L	Industry, PA	(412) 643-8400
New Cumberland	54R	Stratton, OH	(614) 537-2571
Pike Island	84L	Wheeling, WV	(304) 277-2240
Hannibal	126R	Hannibal, OH	(614) 483-2305

Willow Island	162R	Reno, OH	(614) 374-8710
			(304) 665-2520
Belleville	204R	Reedsville, OH	(614) 378-6110
			(304) 863-6331
Racine	238L	New Haven, WV	(304) 882-2118
			(614) 247-2875
Gallipolis	279L	Gallipolis Ferry, WV	(614) 256-6311
			(304) 576-2272
Greenup	341L	Greenup, KY	(606) 473-7441
Capt. Anthony			
Meldahl	436R	Chilo, OH	(513) 876-2921
Markland	532L	Warsaw, KY	(606) 567-7661
McAlpine	607L	Louisville, KY	(502) 774-3514
Cannelton	721R	Cannelton, IN	(812) 547-2962
Newburgh	776R	Newburgh, IN	(812) 853-8470
Uniontown	846R	Mount Vernon, IN	(812) 838-5836
Smithland	919R	Hamletsburg, IL	(618) 564-2315
L&D 52	939R	Brookport, IL	(618) 564-3151
L&D 53	963R	Mound City, IL	(618) 742-6213

Part II
The South Shore

West Virginia

The Northern Panhandle

West Virginia's Northern Panhandle, a neck of land from 5 to 16 miles wide, extends north and south for 60 miles pinched in between the Upper Ohio River and Pennsylvania's western boundary. Because of this panhandle, West Virginia extends north beyond both Pittsburgh, Pennsylvania, and Columbus, Ohio. It is made up of four counties: Hancock, Brooke, Ohio, and Marshall.

Hwy. 2 is West Virginia's road along the Ohio River, and it follows the twisting course of the river as long as that stream forms a border of the Mountain State. This road is often narrower than Hwy. 7 across on the Ohio side, and it goes directly through West Virginia river towns instead of around them. Often, Hwy. 2 leads the traveler close enough that the river is in plain view. There are stretches, especially upstream from New Martinsville, where the riverside is dominated by industrial plants and towering smokestacks. Farther downstream the giant industrial plants give way more frequently to views of the magnificent hills bordering the Ohio.

People living within this panhandle have a kinship with the Ohio, to which their lives are so closely tied. "I love the river," one retired school teacher told us in Chester, West Virginia's northernmost town. We were standing on the neatly trimmed grass above the river as a towboat pushed four barges upstream to the mills in Pennsylvania. "You can see three states here," she added. "That's Pennsylvania right up there."

She suddenly stopped talking to look intently at the Ohio

shore. "Is that a deer or dog?" We watched as a young deer moved out of the shrubs in the back yard of the across-the-river neighbors and nervously flicked its white tail as it munched on leaves.

On this day the river was as clear as it ever gets. The green water reflected the colors of the timbered hills on either side as the Ohio flowed down out of Pennsylvania and into West Virginia.

Chester is a pleasant little river city. This is the home of the Ceramic Products Division of the Anchor Hocking Corporation, and the company offers tours to visitors. Beside the plant is the factory outlet store of Taylor, Smith and Taylor, with bargains in pottery and glassware.

Four miles west of Chester at Newell we found the giant buildings of the Homer Laughlin China Company, the biggest pottery plant in the country in a single location. In the factory outlet store we talked with Ed Carson who greets visitors and organizes plant tours.

Pottery and glassmakers, more than some other industries, have kept the welcome sign out for people wanting to tour their plants. Homer Laughlin offers visitors regular free tours without special appointments. Carson introduced us to Kathleen Kraft, a pleasant woman who doubles as tour guide when not at her work bench putting gold decorations on fine dinnerware.

She led us into the working areas of the giant plant, explained that the soft, gray clay comes primarily from southeastern states and that when properly mixed into a liquid, it is called "slip" and can be poured into molds. There it remains for about an hour before the molds are emptied. The clay that has dried sufficiently to stay in the mold forms the new piece, and the longer the clay remains in the mold the thicker the piece becomes.

This "green ware" is removed from the molds, then trimmed with hand tools before going into the kiln to be fired for two days at 2,200° F. It is then cleaned, glazed, fired, decorated, fired again, and all along the line, inspected. In this age of mass production there is still an impressive amount of handwork required in the making of ceramic products. Handles are attached by hand, trimming, decorating, and cleaning all involve steps performed by hand. Watching the operation helps the visitor appreciate the coffee cup from which he has his morning brew.

At Homer Laughlin pottery, Newell, West Virginia, visitors can watch every step of pottery making, from mixing clay to final decorations (Photo by Homer Laughlin)

Carson explained to us that this pottery company began more than a century ago across the river in East Liverpool, Ohio. Homer, and his brother Shakespeare Laughlin, started the business in 1871. Two years later Shakespeare opted out and Homer carried on. Methods improved, new equipment, including continuous tunnel kilns, was invented, new plants were added, and production continued to climb. The year before we visited the plant its 1,225 employees produced and shipped 35 million pieces of dinnerware. We did our share and bought a set of cereal bowls. At bargain prices.

There were other points of interest in this northern tip of West Virginia. At the junction of Hwy. 30 and Hwy. 8 stands a metal plaque marking the scene of the tragedy that struck Chief Logan of the Mingo Tribe. Here, opposite the Mingo village at the mouth of Yellow Creek, white renegades killed Chief Logan's family, after which Logan retaliated by leading raids against the whites. Then, standing beneath the Logan Elm, that lived until recent years, he delivered perhaps the most eloquent speech ever recorded for an Indian, or any other American.

To the south, on King's Creek Road near Weirton, stands the restored furnace where Peter Tarr cast the iron cannonballs fired by Commodore Perry's ships during the battle of Lake Erie.

If you enjoy watching the ponies or playing golf, you will want to know about Waterford Park, near Chester and 10 miles north of Weirton. Every week of the year the Thoroughbreds run here and racing fans watch from glass-enclosed stands. Most of the three hundred or so racing dates held here each year offer races beneath the lights. The night races from April through December normally get underway at 7:15 P.M.

Also included in this resort complex is a 9-hole golf course, bath and tennis club, and the Waterford Inn with its dining facilities, all of which draw people from Pittsburgh, Youngstown, and other population centers in the three states.

There is a wild side to this northern corner of West Virginia. By leaving Hwy. 2 and driving north for 3 miles on Hwy. 8 we found signs leading to Tomlinson Run State Park. Once in the park the narrow hard-surfaced road drew us into the timbered hills, and suddenly we had escaped the bustling sounds and sights of towns, highways, and industries. We drove down a hill to a narrow lake reaching back into wooded hollows.

Here we hailed a passing green pickup truck and met Dave Lombardo, a friendly young man who is the superintendent.

He was proud of his park and especially of its campground. "There are fourteen hundred acres," Dave said. "We have four trails and a swimming pool, a mini-golf course, picnicking areas, ice skating, and fishing. There is fishing here in the lake for trout and bass, which are stocked every year, and we have four smaller bass ponds that are popular with fishermen. You may not see many people here this morning, but you should be here on a weekend. We draw in a lot of people from Ohio and Pennsylvania." A quarter of a million people a year come here, making Tomlinson Run West Virginia's fifth most popular park. "Before you go," Dave added, "take time to check out our new campground." With a wave of his hand, Dave Lombardo was off again.

The campground lies along a ridge where individual sites for tents or recreational vehicles are screened by vegetation. The plumbing is modern all the way, including showers. There is a dumping station, and there are supplies available at concession stands. Definitely a first-rate camping area.

Another park that also has space for camping is farther downriver in Brooke County on Hwy. 27, four miles east of Wellsburg. This is Brooke Hills Park, covering 700 acres. West Virginia calls it one of its finest county parks. In addition to camping, there are swimming, hiking, picnicking, golf, playgrounds, skiing, ice skating, boating, and even the Brooke Hills Playhouse, a summer theater in a remodeled barn where local theater groups perform. The park, however, is open the year around.

One evening, on Hwy. 27 in Wellsburg, we sought out the Drover's Inn, which is a delight for lovers of good food and/or antiques. Mary Marko bought the old inn in 1965 and set about restoring it. What she bought was a solid structure and a piece of history.

The place was John Fowler's dream when he built it in 1848. He saw the need for an inn that would serve travelers, especially drovers driving their livestock across the toll pikes. The drovers would be offered food and lodging, and their stock, pasture. By 1850 Fowler had the new three-story inn open for business.

At various times Drover's Inn served also as a drugstore, post

office, and general store. Our dinner was excellent and reasonable. Guests are invited to wander through the entire house after
dinner to see the antique furnishings.

South of Wellsburg on Hwy. 67 at Bethany, Alexander Campbell founded Bethany College in 1840. The 27-room mansion
that was his home is today on the National Register of Historic
Places. The mansion is open to the public.

Wheeling: A Splendid Park

Here in the Northern Panhandle is where, in 1861, the state of
West Virginia was born. The country was torn by the conflicts of
the Civil War, and citizens of Virginia's western counties disagreed with the Virginia leaders in Richmond who favored seces-
sion from the Union. They disagreed so violently that they were
determined to form an entirely new state of their own and align
the new state with the North.

Their leaders met at Wheeling in the Custom House, forged their
documents, and reaffirmed their stand. They petitioned Congress
to separate the western part of Virginia into a new state, and the
new state was admitted to the Union in 1863.

The Custom House still stands, and although it was neglected
for a century, it has recently been renovated. It is now West
Virginia Independence Hall, a fine example of Italian Renaissance
Revival architecture, standing in the center of downtown Wheeling, where it is open as a museum.

Wheeling should not be lightly dismissed by travelers. We
stopped one morning at the Caboose, operated on Water Street
near the Civic Auditorium by the Upper Ohio Valley Travel
Council, to see Jim McCracken whose job is selling Wheeling and
the surrounding counties. Jim keeps a stock of circulars on hand
for travelers who ask about the region's attractions. He pointed
out the window toward Wheeling Island, an island a mile and a
half long where 10,000 people live in the center of the Ohio, the
largest population occupying an inland island in the country.

"There's Wheeling Downs," he said, "where the greyhound races bring in thousands of people from all over the area."

Country music? Wheeling has it! And she has it from big names in the business. " 'Jamboree U.S.A.' is held here at Capitol Music Hall, every Saturday night," Jim said. Jamboree U.S.A. has been going on since 1933. It's older than the "Grand Ole Opry." The Capitol fills with country-music lovers from many states and from Canada who come to hear the foot stompin' music of the hills as rendered by Ronnie Milsap, Porter Wagoner, Loretta Lynn, and others.

Then, once a year, the Jamboree moves across the river into the hills of Belmont County, Ohio, and thousands of people flock in for a whole weekend of music. This is "Jamboree in the Hills" and it comes in the middle of July.

Wheeling is proud, and with good reason, of Oglebay Park, a model operation maintained by the city on the hillsides and ridges a few miles from the center of town on Hwy. 88N. This is another of those gifts to the public traceable to the very wealthy, in this case Colonel Earl Oglebay who made his millions mostly from coal.

Oglebay wanted to prove that these steep hills of West Virginia could produce fine livestock and farm crops, so he bought Waddington Farm and established an experimental center. This cost Oglebay a million dollars or so and fell somewhat short of his aims. On his death, he left the estate to the city of Wheeling for public recreation and education. Oglebay Park ranks as a showplace among the nation's municipal parks.

Summer visitors to Oglebay are first impressed with the care given the hundreds of acres that are carefully mowed and tended. Fields and woods get resort-style treatment, perhaps because Oglebay is a resort. There are 34 cabins for rent as well as Wilson Lodge with 200 guest rooms and the Top of the Park Restaurant, perhaps the best dining room in the Wheeling area where visitors can end the day with a locally celebrated drink—"The Wheeling Feeling."

There is an excellent public golf course and driving range. Noted golfers assemble here for tournaments. There are downhill ski slopes, complete with lifts and snow-making machines. Other activities are tennis, swimming, hiking, bicycling, boating, fishing,

In Wheeling, the Old Custom House, where West Virginia chose to become a separate state, is now a museum. (Photo by George Laycock)

and bird watching, plus a children's zoo with a miniature train that chugs through the buffalo enclosure.

The Mansion Museum, Oglebay's summer home, is now a fine museum of furniture, paintings, china, and a glass collection.

Rooms are decorated with furniture of various periods—there is a Federal bedroom, an Empire parlor, and a Victorian parlor.

"The park," as one writer said, "has style without being extravagant and is relaxing without being common."

Wheeling Park is smaller, but also popular with residents of this city. This park has a 9-hole golf course, tennis courts, playground, swimming pool, and ice-skating rink. There are concerts and dances in the park, places to hold a picnic, and even a giant water slide.

Cigars are among the products for which Wheeling is famous, and all who are curious about how stogies are made may visit M. Marsh & Son at 915 Market St. From Monday through Friday, four times a day, visitors are led through the cigar plant on tours.

Among the Wheeling restaurants customarily recommended to visitors are the award-winning Ernie's Esquire Supper Club on Bethlehem Blvd. and Eric's Steak House, Waddle Run Rd.

Oglebay Park, perhaps the valley's finest city park, includes the former owner's mansion, now a museum. (Photo by George Laycock)

Figarettis is a good family restaurant offering Italian food and
perhaps the best spumoni ice cream in the entire Ohio Valley.
Mr. Figaretti takes great pride in the spumoni, which he himself
makes.

The most famous of Wheeling's bridges spanning the Ohio
River is her historic suspension bridge. When a suspension bridge
was built here in 1849 it became the first bridge to span the
mighty Ohio. All of Wheeling was proud of this magnificent
structure suspended from its wire cables.

Then, during a violent spring storm in 1854, the bridge first
rose up, then came crashing down in ruin into the river. The
bridge was rebuilt and opened in 1860. It still stands. The tower
on one end rises 20 feet higher than its twin on the other side; the
bridge, like most roads in West Virginia, goes uphill and downhill.

Moundsville: And the Highest Mound

In the heart of the next county seat downriver, and across from
the West Virginia State Penitentiary, stands one of the state's
most famous man-made landmarks, and one of its oldest: the
Grave Creek Mound. This mound was built by the Adena people
between 250 and 150 B.C. It is 69 feet high and had a base diameter of 295 feet. A moat 40 feet wide and 5 feet deep once surrounded it. We traced the history of the mound and the Adena
people in the halls of the recently opened Delf Norona Museum
beside the mound. There was once a building erected on top of
the mound because of the view it commanded of the surrounding
area. There is even a report that in 1860 a saloon was built on
top of the mound, but that the business did poorly because, in
those pre-elevator days, it was too far to climb for a drink.

In 1838 amateurs dug into the mound in search of buried treasure. They found some bones plus a strange stone bearing hiero-

This famous mound at Moundsville, West Virginia, was a burial site for prehistoric people. (Photo by George Laycock)

glyphic characters that to this day are indecipherable. This still leads to occasional speculation that ancient Norsemen came to the banks of the Ohio long before Christopher Columbus ever reached the New World.

Marshall County has a county park near Moundsville, Grand Vue Park, which is reached by following Hwy. 250NE to Grand-view Road. Once there you can play tennis, golf, take a swim, or have a picnic. In winter, cross-country skiing is popular. There are four fully equipped cabins for rent.

The most popular factory tour in this area is a visit to the Fostoria Glass Company, First St. in Moundsville. There we met Harry Carney, retired after more than half a century in the factory making glassware. "I started in the plant when I was four-teen," he told us. "Then came the labor law and I had to give my age. I changed my age on my papers and went on working. We took pride in what we did. If they brought us a hard job, we'd say, 'Yeah, we'll try.'"

He led us down the steps into the hot and noisy room where craftsmen work around huge furnaces fired by natural gas to temperatures of 2,200° F. Glowing dabs of red and orange molten sand are lifted from the furnaces on the ends of long hollow steel tubes, rolled gently and knowingly, then blown into a glass bubble with a gentle pressure by the craftsman who next places the bulb into a form that helps shape it into a thin piece of fine crystal. The amount of handwork that still goes into these pieces left us with an added sense of appreciation for the product and skills of the craftsmen.

Glass blowing is an ancient art. The Egyptians were making glass some 4,000 years ago and were blowing glass not too long afterwards. Much of the strength of modern glassware comes from the slow cooling in the long tunnel-like ovens called the "lehr." In 1608 the first industry in the United States, a glasshouse, was built outside the Jamestown settlement. Fostoria began operations in 1887. Many of its skilled workers, like Harry Carney, have labored in the factory for thirty or forty years or more, and afterward can never get it fully off their minds. "I dream about this place," Carney told us quietly.

Fostoria maintains two clearance outlets, one next to Howard Johnson's Lodge in Wheeling; the other across the street from its factory in Moundsville.

Glass Factories You Can Visit

The Ohio Valley is the glassmaking capital of the United States and tours through the factories where glass is blown and craftsmen create handmade glassware are highly popular with tourists. Visitors should remember that many glass factories close the first two weeks of July for vacations.

Factories that welcome visitors include the following:

PENNSYLVANIA

Lenox Crystal
  Mount Pleasant, PA
  On Hwy. 31
  Phone: (412) 547-4541
L. E. Smith Glass
  Mount Pleasant, PA
  On Hwy. 31
  Phone: (412) 834-9123

Westmoreland Glass Co.
  Grapeville, PA
  1 mi. E. of Jeanette off Hwy. 30
  Phone: (412) 523-5481

OHIO

Imperial Glass
  Bellaire, OH
  5 mi. S. on Hwy. 7
  Phone: (614) 676-3511

WEST VIRGINIA

Blenko Glass Co., Inc.
  P. O. Box 67, Henry Rd.
  Milton, WV
  Phone: (304) 743-9081
Fenton Art Glass Co.
  P. O. Box 156
  Williamstown, WV 26187
  Phone: (304) 375-6122
Fostoria Glass Co.
  1200 First St.
  Moundsville, WV
  Phone: (304) 845-1050
Gentile Glass Co.
  425 Industrial Ave.
  Star City, WV
  Phone: (304) 599-2750
Hamon Glass & Visitors' Center
  102 Hamon Dr.
  Scott Depot, WV
  Phone: (304) 755-3381 or 755-2025

Mid-Atlantic Glass Co.
  Ellenboro, WV
  Phone: (304) 869-3351
Pennsboro Glass Co.
  P. O. Box 487
  Pennsboro, WV
  Phone: (304) 659-2871
Pilgrim Glass Corp.
  P. O. Box 395
  Ceredo, WV
  Phone: (304) 453-3553
Viking Glass Co., Plant 1
  P. O. Box 29, Parkway St.
  New Martinsville, WV
  Phone: (304) 455-2900
Viking Glass Co., Plant 2
  P. O. Box 9246
  Huntington, WV
  Phone: (304) 429-1321

INDIANA

Zimmerman's Art Glass Co.
  Corydon, IN
  Phone: (812) 738-2206

Wetzel County: Country Roads

In the course of a year, two major events bring people into this rugged hill county and its county seat, New Martinsville. In September comes the annual New Martinsville Inboard Regatta attracting speedboaters from around the country because this regatta on the Ohio is famous as one of the country's fastest races. The hills are alive with the sound of engines. Music to the local merchants.

The other giant event is Town and Country Days in mid-August, and this is more than a run-of-the-mill country fair. In Wetzel County, folks look upon Town and Country Days as a revival of activities popular in their grandparents' time. From square dancing and country music, entertainment goes to fiddling contests and arm wrestling, with now and then a sky-diver or tractor-pulling contest thrown in for a modern touch. There is something happening all the time, and most of the action is centered 2 miles

This mountain scene near Proctor is typical of vistas along West Virginia back roads. (Photo by George Laycock)

east of New Martinsville on the 4-H grounds. If you want to bring your family and camp, there is space available for family tents or recreational vehicles.

Wetzel County also offers an excellent opportunity to visit a glass factory. The Viking Glass Company in New Martinsville has been creating treasured glassware since the turn of the century, and four times a day it offers free tours for visitors.

One of our favorite activities in West Virginia, in any season, is exploring country roads. Whenever possible we leave the main highways and escape into the hills.

The rules for exploring country roads are simple. Before heading out into the country, check your fuel supply. Agree with your traveling companions that you are not on a tight schedule and that getting lost will be part of the adventure. Attitude is important. Country roads are an adventure, especially in the mountains of West Virginia. Travelers prone to worry can always stop ahead of time at the county engineer's office in the courthouse and buy, at modest price, a county map.

On Hwy. 89 the narrow blacktop road soon led us through a maze of twists and turns into deep hollows, out onto ridges, and down through the forests. Little farms and modest country homes beside the roads were well tended and pleasant looking. There were picture postcard views from every ridgetop. Lines of ridges stack up behind each other until the last is lost in the distant blue haze of the Appalachians.

Wondering where we were, we stopped at one point to talk with an elderly couple trimming grave sites in a hilltop cemetery, but they did not really know where we were either. One lady told us, "Eighty-nine comes out on one of them hills on yon side of Belton." Oh well! Away we go. More adventure.

When you come here, allow time for a circle drive, and we'll now guide you onto a good one through country as scenic as any we know throughout the length of the Ohio Valley. Give yourself at least an hour. But that's approximate. Follow Hwy. 89 from New Martinsville eastward to Doolin Run Rd., then turn south on Doolin to American Ridge Rd., and follow that back into town. Some call this section New Switzerland, and the resemblance was even more pronounced after we discovered Dick Schnacke who makes Whimmy Diddles for a living.

West Virginia's back roads offer scenery that changes little through the years. (Photo by George Laycock)

Dick, a tall, pleasant man with a slightly ruddy complexion, came out of his home state of Kansas three decades ago with a degree in engineering. He arrived in West Virginia to work at a massive new chemical plant being built on the banks of the Ohio River, liked the hills and the folklore of the state, and was especially intrigued by the toys that mountaineers have made for their children for many generations.

You can see what Dick and mountain toys have done for each other if you drive out onto American Ridge. (Dick says the easiest way to find him is turn off Hwy. 2 at Newman's Exxon station in New Martinsville and follow Doolin Run Rd. for 5½ miles to the top of the hill. Make a sharp turn left onto American Ridge, and from there it's only a quarter of a mile.)

A sign over the door reads, "Mountain Craft Shop." The place

Old-time folk toys, fashioned in the homes of mountain craftsmen, are shipped from the Mountain Craft Shop to stores throughout the country. (Photo by George Laycock)

High on a West Virginia mountain Dick Schnacke created this chalet and a new industry in old toys. (Photo by George Laycock)

was strangely quiet, but Dick was in a back room. His help had this day off. Dick was happy to show us his wares and tell us about his unusual business. The shelves were filled with wooden toys, some of which I recognized from my childhood in the hills of southern Ohio. But I had seen none of these toys for years.

"I have fifty neighbors out along these ridges making toys in their homes," Dick explained. "It's a cottage industry. I tell them what I can sell, they make the toys according to my plans, and I buy what they make. This has brought new prosperity to a lot of families." In addition, Dick employs five people in the shop, helping pack and ship the toys that must go out to fill the orders. Business has been building up for Dick and his mountain craftspeople for two decades. Orders come from stores, shops, and individuals in every state, as well as some foreign countries, making Dick the biggest producer anywhere of authentic folk toys.

"Everything we make," he said, "is an 'old' toy—an idea that has been around in these mountains for a long time. We're finding new ones every week—new old ones, that is." He walked along one long shelf, picking up toys and demonstrating them. The Whimmy Diddle is a stick with notches cut in the top and a little propeller tacked onto one end. Rub another stick along the notches and the propeller whirls around, first in one direction, then the other. Also, there were the Limber Jack, Spindle Top, Bull Roarer, Flipper Dinger, and the Do Nothing Machine—177 in all, and all handmade by Dick's mountain craftsmen. Also on the shelves was a supply of the books that Dick Schnacke has written. They have made him known as the leading authority on American folk toys.

Dick also invited us to see the home he and his wife, Jean, have built near the shop. The tall Swiss chalet can be seen from other ridges round about. When Dick is not at work in his shop, he can be found in the chalet, enjoying perhaps the best view in the Ohio Valley.

Tyler County: Oil Country

Tyler County stretches along the Ohio from Paden City to Ben's Run. About 8 miles downriver of Paden City is Sistersville. There is a solid feeling about Sistersville. Its turn-of-the-century mansions are a constant reminder of the oil boom that brought wealth to the town.

Charles Wells settled here in 1776, and Wells is still a prominent name in the area. The town was laid out in 1815 on land owned by two sisters, Sarah and Delila Wells.

The Wells Inn, built in 1894 by Ephraim Wells, is on the National Register of Historic Places. Furnished and decorated in Victorian style, it is still operated as an inn (by Ephriam's great-grandson, John Wells Kinkaid, Jr.), and you may stay there as we did, enjoying turn-of-the-century splendor plus every modern convenience—even sauna baths. Dining rooms are open for all three meals. Since the Sistersville Municipal Park is located just behind the Inn, you can go over for a dip in the pool before dinner. Write: Wells Inn, 316 Charles St., Sistersville, WV 26175 or phone: (304) 652-3111.

Later in the evening, we strolled through this historic river town, noted for its peaceful atmosphere and Victorian and Greek Revival architecture. The Town Hall, hexagonal in shape, is also on the National Register of Historic Places. On Riverside Dr. we found the Sistersville Historic District Oil Well Park with an oil derrick (the only one we saw). Beside the Park is the Sistersville Ferry landing.

The days of river ferryboats are passing, and tourists drive miles out of their way to find these little boats still at work. Here and there a ferry still goes back and forth across the Ohio. One of these is the *Elinor D.*

We came upon the *Elinor D,* secured to the riverbank for the night. She had run her 13 hours, as she does 7 days a week, and there was a "Closed" sign hanging on an oil drum that blocked the steep ramp leading down to the water's edge.

The following morning, the *Elinor D* was back at work early, keeping up a river tradition that has gone on continuously at this crossing since 1818. This ferry operates between Sistersville, West Virginia, and Fly, Ohio. We watched as two vehicles boarded her, a loaded red Coca-Cola truck and a small car carrying a traveling family. We heard a deckhand tell them loudly as we brought a camera into position, "Yer gonna get yer picture tooken."

Ten minutes later the ferry returned and this time the photographer walked aboard. Captain Gilbert L. Harmon invited him up to the pilothouse to take pictures. The captain explained, "I used to work on the bigger boats. Maybe I will again. But this job keeps me closer to home." His home is beside the river. Six days a week he runs the ferry, alternating shifts with his father, a veteran of thirty-seven years on the Ohio. On his day of rest he goes back to the river, this time taking his son out in his own motorboat.

Nobody knows how long the ferry will operate between Fly and Sistersville. Traffic is light sometimes. There is a bridge 12 miles upstream at New Martinsville. "I'd sure miss the ole river if I couldn't work boats no more." Gilbert Harmon waved, and the ferryboat churned off on its next trip across the river.

Highway 18 is another of West Virginia's country roads, winding up a narrow valley past neat, small farms. About 12 miles from Sistersville, we came to Middlebourne, the county seat, founded about 1812 and given the name because it was midway between Pennsylvania and the old salt wells on the Kanawha.

The lady on duty at the library, a lifelong Middlebourne resident, assured us that "a lot of nice people came from Tyler County, but nobody famous that I can think of." After a few minutes, however, she recalled that long before her time, the first governor of West Virginia, Arthur Boreman, lived here, and that former Governor Cecil Underwood came from Tyler County.

The ferryboat at Sistersville, West Virginia, is one of the few still operating on the Ohio River. (Photo by George Laycock)

Wells Inn is a famous nineteenth-century hotel still in business at Sistersville, West Virginia. (Photo by George Laycock)

Conway Lake lies 8 miles south of Middlebourne, and signs on Hwy. 18 at Centerville (formerly Alma) point the way. Conway Lake and the surrounding area is maintained by the West Virginia Department of Natural Resources as a public hunting and fishing area. There were a few fishermen around the lake. The small campground (with pit toilets) was empty on the mid-summer day we were there.

Middle Island Creek, which flows up out of this hill country toward the Ohio River, is famous among local people as the "longest and crookedest creek in the world." They tell you about "the jug," the section where Middle Island Creek makes a 7-mile-long curve and comes right back within 90 feet of itself.

Oil is still the major topic of conversation among citizens of this county. The rising prices of petroleum brought a renewed interest in exploring and drilling. The weekly newspaper lists the

The historic ferryboat between Sistersville, West Virginia, and Fly, Ohio, is a popular ride for tourists. (Photo by George Laycock)

This city park at Sistersville, an important early oil-drilling center, celebrates the story of a famous well. (Photo by George Laycock)

new strikes as well as other oil industry news. Even those who do not strike oil can look forward in September to the annual Oil and Gas Festival in Sistersville, when the town fills with visitors and there are exhibits, contests, and activities rooted in the oil and gas industry.

AUTOMOBILE FERRIES OVER THE OHIO RIVER

Moundsville, West Virginia
   Connects Moundsville with Powhatan Point, Ohio.

Sistersville, West Virginia
   Connects Sistersville with Fly, Ohio (new bridge will replace ferry).

Augusta, Kentucky
   Connects Augusta with Hwy. 52 in Ohio.

Anderson Ferry, Ohio
   Connects Ohio shore, downriver from Cincinnati with Constance, Kentucky.

Cave-in-Rock, Illinois
   Connects Cave-in-Rock with terminus of Hwy. 91 in Crittenden County, Kentucky.

Pleasants County: Fishing Tournaments

Driving southwestward on Hwy. 2 the traveler comes into the county at Ben's Run and along the way has frequent pleasing views of the river and the surrounding hills.

The only town of significant size is the county seat, Saint Mary's, which was founded by Alexander H. Creel. His two-story brick house still stands, serving today as the Masonic Hall. The house is on the National Register of Historic Places, and a plaque on the front tells us that in 1851 Pleasants County was organized here and the first court was held in the house that same year.

The modern courthouse stands at the top of a steep hill at the end of its own wide boulevard.

Popular with local people, Pleasants County Park is at the end of Cherry St. in Saint Mary's. Spread over 68 acres of parklands are hiking trails, swimming pool, picnic grounds, miniature golf course, and playgrounds, a good midday stop for the family looking for a picnic area, and a place for the kids to work off some energy.

At times skilled bass fishermen congregate in Saint Mary's to participate in bass tournaments on the Ohio River and Middle Island Creek. One of the attractions for river users, whether fishermen or boaters, is the launching area and marina right in town.

There is industry in Saint Mary's, and the city has an air of prosperity. A bridge links it with the Ohio village of Newport.

Up the Road

North Bend State Park

The best known tourist attraction around Pleasants County is up the road. Take Hwy. 16 to Harrisville and turn west toward Cairo, following signs to North Bend State Park. If you are approaching from U.S. 50, exit on Hwy. 31.

There is a first-class campground with hot showers, laundry facilities, and dumping station. The campground lies along the river and some campers can fish from their sites.

Non-campers stay in wooded settings in deluxe vacation cabins with either two or three bedrooms, fireplaces, and modern kitchens including built-in appliances. Bring only your food.

Another option is to stay at the lodge, which has 30 modern rooms and a dining room offering striking views of the West Virginia mountains.

There are tennis courts, a swimming pool, miniature golf course, hiking trails, picnic grounds, and playgrounds with game courts.

The address is: North Bend State Park, Cairo, WV 26337. Phone: (304) 643-2931. The toll-free number from West Virginia is (800) 642-9058, and from nearby states (800) 624-8632.

Parkersburg: And a Famous Island

A couple of miles south of Parkersburg is a ridgetop offering a magnificent view of the valley. One pleasant summer evening we drove out on this ridge to the Point of View Restaurant (which we rate as excellent), and from our corner table in the glass-enclosed dining room we could see for miles. Upstream was Parkersburg with its bridges over the Ohio. Across from us on the Ohio side was Belpre, and beyond that the wooded green hills. Below us, in the middle of the river lay Blennerhassett, the most historic island in the valley, an island that became world famous during the 1800s.

In the late evening sun a large riverboat, pushing thirteen

Blennerhassett Island, site of a strange conspiracy, attracts boat-loads of visitors. (Blennerhassett Historical Park Commission photo)

heavily loaded coal barges, moved downstream on the south side of the island, while another pushed its barges upstream on the north side. At the upper end of the island a party boat moved out, and we could see the little sternwheeler plowing upstream in the sunset toward Parkersburg with its last load of passengers returning from Blennerhassett.

Going out to the island the next afternoon turned out to be easily arranged. At the point where the Little Kanawha enters the Ohio at Parkersburg, there is a ramp where the sternwheeler loads and unloads her passengers, and the captain was ready to depart. When the boat is in service, normally May through October on weekends and holidays, she leaves on the hour beginning at 1 P.M. and returns on the half hour.

Standing at the head of the ramp was Captain Everett Ruble, Jr. Selling tickets just inside the lower deck was his wife, and his son was at the wheel up in the pilothouse. The boat is Ruble's dream, and he built it himself in his back yard in Belpre. "It took eighteen months," he said. "It was just something I'd always wanted to do." He launched the boat in 1976 and for that reason called it the *Centennial.* She is rated to carry 125 passengers.

The *Centennial,* traveling at 6 miles an hour, moved off downstream and 20 minutes later eased into the landing at the island. Her passengers filed off. Some local people carried picnic baskets; other passengers were from out of town; visitors who wanted to tour the island.

Also aboard was Dr. Ray Swick, who must know more about Blennerhassett Island than anyone else alive does. When he was a small boy, living across the river in Belpre, the mysterious island haunted his thoughts. "When I was in the sixth grade," he told us, "I asked my father about the island. He said there was some kind of scandal connected with it." Young Ray Swick then talked to the local librarian and began to learn about the series of events that brought the island its notoriety.

This information was only the beginning for Swick. He later enrolled at Marietta College and continued his long search for more information about the island and the surrounding valley until he had earned two advanced degrees in history. Swick, who today is historian for the Blennerhassett Historical Park Commission, stood on the roots of the biggest tulip poplar tree we had

Beneath one of the world's largest tulip poplar trees, historian Dr. Ray Swick talks with visitors about Blennerhassett. (Photo by George Laycock)

ever seen and told the story of the island to the people assembled around him.

Harman Blennerhassett, an Irish aristocrat, was in disgrace with his family for marrying his niece, Margaret Agnew. In addition, he had earned disfavor for joining an outlawed political group fighting for the freedom of Ireland. Under pressure for these acts, Blennerhassett sold his estate and, with Margaret, left for America to begin a new life.

They arrived in New York in August 1796 with a retinue of servants and made their way across the mountains to Pittsburgh. The following summer they descended the river to Marietta.

With its cultivated New England settlers and its lovely surroundings, Marietta was charming to the Blennerhassetts who decided to look no further. Fourteen miles downstream, in the middle of the Ohio River, was an island for sale. Furthermore, the island was in Virginia, and here Blennerhassett could own the slaves he felt necessary for plantation life.

Blennerhassett's mansion, which took two years to complete, was overwhelming. The main house was two stories high and on each side there were rectangular wings connected to the main house by curved porticos. The entire front of the great white mansion measured 132 feet.

There was a parklike front lawn, and behind the house were extensive flower gardens with winding gravel paths leading to beautiful vistas. The mansion was as splendid inside as it was grand outside. Blennerhassett had spared no expense.

The first sight of the estate was breathtaking for settlers and travelers coming downriver. Visitors came from far and near and were always welcome. The word most often used to describe the island was "enchanted." But the enchantment was to be short lived.

Aaron Burr, the former Vice-President who had killed Alexander Hamilton in a duel, arrived here in 1805. Burr had been forced out of politics and was consumed by jealousy and frustrated ambition.

A few days later another Blennerhassett visitor was General Wilkinson on his way to St. Louis to become Governor of Upper Louisiana. Farther downstream, Burr and Wilkinson rendezvoused and plotted.

The next year the Blennerhassetts were drawn into Burr's web. His plan, it was believed, was to invade the Southwest or perhaps Mexico and set up a new country. But President Jefferson got wind of the plot and Burr was captured and tried for treason. The local Virginia militia took over the island, and the Blennerhassetts, with their two sons born on the island, fled to Louisiana. They had lost their fortune. They lived in Canada and finally went to England, where they died in poverty.

In 1811 their mansion was burned by slaves working on the island. Today the foundation has been excavated, and Ray Swick showed us where the building once stood. This and a few of the oldest trees are all that remain.

We hiked along the carriageway (called Lovers' Lane) to the interior of the island and viewed the site of the blockhouse where Harman and Margaret had lived before the mansion was finished. An abandoned old brick house stands here too. A farmer named Neale and his family lived here for many years. Now the island, owned by the Du Pont Company, is leased to the Blennerhassett Historical Park Commission. It is a state park and is on the National Register of Historic Places.

Plans call for added improvements that will make Blennerhassett Island increasingly interesting for those who want to come over for picnics and see where it was that the hapless Blennerhassett listened to the treasonous plans of Aaron Burr.

For information, call the Blennerhassett Historical Park Commission in Parkersburg, (304) 428-3000.

Early one morning we drove north out of Parkersburg, following Hwy. 14. This could be called a highway of artists. Don Whitlach has a gallery on highways 14 and 68 near downtown Parkersburg. In Vienna, just north of Grand Central Mall, which calls itself "The Showplace of West Virginia," is the Linda Myers Gallery. Prints and originals are for sale. And in Williamstown you will find the Marj Teague Art Gallery, where the artist sells originals, prints, and a large selection of West Virginia craft items.

At the Fenton Art Glass Company in Williamstown, visitors are led, in small groups, from the factory outlet store through the clean plant to see skilled workers turning out handmade glass objects. This is a very popular stop on a tour of the valley. And there are bargains in the outlet store. Upstairs is a museum of glass with a slide show about glassmaking.

In the city of Parkersburg there are several things of interest. On Juliann St. there is the Julia-ann Square Historical District, with old homes on the National Register of Historic Places. Nearby at 1334 Market St. is the Hills 'n' Hollows Gift Shop with West Virginia rural crafts for sale.

The City Park, a few blocks north of Hwy. 50, is a good place for a picnic. There's an entrance at Park and Seventeenth streets. You will find a lake, a swimming pool, and trails for jogging and bicycling. The Centennial Cabin and Museum in the park is open in the afternoons on Sundays and holidays, May to September.

City Park is the site for two festivals during the year. First is the West Virginia Honey Festival in mid-August. If you like honey, you'll love this festival with its homemade food and drinks prepared with honey. There are also exhibits, movies, a

Glass factories are popular tourist attractions in the Ohio Valley. This craftsman shapes glassware in the Fenton Art Glass Co. at Williamstown, West Virginia. (Photo by George Laycock)

10,000-meter "Honey Run," and the man with the honey-bee beard.

The other festival in City Park is the Harvest Moon Festival on the third weekend in September. Arts-and-crafts people from six states bring their displays and demonstrations. The Choral Society, Theatre Group, and dance groups all perform.

In the Grand Central Mall at Vienna, there is Eli's, if you want a pleasant spot for an inexpensive meal. Lodging and eating places in Parkersburg are concentrated at the junction of highways 50 and 77. But the best restaurant, as we said, and perhaps the most expensive, is the Point of View, on Ridge Hill Road, off Hwy. 68 south of town.

The captain and owner of the sternwheeler Centennial *built this boat in his back yard for hauling passengers to Blennerhassett Island.* (Photo by George Laycock)

Jackson County: And G.W.'s Lands

On the Fourth of July weekend each year, Ripley, the quiet county seat of Jackson County, West Virginia, awakens. More than one hundred artists and artisans—whittlers, stitchers, weavers, potters, glassblowers, and blacksmiths—invade Ripley for the huge annual Mountain State Art and Craft Fair just out-side town at Cedar Lakes. Visitors by the thousands gather from all parts of West Virginia and from surrounding states. Dancers and musicians stroll around the fairground performing for onlookers, while everyone enjoys the homemade ice cream, buck-wheat cakes, sausage, and West Virginia-style roast beef. In Ripley, McCoy's Best Western Motel, a favorite stop between Parkersburg and Charleston, and other motels fill to capacity.

One summer day we sought out the Armstrong House on North St., built in 1820 and on the National Register of Historic Places, then stopped at the public library searching for other points of in-terest in Jackson County. Dewitt Williams, who was in charge of the library that day, mentioned two things for which Jackson County is famous. "It was the scene of the last public hanging in West Virginia," he said, "and George Washington at one time owned a good part of the county."

Because the hanging of Morgan, a handyman who slew his em-ployer and her daughter by chopping them up with a hatchet, seemed no longer to be the tourist attraction it once was, we inquired about Washington's lands.

"Washington was an excellent judge of land," Williams told us. "He chose extensive bottomlands here as payment for his military services."

We drove down to Ravenswood, which was included in Wash-ington's holdings. This is a small river town, clean and prosper-

Craftsmen, musicians, and artists come from miles around to participate in the Annual Arts and Crafts Fair at Ripley, West Virginia. (Photograph by Tom Evans)

ous with some fine old homes. Down by the Ohio River, we found Washington's Lands Park where a two-story brick building that once served as the lockmaster's house is now the Washington's Lands Museum. The historic marker tells us that there was

These West Virginia ladies spin wool as their grandmothers did.
(Photograph by Gerald S. Ratliff)

a riffle at this point on the river, and that Indian bands and early white settlers used this spot to ford the stream. Also, during the War Between the States, a Confederate General and his men carried their flag across the river here on a short foray. The park also has a boat-launching ramp and picnic ground.

This is the scene, in mid-August, of the Ohio River Festival, Ravenswood's big event of the year.

About 3 miles north on Hwy. 68, stands Coleman Chapel, a

The annual New Martinsville Regatta is one of the popular boat-racing events on the Ohio River. (Photograph by Gerald S. Ratliff)

United Methodist Church, built in 1860, and on the National Register of Historic Places.

There are two covered bridges in Jackson County. One is on the Left Fork of Sandy Creek. If you're traveling I-77, use the Ravenswood exit, and go east to Hwy. 21, then left to the north side of Sandyville, and turn right on secondary road 15.

The other bridge is over Tug Fork Creek at Statts Mill—exit I-77 at Fair Plains, north to County Rd. 36, and east 5.3 miles to Statts Mill.

Mason County:
Beginning of a Revolution

When American colonists first engaged the British regulars at Lexington, Massachusetts, on April 19, 1775, the people of New England were quick to proclaim this "shot heard round the world" as the first battle of the Revolution. There was no way they could know that the honor would eventually be claimed for a battle six months earlier far to the west on the banks of the Ohio. Today the site of this historic battle on the Ohio is a shrine visited by thousands of people every year.

The Kanawha River, a major Ohio River tributary formed by the New and Gauley rivers, reaches back into the mountains, and comes down through Charleston, the capital city of West Virginia, to empty into the Ohio at Point Pleasant. Travelers crossing the high bridge over the Kanawha River into Point Pleasant, see a towering marble monument in a little green park where the two rivers meet. This, say many historians, is really where the first battle of the Revolution was fought.

Lord Dunmore was Governor of Virginia from 1771 to 1776, and his loyalties naturally lay with the British king who appointed him. He may have viewed conflict between the Indians and colonists as one way to keep the colonists from uprising against Great Britain.

Lord Dunmore ordered that an army be recruited for a march to the mouth of the Kanawha, and there this division, led by General Andrew Lewis, was to join with another force commanded by Dunmore himself. Then the combined army would cross the Ohio to attack the Shawnees in their own territory.

Lord Dunmore, however, instead of going to the Kanawha, struck out into Indian country north of the Ohio, where he went into conference with the Indians. At about the same time, on Oc-

The military engagement at Point Pleasant is said to have been the first battle of the Revolution. (Photo by George Laycock)

tober 10, 1774, Chief Cornstalk, aware that the forces of the "long knives" were now divided, led some 1,100 warriors from several federated tribes across the river to attack Lewis. After a bloody all-day battle, much of it hand-to-hand fighting, many on both sides lay dead and dying on the point of land at the mouth of the Kanawha.

After defeating Chief Cornstalk, Lewis and his Virginia recruits marched north toward the Indian country, disillusioned completely with Governor Dunmore. The Governor, who claimed to be working out a treaty with the Indians, learned of Lewis's approach and dispatched a messenger ordering Lewis to turn back. Instead, Lewis became the first American officer to defy a direct order of a superior British officer. He marched on.

Because Dunmore was now considered by Lewis to be an enemy of Virginia, Lewis made no direct report of the battle at Point Pleasant. But others wrote of it, among them Colonel John Stuart who fought there. "The battle of Point Pleasant," he wrote, "was, in fact, the beginning of the Revolutionary War that obtained for our country the liberty and independence enjoyed by the United States."

Today this historic battlesite is maintained by West Virginia as Tu-Endie-Wei Park, the Indian name said to have meant "mingling of the waters." Commanding this 2-acre park is a granite shaft 84 feet high, the Point Pleasant Battle Monument so often photographed by modern tourists.

Here also, overlooking the Ohio, is the first building in Mason County made of hewn logs. The 1796 building, known as the Mansion House, stands on its original site in remarkably solid condition nearly two centuries after Walter Newman erected it as a tavern. The museum, managed by the local chapter of the DAR, contains an excellent collection of old dishes and colonial furniture as well as Indian artifacts.

The park at Point Pleasant is open free of charge from early spring to late fall.

Four miles north of Point Pleasant, off Hwy. 62 and across from the Mason County Fairgrounds is the Mason County Regional State Farm Museum where Walden F. Roush leads a little group of volunteers in efforts to preserve the tools and techniques known to yesterday's farm families. Roush grew up on a farm nearby then went on to become a school teacher and County Superintendent of Schools. After his retirement, he started work on a project he had long planned. "We were losing our farm heritage," Roush explained, as we sat at a table on which he had spread articles and pictures about the museum. "In 1975, we organized a nonprofit corporation to start working on a farm museum. I told them, 'We are fifty years late, but not too late.'"

The Mason County Commission provided 50 acres of land adjacent to the Fairgrounds. Word went out. Donations of tools and pioneer furniture began to arrive.

First, a large metal building was completed to house many of the antiques. There are hundreds of antique farm tools as well as old steam engines and collections of ancient musical instruments and tools used by carpenters and coopers.

Another building is a Blacksmith Shop. A blacksmith works here when the museum is open. This is one of the best-equipped shops anywhere.

There are 24 buildings on the museum grounds; 3 of them are restored log buildings. One of the log structures is a replica of the earliest Lutheran Church west of the Alleghenies where Mason County pioneers worshipped. There is also the Mission Ridge one-room schoolhouse, complete with all fixtures including textbooks. Another building contains Morgan's Museum, a collection of stuffed animals.

The museum has a country kitchen where farm meals are still prepared and served on special occasions.

Roush says, "A farm museum should be more than a collection of antique tools. It should preserve the methods practiced by our ancestors, and that's why we have several events throughout the year that make this a living, working museum." These demonstrations include: grinding sorghum in the museum's mill, then boiling down the syrup; local women assemble to make apple butter; the museum grows grain crops, which it then harvests with antique equipment and threshes by a stream-driven thresher. "We want the old methods to come to life," Roush explains.

The annual list of special events includes shooting matches by muzzle-loading rifle clubs. Or there may be demonstrations with the livestock kept on the grounds, including Jerry and Buck, the oxen, or the giant Belgian gelding, "General," standing 19½ hands high.

A favorite time to visit the Farm Museum is the second week in August during the Mason County Fair, the biggest county fair in West Virginia.

A Country Festival is held the first weekend in October when cider and apple butter are made, and visitors square dance to country music. The first weekend in May brings the Antique Steam and Gasoline Engine Show with bluegrass music, pioneer crafts, and country foods.

On any of these special days Roush's wife, Louise, may be

found heading up a crew of volunteer cooks in the Country Kitchen, where emphasis is on old-time West Virginia foods. The following recipes are a few of the favorites from Louise B. Roush.

CORN BREAD

2 cups corn meal	3 tblsp. sugar
1 cup flour	2 eggs, beaten
4 tsp. baking powder	2 cups milk
¼ tsp. salt	

Mix all together. Bake 20 to 25 minutes at 400 degrees. A little more milk can be added if mixture seems too stiff. Bake in a 9 × 12 pan.

PINTO BEAN PIE

1 unbaked pie shell	3 eggs, beaten
1 cup mashed pinto beans	1 tsp. nutmeg
1 cup sugar	2 tblsp. melted butter

Mash beans well. Mix nutmeg with sugar and add to beans. Stir in beaten eggs and mix well. Add butter, pour into unbaked pie shell. Bake at 350 degrees for 45 to 50 minutes (until inserted toothpick comes out clean).

CORN MEAL PIE

2 unbaked pie shells	8 tblsp. corn meal
1 cup butter	3 tblsp. flour
2 cups sugar	1 cup milk
3 eggs	1 tsp. vanilla

Mix all ingredients and bring to a boil, stirring constantly. Boil 3 minutes. Pour into pie shells and bake at 375 degrees for 35 to 40 minutes.

The Farm Museum is normally open every weekend, but visitors at other times will be led through the exhibits by Roush or other volunteers if they call in advance. Admission is free. Phone: (304) 675-2834.

Accommodations

Mason County has facilities for travelers. There is lodging on Hwy. 62 a short distance north of Point Pleasant. Campers can find space at Krodel Park on highways 2 and 62 east of town. There are full hookups for RVs, and there are fishing, swimming, and game areas. A more rustic campground is located on the Chief Cornstalk Public Hunting and Fishing Area maintained by West Virginia's Division of Wildlife. Four and a half miles from Point Pleasant on Hwy. 35, turn right at Beech Hill at entrance to Cornstalk Area. There is good pond fishing here, and hunters use the area in season for hunting deer and grouse.

Huntington: River City with Class

Huntington, in Cabell County, is West Virginia's largest city, an attractive municipality of 68,000, where it is remarkably easy to find your way around. The streets run north and south, the avenues east and west, and all of them are wide thoroughfares that cross at right angles with few of those tortuous routes or multiple junctions found in many river cities.

Huntington makes no claim to being a venerable city in the valley. The earliest settlement here was Holderby's Landing where a few people lived by selling supplies to the riverboat crews. In 1869 Collis P. Huntington arrived, leading a survey party. Huntington, a civil engineer, drew up his plan for the city with its wide streets and parklands.

The arrival of the railroads brought prosperity, and within four years after Huntington arrived, 4,000 people lived in his town. Huntington later became president of the Chesapeake & Ohio Railroad. Coal, natural gas, and river shipping nourished the economy. Today Huntington has 400 plants whose products include metal alloys, railroad cars, chemicals, glassware, furniture, clothing, and electrical equipment.

Even before Huntington was here, there was Marshall University, which was founded in 1837 as Marshall Academy and named for Supreme Court Justice, John Marshall. Today Marshall University's campus covers 50 acres where 11,800 students work toward degrees in many fields, including medicine. The university brings the Huntington area important cultural and sports events.

Instead of tearing down old landmarks, Huntington converts them into cultural and historic community assets. A visit to Heritage Village emphasizes the point. Heritage Village, at Eleventh St. and Veteran's Memorial Blvd., is built around the old Baltimore & Ohio passenger station. The depot has been converted to a fine restaurant where we arrived one day at lunchtime. Cold beer is drunk from frosted pint jars; the Reuben sandwiches rate a ten. We also sampled the open-face crabmeat sandwiches with cheese sauce, served with fresh fruit. The food ranks with the best we've found up and down the valley. This is a popular stop in Huntington for both lunch and dinner.

Outside the station, railroad engines and cars are on permanent display, and around the courtyard are old freight warehouses that are now shops and galleries. Another of these buildings is the old Bank of Huntington, which opened in 1875.

Every town has its cherished memories, and Huntington has never quite forgotten the excitement created when members of the James Gang came to town two months after the bank opened. At the time, the Methodists were holding a conference in the church at Fourth Ave. and Tenth St., and strangers were arriving so frequently that the gang members were viewed as four more Methodists.

At noon on Monday, when cashier Robert Oney was alone in the bank, two of the gang sauntered into the building, vaulted the counter, and pointed their six-shooters at Oney's head, leaving him little choice but to hand them the money bags. Soon after the quartet of robbers rode out of town, a determined posse, led by the bank president, pursued them, spurring their West Virginia mounts to such speeds that the James Gang may have developed a new respect for mountaineer horsemen. Two of the robbers es-

This statue of Huntington's founder stands on Heritage Square.
(Photo by George Laycock)

caped and made their way back to Missouri. A third, however, was mortally wounded while being chased through Kentucky. The fourth was captured in Tennessee and spent the next twelve years in the West Virginia Penitentiary. Thereafter, the James Gang seems to have lost its stomach for robbing banks in West Virginia or elsewhere in the East. The bank the James Gang robbed is now an ice-cream parlor in Heritage Village.

The most popular city park in Huntington is Ritter Park, 150 acres of fields and woods south of town, a favorite place for strolling through the famous rose garden, picnicking, jogging, or playing tennis. Huntington has other parks, including Wallace Park, Memorial Park, and Rotary Park.

This is a good city for golfers too. There are 12 golf courses spotted on the hillsides around Huntington, all within a 15-minute drive of the downtown area. The Huntington Convention and Visitors' Bureau offers a list of golf courses. Phone: (304) 525-5131.

Boating is big here; outboards and sailboats launch on Beech Fork Lake in the nearby state park and on the Ohio River. These are also excellent fishing waters.

The Ohio Valley is not among the nation's top skiing areas, but skiers in Huntington find ski slopes within half an hour of downtown.

For the roller-coaster crowd there is Camden Park, reached by following Hwy. 60 west of town a short distance. In addition to rides and other attractions, the park has an Ohio River landing where the paddlewheel-driven *Camden Queen* is docked and from which she makes 1-hour tours several times a day (except Monday) from May through Labor Day. The phone number at Camden Park is: (304) 429-4231.

Huntington Galleries is a major cultural center. Works of art are displayed in its 10 exhibition rooms. There are also studio workshops for classes, a 300-seat auditorium, museum store, a sculpture garden, and 2½ miles of nature trails. The Huntington Chamber Orchestra performs here. There are special exhibits of regional art and each summer an invitational exhibit of handmade glass.

Other cultural attractions include regular performances of the Greater Huntington Symphonic Band and the Community Players, a dramatics group.

For the events that draw truly large crowds, name performers, visiting rodeos, the circus, trade shows, or the annual Dogwood Arts and Crafts Festival held each spring, Huntington has a new Civic Center downtown.

Dining Out

Huntington has excellent places for dining out, and the following are special favorites:

Club Pompeii and Holderby's Landing at the Holiday Inn Convention Center, 1033 Third Ave.

Heritage Station, Eleventh St. and Veteran's Memorial Blvd. Especially sandwiches, soups, salads, cheesecake.

The Ma-Kiki Club, 3325 Hwy. 60E. Polynesian restaurant, local residents recommend.

Ming's Restaurant, Fourth Ave. and Tenth St., in the Frederick Building. A favorite for Chinese food.

Rebels & Redcoats Tavern, named as one of the 10 best restaurants in West Virginia, 625 W. Fifth St. Seafoods and steak.

Upstairs Rooms & Fine Accessory Shop, 1426 Third Ave.

The Mountaineer Dinner Theatre is at 3973 Teays Valley Road, Hurricane, WV.

The big concentration of motels serving the Huntington area is on Hwy. 60E. Several other motels and hotels are downtown, including the Holiday Inn-Downtown.

The Blenko Glass Co. factory showroom at Milton is a popular West Virginia tourist attraction. (Photo by George Laycock)

This part of the state maintains West Virginia's reputation as the leading center for handmade glassware. There are two glass factories in Cabell County. One is Viking Glass Company's Plant No. 2 at 1500 Adams St. or Hwy. 60 just off I-64, Huntington. The other is the Blenko Glass Co. at Milton, east of Huntington off highways 60 and I-64. Both offer visitors the opportunity to see craftsmen at work blowing glass. The Blenko Visitors' Center has a special display of stained glass.

A quarter of a mile from the Blenko Glass Visitors' Center is an old covered bridge. This red covered bridge across the Mud River remains in use and is in excellent condition. It is 112 feet long and was built in 1875, following a design by the bridge engineer William Howe.

Up the Road

Charleston—The Capital City

On the edge of the historic Kanawha River, 35 miles south of Ripley is West Virginia's sparkling capital city, Charleston. The city is easily reached either from the north by following the scenic I-77 south from Ripley, through steep timbered hills, or from the west by traveling I-64 from Huntington 50 miles away.

Two of the major attractions in Charleston are on the Capitol grounds. The most prominent of these is the impressive Capitol building standing on Kanawha Blvd. East. The golden dome of the Capitol is visible from a distance as you approach the center of the city. Inside this building, designed by the architect Cass Gilbert, visitors stand looking up at the rotunda and the massive 2-ton chandelier made of 3,300 pieces of hand-cut Czechoslovakian crystal. There is a guide service and visiting the Capitol is free.

The other outstanding tourist attraction on the Capitol grounds is the Science and Culture Center at Greenbrier and Washington streets, housing the state library, archives, and museum with displays of Civil War materials, as well as a settler's cabin and country store. There is also a craft shop open daily in the Center.

Coonskin Park, near the airport, covers 1,000 acres and has a driving range, skeet shooting, trails, and horseback riding.

Sunrise, 746 Myrtle Rd., is a restored mansion featuring a collection of artworks, garden center, live animal display for children, films, and planetarium. Admission is charged for the planetarium, but other exhibits are free.

Charleston has a wide range of attractions for those interested in ballet, opera, symphony, and theater. Details available from Kanawha Arts Alliance. Phone: (304) 744-5301.

West Virginia's Capitol building in Charleston. (Photo by George Laycock)

Wayne County: Two Lakes

From Huntington downriver into Wayne County, the traveler is in the hills at once—steep hills covered with hardwood forests and narrow hollows through which little creeks run. Highway 152 is a scenic route following Twelvepole Creek into Wayne, the county seat, population about 1,500.

The courthouse sits in the middle of town, and a friendly lady there thought the person most likely to have answers to our questions would be Otis Skeans, the Mayor of Wayne. We soon discovered that Skeans, who also heads up the Chamber of Commerce, might be any of several places including his restaurant, his office in the little white City Hall, his home on the edge of Wayne, or any number of businesses where he might have chores to do or people to see. We pursued him from one place to the other, "just missing Otis" at every stop until, on the third trip back to the City Hall, we reached him on the telephone and he said, "Just stay right there and I'll come over." He arrived carrying a circular with advertisements in it from all the local businessmen and some editorial material on the advantages of Wayne to any industry that might discover it. (None has.) There was a picture of the dedication of the new swimming pool with Mayor Skeans being pushed in, clothes and all. "I think they had it all planned." A broad grin lighted up the round face of the mayor.

The mayor believes Wayne County is a healthful place to live. One of his neighbor ladies he said was 103 years old and still going strong. We asked about historic old homes in the area. "They're all old," the mayor said, laughing, "but I don't know that any of 'em's historic."

Wayne County, however, has appeal to visitors, and two of the biggest attractions are the lakes. "Both of 'em has good fishing," said the mayor, "and lots of folks use them."

Beech Fork Lake is just north of Wayne. A Corps of Engineers impoundment, it offers fishing, boating, swimming, and camping. There are also picnic areas. Beech Fork has 720 surface acres and a 31-mile shoreline in summer. In winter it is drawn down about 6 feet to allow storage space for flood waters.

About 10 miles southeast of Wayne, off Hwy. 37, the traveler comes to East Lynn Lake backed up behind an earthen dam 133 feet high and 652 feet long, another Corps of Engineers structure. East Lynn Lake, on the east fork of Twelvepole Creek, is 12 miles long. You may swim, fish, boat, camp, and picnic here.

Cabwaylingo State Forest is located in the southern part of Wayne County on Hwy. 152 near Dunlow. There are 13 standard cabins for rent, fully equipped. Advance reservations are necessary. The toll-free number inside West Virginia is: (800) 642-9058. The number from surrounding states (Indiana, Ohio, Kentucky, Pennsylvania, western New York, Maryland, Virginia, New Jersey, Delaware, the Carolinas, and Washington D.C.) is: (800) 624-8632.

Ceredo, off Hwy. I-64 west of Huntington in Wayne County, is widely known as a center of glassmaking. The Pilgrim Glass Corporation is located here adjacent to the Huntington Airport, and thousands of tourists stop at the plant's visitors' center each year. Tours are anytime during working hours, and they start whenever visitors arrive.

At roadside stands, like this one on the banks of Twelvepole Creek, near Wayne, West Virginia, farmers offer pumpkins, apples, honey, and cider for sale. (Photo by George Laycock)

Fishing the Ohio

Early settlers drifting down the broad Ohio were struck with
the natural beauty and the wildlife on shore, but they also wrote
of giant catfish thumping against their flatboats at night until they
could not sleep. There were also bass, pike, and other species of
fish. The waters were still clean, and because they were fast moving, they were rich in the life-giving oxygen needed by game fish.

The river changed as the human population grew throughout
the watershed. And as surely as the water quality was altered, so
was the list of fish living in it. But in recent decades there has
been a campaign to clean up the river. The result is that today
fishing in the Ohio River, although different from what it once

*Fishing is good in the Ohio River and biologists say the big
stream is underfished.* (Photo by George Laycock)

was, remains excellent both for the number of species caught and total pounds that can be taken.

One of the big appeals is that here is a major river that is *underfished*. Biologists working with the Ohio River say so, and the fact that there are few fishermen on the Ohio is evident to those traveling the valley. As a result, those who fish find unlimited opportunities along the Ohio and in the mouths of its tributaries where fish seem to concentrate. As Arnold Mitchell, a sport fisherman and former commissioner for fish and game for the state of Kentucky, told us, "We feel that the Ohio has a lot of good fishing going to waste."

Kentucky, which owns three fourths of the Ohio River, has worked for years to bring these waters to the attention of more anglers. The state fisheries people have stocked rockfish, and on occasion these giants are caught.

But the species commonly sought by Ohio River fishermen are black bass. Some anglers go especially for catfish, crappie, or sauger. Sauger is a member of the pike family and often caught

Because of the new high-level pools, fishing is especially good in the mouths of tributary streams. (Photo by George Laycock)

below the dams. Ohio River bass fishing has become productive enough to attract fishing tournaments in which the professionals compete.

You need a fishing license for fishing the Ohio River, and the license required depends on the part of the river you fish. As we traveled the valley, working on this book, the legal standing of the Ohio River was in question. Historically, it belonged to Virginia as far as the low-water mark on the north shore, which meant that Kentucky and West Virginia, when carved out of Old Virginia, inherited the Ohio River for its entire length. But the new high-level dams moved the low-water mark up onto land that had belonged to Ohio, Indiana, and Illinois, and until this question of ownership is settled once and for all—if it ever is—the fisherman puzzled by how to fish the Ohio River legally should inquire in the nearest county courthouse along the river. Find the local conservation officer, or check with operators of sporting goods stores and fishing docks.

West Virginia and Kentucky fishing licenses will continue to cover the situation in their respective states. These states have long offered non-residents a special Ohio River Fishing License that sells for less than the state-wide fishing licenses. On the north shore, fishing from the bank is legal, providing the angler has a current fishing license from the state in which he or she stands.

Kentucky

Boyd County: Mountain Music

Catlettsburg, Kentucky, is a town of 3,000 on Hwy. 23, a short distance from the West Virginia line. Industry is concentrated around the mouth of the Big Sandy and for 10 miles or so up the river along Hwy. 23. Catlettsburg is an old town and was once the largest timber center in the world. One of the most historic buildings here is the old bank building which now serves as the home of WCAK radio.

Catlettsburg, each year, has a Fourth of July Celebration and Homecoming, which is a major event of the year.

Lakewood Village, Kentucky's only ski resort, is located outside Catlettsburg. Drive south from I-64 at the Cannonsburg exit to Hwy. 3N. Skiing lessons and rental equipment are available.

Although Catlettsburg is the county seat of Boyd County, Ashland, 5 miles down the Ohio River, is the largest population center in eastern Kentucky. The Poage brothers arrived here from Virginia in 1815, settled on land where the center of Ashland now stands, and this was the beginning of the city. From its early days this region became important for iron, charcoal, and lumber, followed in recent years by steel, petroleum, and chemical products.

In 1978 The Appalachian Heritage Park opened on the south edge of Ashland, on McCullough Drive off Hwy. 60, to preserve the works of Jean Thomas who gained fame by traveling through the hills and recording mountain music before radio and television invaded every hollow. The mountain people of eastern Kentucky played fiddles, dulcimers, banjos, and guitars, and sang ancient ballads brought from England, Ireland, and Scotland by their ancestors. Jean Thomas played and sang, but in addition she wanted to preserve the Appalachian music. She traveled around the hills so much that she was known among mountain people as "The Traipsin' Woman." Her home was in Ashland, where she lived beyond her hundredth birthday.

As The Traipsin' Woman grew older, she worried about the possible loss of the music she had preserved, and the Ashland Foundation created the Jean Thomas Museum as part of the Appalachian Heritage Park. The museum is as nearly like Jean Thomas' home as it could be made with her furniture and possessions, musical instruments, notes, and the nine books she authored.

For more than thirty years Jean Thomas organized an annual folk song festival that brought crowds of visitors and widespread attention to Ashland. The last of these festivals was held in 1972. In recent times leaders in Ashland have reorganized the American Folk Song Festival as an annual event.

Also being developed at Appalachian Heritage Park is a reconstructed one-room log schoolhouse, the McGuffey School Museum, housing McGuffey's books and furnished with typical early school furniture.

At Central Ave. and Seventeenth St., in the heart of Ashland, Central Park covers about 50 acres. Within this park there are half a dozen Indian burial mounds.

In Ashland the place to attend music and dramatic presentations is the Paramount Art Center downtown at Thirteenth St. and Winchester Ave. This Art Deco movie palace, built in 1930–31, has been renovated by the Greater Ashland Foundation.

There are many historic old homes in Ashland, homes built by early leaders in the iron and coal industries. These are occupied, but a map for a walking tour of the area where the old homes are concentrated is available at the public library. These homes, on the National Register of Historic Places, are concentrated along several blocks of Bath Ave. between Thirteenth and Seventeenth streets.

Several noteworthy restaurants are in Ashland. One is the

Camelot, a supper club and lounge serving prime rib, steaks, and seafood at 2275 Winchester Ave. Another is the Chimney Corner at 1624 Carter Ave., where southern fried chicken is a specialty, as well as steaks and seafood.

Greenup County: Hiking Trails

All the way across northern Greenup County the major highway, U.S. 23, flanks the Ohio with a divided 4-lane thoroughfare allowing occasional glimpses of the river through the trees. Greenup is a little rural county-seat town with its full quota of pickup trucks parked along the street. There are several fine old homes along the two blocks of Front St. facing the Ohio River.

In a branch of the county library across from the courthouse we searched for details of the Jenny Wiley story.

Jenny Wiley would never have guessed that one day there would be a splendid mountain hiking trail named for her or that two hundred years later people would remember her adventure.

Jenny was at home in the family cabin in Virginia, alone except for her children, when the Indians came. The Indians massacred the Wiley children, then dragged Jenny off through the forest to slavedom. Months later she escaped and slipped back along the woodland trails to a reunion with her husband. The Jenny Wiley story has since been told and retold.

When hikers and backpackers of Kentucky began surveying the mountains for suitable trails they naturally enough scouted out the return route Jenny Wiley followed. Through the remote hollows and along the ridges they obtained easements from landowners allowing hikers to pass through country that most people never see.

When the Jenny Wiley Trail opened, after five years of work, there were trailside shelters every 10 miles or so along the entire 180 miles, and trees were blazed with blue paint to keep hikers on their route. The trail begins at South Portsmouth, Kentucky, across the river from Portsmouth, Ohio, and winds through the mountains south to Jenny Wiley State Park near Prestonburg.

In addition, there is a connecting trail linking the Jenny Wiley Trail with Greenbo Lake State Resort Park. This link is the Michael Tygart Trail, and it is blazed in yellow. Meanwhile, the Simon Kenton Trail, blazed in white, connects the Jenny Wiley with Carter Caves State Resort Park.

Jenny Wiley needed nine days to hike the length of the Jenny Wiley Trail, but thirty-five-year-old Carl Curnutte, an Ashland, Kentucky, scoutmaster, made it in seven days hiking alone at a leisurely pace. Curnutte reported scenic overlooks, acres of wild flowers, and rock gorges. "It's rough terrain south of Route 7," said Curnutte. "You start running ridge lines all the way into Jenny Wiley State Park." Write Jenny Wiley Trails Conference, Trail Director, c/o FIVCO, P. O. Box 636, Catlettsburg, KY 41129.

In Greenup County, the major attraction is Greenbo Lake State Resort Park, 8 miles southwest of Greenup on Hwy. 1. We talked with the Park Superintendent, Kelly Newton, who told us about a

This nature preserve is maintained in W Hollow, Greenup County, Kentucky, as a monument to Jesse Stuart who grew up here and became one of the state's most honored authors. (Photo by George Laycock)

recent "Ski Weekend" when there was no snow and temperatures were a springlike 50 degrees. "I'm beginning to think we'll have to change the name," he said seriously. "We've had snow only one weekend the first three years we've had our ski weekend." But people came anyhow. They hiked the trails, enjoyed the Saturday night meal that has become a local tradition, and listened to bluegrass music. "We fed four hundred," said Newton. This Chuckwagon Dinner, with bluegrass music is held every Saturday evening, the year around.

The rooms of the lodge at Greenbo are generally booked full on weekends and through the summer and fall. There is a Class-A campground with 63 RV sites, and an adjoining campground where the facilities are slightly more primitive and the prices a dollar less per night. There is nearly always room, at least in the "primitive" campground, and according to the official Kentucky Campground Directory, this is the only camping place in Greenup County.

Greenbo's visitors hike trails that range in length from 1 to 7 miles. They play tennis and swim, use the miniature golf course, and go horseback riding. They also fish the 225-acre Greenbo Lake which, Kelly Newton tells us proudly, yielded the state record largemouth bass, a 13-pound 8-ounce fish that fell to local fisherman Delbert Grizzle in August 1966.

Address: Greenbo Lake Resort Park, Greenup, KY 41144. Phone: (606) 473-7324.

The best-known citizen of Greenup County, and perhaps of all Kentucky, is author Jesse Stuart, whose home is in W Hollow just over the hills from Greenbo State Park. Stuart grew up in this hollow and returned to buy up most of it with the earnings from his prolific writings. Among his fifty books are such titles as *Taps for Private Tussie, Man with the Bull-tongue Plow,* and *The Thread that Runs So True,* which is the widely translated story of Jesse Stuart's years of teaching in local schools.

A foundation now manages W Hollow as the Jesse Stuart Nature Preserve where future generations will see a corner of Eastern Kentucky reverting to the way this land looked before the arrival of Jesse Stuart's ancestors. A 3-mile loop trail begins at Charlies Cabin, and an 8-mile foot trail connects W Hollow with

Greenbo State Park. Maps are available at the park. A narrow paved road runs the length of W Hollow between Hwy. 1 and Hwy. 2 to the west, and signs mark it on both of these highways.

From Greenbo State Park we drove out Hwy. 1 to the Old Town Covered Bridge, spanning the Little Sandy River. The bridge, built in 1880, still rests on its original stone piers and carries traffic daily. It is on the National Register of Historic Places.

This country was famous in the 1800s for its iron furnaces, and plaques along the country roads tell the stories of these furnaces. The remains of an old stone furnace still stands near the campground in Greenbo State Park.

Up the Road

Another of Kentucky's famous state parks, Carter Caves State Resort Park is within an easy drive of Greenbo. The lodge, open the year around, has 28 rooms with wall-to-wall carpeting, color television, and air-conditioning. There are, in addition, 8 fully equipped efficiency cottages set back among the trees, plus a campground with sites for 86 recreational vehicles or tents, all with electric and water hookups.

Carter Caves covers 1,239 acres laced with several miles of trails. The 9-hole regulation golf course offers rental clubs and carts year around. There are tennis courts. Lodge and cabin guests have the use of a swimming pool, and there is a community pool ¼ mile from the campground.

A big attraction here are the caves. Cave tours are organized at the Trading Post.

Nearby Tygarts Creek is a popular canoe stream, and canoe trips are organized by the park. Tygarts Creek is a favorite for catching muskies and bass.

Carter Caves State Resort Park is 4 miles north of I-64, and 8 miles from Olive Hill, Kentucky, on Hwy. 182. Address: Carter Caves State Resort Park, Olive Hill, KY 41164. Phone: (606) 286-4411.

The Quiet of Lewis County

Those who feel a need to escape the fast-paced tempo of crowded cities should travel to Vanceburg. It is the county seat of Lewis County, which stretches for 40 miles along the south shore of the Ohio River. This is peaceful country, perhaps too peaceful for some tastes.

On the courthouse lawn in Vanceburg you can photograph the only monument south of the Ohio River dedicated to Union troops. Then you can drive out Hwy. 984 to see the old covered bridge where it has stood over Cabin Creek since 1875.

If you are checking out old homes, look up the Sexton House in Tollesboro. Magistrate Isele Grigsby built this house in the 1840s. The old Halbert House, 827 Front St., in Vanceburg was once the boys' dormitory for Riverside Seminary.

Lewis County may be best known for Kinniconick Creek, home of a freshwater fish that grows large enough to scare people. The fish is a species of pike, the muskellunge, ordinarily called "musky." Not until one of these fish is 30 inches long is it a legal-sized keeper, and it needs nearly five years to reach this length. The official state-record musky weighed 43 pounds, and there is evidence that Kentucky waters have yielded much larger muskies that were never officially recognized. Some years ago a fisherman showed me a mounted specimen of a 51-pound musky taken from the Little Barren River.

Even this fish might not be the state's largest. One Kentuckian told me, "Hell, there's been a lot caught bigger than that." The Kentucky musky fisherman is caught between a rock and a hard place. On the one hand, he never shrinks a fish, especially a musky. On the other, he really doesn't want word to get out that there are trophy fish of these proportions lurking in Kentucky waters.

Biologists studying Kentucky's fisheries have found muskies living in all the long pools of Kinniconick Creek, and fishermen come here trying to tempt the surly giants to attack oversized plugs or spinning lures. But the musky is reluctant to do this, so a confirmed musky fisherman may cast all day without a strike, then go back and cast all day tomorrow. I once had a musky simply come out and follow the lure on a pool in Kinniconick and even that was unforgettable.

The problem with fishing for the muskies of Kinniconick is gaining access. There are places where country roads cross the creek. If these locations are not posted against trespass, fishermen use them as access. But the safest plan is to ask permission of the landowner.

The fisherman nursing an unfulfilled urge to catch a musky may stand a better chance at Cave Run Lake about 40 miles south of Vanceburg near Morehead. A Kentucky biologist told us, "Cave Run is the best bet by far." The state stocks it each year. Cave Run has launching ramps, marinas, and musky-fishing guides.

Muskies have suffered from impoundments, pollution, and overfishing. Other Kentucky waters where these trophy fish still live include Tygarts Creek, the Little Sandy River, Red River, Licking River (including Cave Run Lake), North Fork of Triplett Creek, Station Camp Creek, Sturgeon Creek, parts of the Kentucky River, Barren River, and 130 miles of the Green River.

Bluegills are better to eat. So what do you do with a musky? Most fishermen release them, quickly and gently—after they've had a picture taken.

Mason County: Early Kentucky

Maysville is a picturesque old town that resembles a village along the Rhine.

There are really two Maysvilles—the old and the new. And Maysville is proud of its past. Drive toward the city from north, east, or west, and you see none of the shopping centers or fast-food franchises that stamp so many American cities into similar molds. Maysville has them, but they are hidden beyond the crest of the hill that forms the backdrop for the historic downtown section. There is little room for expansion in the narrow flood plain between the Ohio River and the hill; it is already crowded with beautiful old buildings. Behind the downtown streets on terraced hillsides, stand historic mansions commanding sweeping views of the river and the Ohio hills beyond.

The iron railings and ornamentation on the old buildings have a story to tell. Maysville was once a bustling center of shipping and trade; a market for tobacco and cotton. Steamboats from Pittsburgh, St. Louis, and New Orleans tied up at Maysville docks for loading and unloading. The iron balconies reflect a New Orleans influence brought to Maysville by riverboat captains and other travelers.

Architectural students come to Maysville to study the buildings. It is said that examples of all periods of American architecture are found here. There are Spanish, French, English, and German cultural influences to be noted.

Visitors can stop at the Chamber of Commerce, 115 E. Third St., for a tour map. We found the best place to begin a tour is the Mason County Museum, 215 Sutton St. The museum was built about 1876, and is on the Register of Historic Places. There are genealogical records and rare books upstairs, displays, dioramas, and slide presentations on the ground floor.

The Public Library next door has a collection of rare books of local history. The library also displays a self-portrait of Aaron Corwine, a famous artist born here.

The house on the corner is "Phillips' Folly," so called because William B. Phillips ran out of money in 1824 before he finished it. Legend has it that he recouped his fortune by gambling and completed the house in 1828.

The Sheriff's Office on Third St., built prior to 1817, was the home of Pleasant H. Baird, a jeweler in early Maysville.

Next is "Old Tip" on the courthouse lawn. Old Tip is a cannon, brought back from the Battle of Tippecanoe after the War of 1812. The gun was infamous for kicking so hard when fired that it injured several men. So it was retired to the courthouse lawn where it served as a hitching post.

The courthouse, with towering white columns, was built in 1844, as the Maysville City Hall. Four years later the county seat of Mason County was moved from Washington to Maysville, and city hall became the Mason County Courthouse. Check your watch against the clock in the tower. The clock was built by a Flemingsburg blacksmith in 1850, using wooden parts, and it still runs.

On the corner of Court and Third streets stands the Presbyterian Church. It was erected in 1850. In 1854 an explosion half a mile away knocked a hole in the side of the new church, and the hole can still be seen.

Beyond the church is Olde Mechanics Row, built about 1850 by John Armstrong who came here as a peddler, liked the bustling little city, and stayed to make his fortune. Note the iron grillwork. These row houses were built for tradespeople and artisans.

The Rev. Edgar House across Third St. was built in the 1820s of logs and later covered with clapboards.

The Dr. John Shackleford House was built as an office for an early Maysville physician, before 1850.

West of the bank is the Isaiah Wilson House, built in 1824. The Rhoden Hord House next door was built in 1822, and is the oldest brick house in the block.

The A. M. January House was built in 1838 and is still occupied by the builder's descendants. Farther west on Third St. is the Dr. Louis Frazee House, built in 1856 as a home and office.

The George Cox-Russell House, an American Romanesque, built in 1888, is on E. Third St., just east of Market St.

At 128 E. Third St. stands the Cox-Hord House, built in 1880 by Andrew T. Cox. In 1886, Cox Row was built on Market St. between Third and Fourth streets.

More recently Maysville was the girlhood home of singer and actress Rosemary Clooney. The world premier of her first movie was held here in 1953, and Maysville changed the name of Lower Street where the Clooney house stands, to Rosemary Clooney Street.

Maysville's most famous restaurant is Caproni's down by the river near the railroad station. It is a favorite with local people and visitors alike.

Maysville has seen its share of devastating floods. Homes and

businesses were built close to the Ohio River and a walk along
Front Street reveals the latest answer to the flood problem. This is
a walk by the riverside but without a scenic view. From the windows of the fine old Front Street buildings one sees, across the
narrow street, only the high concrete wall built to keep the river
out of town.

Many visitors plan to be in Maysville on one of its special days.
Court Day each month was a Kentucky tradition, bringing citizens to county seats by mule and spring wagon from miles
around. The streets turned into trading centers as farmers
swapped everything from pocketknives to hound dogs. Once a
year Maysville relives those times. Court Day is the first Monday
in October. The flea market is open. Crafts and other goods are
sold to thousands of visitors.

The story of Maysville as a gateway to Kentucky begins with
herds of bison that once lumbered over the hills and waded the
shallow streams. Their main trail, one they followed for centuries,
crossed the riffles of the Ohio River here, and led southward to
the salt licks. Where the buffalo walked they packed the trail into
a hard, bare thoroughfare, and this natural road was first used by
Indians and later by early settlers who called it the Buffalo
Trace. Today it remains a thoroughfare, and those who drive
south on Hwy. 68 out of Maysville are following the old Buffalo
Trace.

This route was followed by Simon Kenton who ranked with
Daniel Boone as Indian fighter and frontier scout. Kenton left
Virginia at the age of sixteen, convinced that he had killed a man
in a fight over a girl and would be tried for murder. He fled, bare-
footed, it is said, without gun or money. His victim recovered, but
Kenton had found his place in the wilderness.

Eventually, Kenton reached the wild and beautiful Ohio Valley. By now he had learned to shoot with deadly accuracy, read
every track in the wilderness, and support himself by hunting and
trapping. He became a famous scout, Indian fighter, and a hero
among the settlers.

Kenton dreamed, as most frontiersmen did, of owning his share
of the wilderness. He wanted land where the cane grew; the native bamboo. The cane of "Caintuckee," would support livestock
through the hard winters, and these fields could also be more eas-

ily cleared for corn than the towering forests could. This search brought him down the Ohio to the mouth of a little creek where there was a natural harbor for river landings. Limestone cliffs along the creek gave it a name, "Limestone." Later Limestone would become Maysville.

Kenton came to Limestone in 1774 accompanied by his friend, Thomas Williams. Together they followed the Buffalo Trace south and at last found the canebreaks about which they had heard. Living in a half-face shelter made of brush, the two men cleared an acre of land and planted the first corn crop in this part of Kentucky.

This is also where Kenton built Kenton's Station, a fort and trading post a mile and a half west of the Buffalo Trace and four miles south of the Ohio River. Word spread. Flatboats brought more families seeking land in the wilderness. After their boats pulled into the harbor at the mouth of Limestone Creek they moved inland, fearing Indian attacks, to Washington, the new town rising on land Kenton had sold to Arthur Fox and William Wood. The Buffalo Trace was the town's main street.

Eventually Kenton lost thousands of acres of land because of faulty claims. He operated a general store in Washington for a while, but he was restless. He had a series of miraculous escapes from the Shawnees, ran the gauntlet repeatedly, and even survived being tied backward on the back of a wild, unbroken horse that raced through the woods with him.

Kenton lived to be 81. He died in Urbana, Ohio, but Mason County, Kentucky, always claimed him as its first and one of its most famous citizens. The memory of Simon Kenton, the ultimate woodsman and scout, is still strong both in Maysville and Old Washington out on the Buffalo Trace.

When the county seat moved from Washington to Maysville in 1848, Washington residents predicted their town would wither on the vine. It did, but it did not disappear. In recent years Washington has discovered new promise in the flow of tourists.

Drive over the hill and south on Hwy. 68 to Old Washington, only 4 miles away. From April 1 to early September, and later on autumn weekends, Washington's shops and historic buildings are open. Guided tours can be arranged at the Visitors' Center. Also, there are circulars to explain the town's background and lead visitors on walking tours.

Behind Washington stands Federal Hill, the 1800 home of Captain Thomas Marshall, Jr., who came down the Ohio on a flatboat with his family in 1780. Thomas became a famous lawyer; his brother, John, was Chief Justice of the U. S. Supreme Court for thirty-four years beginning in 1801. Their mother lies in a privately owned family cemetery. Inscribed on Mary Marshall's tombstone is "b. 1737. She was good, not brilliant, useful, not ornamental, and the mother of 15 children."

Most of Washington's other buildings of historic interest may be seen along Main Street. Take time to wander through the shops that offer antiques and craft items. Visit the Paxton Inn, which welcomed travelers in the 1800s. The Albert Sidney Johnson Home, built in 1797, is restored, furnished, and open to the public. Admission charged. Medford's Fort was built by George Medford in 1787, one of the last homes constructed from planks salvaged from the flatboats that brought families down the Ohio. The Old Church Museum, built in 1848 and originally Methodist, is now used by all faiths and houses collections of church history.

At lunchtime, find your way to Broderick's Tavern, dating back to 1794. It may be the oldest Kentucky restaurant still in business. We found it a pleasant place, and the food was excellent.

The Old Washington Antique Festival is held the third weekend of September, an event not to be missed by antique hunters.

The biggest annual event in Washington is Frontier Christmas which comes each year on the first weekend in December. There is no charge for visiting the historic houses during Frontier Christmas. Washington welcomes its guests and celebrates Christmas as it was celebrated long ago. After this event, the historic buildings and the shops close until the following April.

Washington is on the National Register of Historic Places and deserves to be.

KENTUCKY117

Up the Road

Blue Licks Battlefield State Park

When buffalo waded the Ohio River at Maysville, they were headed for the mineral springs 23 miles south on what is today Hwy. 68. Long after the last of the buffalo were gone, people came to the springs, also in large numbers, and for the same purpose—to take the waters. Prior to the Civil War, stages brought them to the hotel that stood at Blue Licks. This was also the site of the battle known as the last battle of the Revolutionary War, and a granite shaft lists the names of the 60 pioneers, including the son of Daniel Boone, who fell here in 1782.

Today travelers still come. Kentucky maintains Blue Licks Battlefield State Park with campground, swimming pool, bathhouse, playground, and hiking trails. There is also a museum with collections of historical and paleontological treasures. Address: Mount Olivet, KY 41064.

Three and a half miles north of the state park on Hwy. 1029 is a 108-foot-long covered bridge.

Augusta and Its Ferry

From Maysville, we drove downriver, following Hwy. 8, a narrow sometimes winding road through a rural area. Now and then there was a view of the river on our right. Where the road crosses from Mason County into Bracken County, we stopped to read the historic plaque that marks the location of the last formal duel fought on Kentucky soil. It was here that former Maysville

Mayor, William T. Castro, who had been arrested by Colonel Leonidas Metcalfe as a secessionist, was killed by Metcalfe.

Eighteen miles west of Maysville we came to Augusta, a quaint river village, one of the prettiest anywhere along the Ohio. This historic row of houses on the riverfront served some years ago as a Hollywood movie set. When the movie *Centennial* was filmed, the Augusta riverfront was just right as St. Louis of the mid-1800s. Much of Augusta is on the National Register of Historic Places. Its architecture is varied, but one of the most impressive buildings is the old Baker Wine Cellar at the junction of highways 8 and 19. It is 105 feet long, 22 feet wide, and has walls 46 inches thick. Built in the 1800s, it stands as a reminder of the era when Bracken was a major wine producing county.

Riverside Drive, also known as Water Street, is an excellent place to begin a walking tour. Starting at the west end, the General John Payne Home, built about 1792, was visited by President-elect William Henry Harrison on the way to his inauguration. This house was the birthplace of General George C. Marshall's mother, Laura Bradford.

Birthplace of Stuart Armstrong Walker, 321 Riverside. Born in 1880. Walker was a playwright and producer who patented the portable theater and introduced the individual spotlight system.

At 213 Riverside is the Robert Schoolfield log school, built prior to 1795, the first schoolhouse in Bracken County.

Tom Broshear's Tavern, 209 W. Riverside has been traced back to 1795 and is believed to be the oldest three-story brick residence in northern Kentucky. It is said that the log cabin behind the house was once Simon Kenton's home.

205 W. Riverside was built by W. C. Marshall, grandfather of General George C. Marshall, about 1800. At 213 W. Riverside, the Robert Davis Home was built about 1797.

The Robert Mains Home, 201 W. Riverside, built in 1797, was owned by John Boude, owner of Augusta's first ferry. This home is now a memorial to the Mains family. In the next block on Riverside stands the Early Kentucky Row House. The Piedmont House, 109 W. Riverside, was built in 1797. Its famous Piedmont door was brought from Virginia. Dr. Joshua Tayler Bradford, a noted American surgeon, once lived here. At 108 E. Riverside is the old Bradford Hotel, built about 1850.

The Thornton F. Marshall Home, 204 E. Riverside, was built in 1860. Marshall, when a Kentucky Senator, cast the deciding vote that kept Kentucky in the Union. The old Methodist Church at the corner of Riverside and Bracken St. was built in 1819.

Turn north to the Dr. Joseph Tomlinson Home at 210 Bracken St. This house, built in 1823, was the home of the first president of Augusta College. Dr. Tomlinson's nephew, Stephen Foster, visited here, and it is said by some that the pleasant view inspired "My Old Kentucky Home."

The First Baptist Church, Third and Bracken streets, was built in 1820.

The R. W. Winters House, 306 Elizabeth St, was built by Winters about 1850 after the style of town houses in the Carolinas. It now houses an antique shop.

White Hall, Third and W. Elizabeth streets, built in the early 1800s, is the ancestral home of General George C. Marshall.

If you come to Augusta on Labor Day weekend, you will find crowds visiting the annual Augusta Flea Market. Arts, crafts, and antiques abound, and some of the historic buildings are open for tours.

There is no bridge connecting Augusta with Ohio, but the famous ferry, *Ole Augusta,* still plies the river from West Riverside to Boude's Ferry Landing on Ohio Hwy. 52. The historic ferry operates daily, except Wednesday or during bad weather, from 8 A.M. to 6 P.M. The crossing takes 7 minutes, and the view is considered one of the most beautiful on the river. The ferry ride is a special favorite of traveling families with children.

Brooksville, located south of Augusta on highways 19 and 10, is the county seat of Bracken County. The impressive courthouse was built in 1915, and the original jail, built in 1833, is still in service. The Ware Hotel, built before 1800, is one of the oldest buildings. Jett Memorial Park has a picnic area, tennis court, swimming pool, and miniature golf.

The Walcott covered bridge, on Hwy. 1159 between Brooksville and Wellsburg, was built in 1824. This is thought to be the oldest of Kentucky's remaining covered bridges.

Pendleton County and
Kincaid Lake

The seat of government for Pendleton County is the quiet, old town of Falmouth, settled in 1776 by settlers from Virginia who named it for Falmouth, Virginia. The major recreation area in this county is Kincaid Lake State Park, on Hwy. 159, northwest of Falmouth. The park covers 502 acres and has a 250-acre lake that is locally famous for excellent populations of bass, bluegills, crappie, and catfish. Boats are limited to 10-hp motors.

There are hiking trails, playground, badminton, shuffleboard, tennis, and paddle-tennis courts, swimming beach, and picnic areas. There are also bicycle trails.

Campers visiting Kincaid Lake State Park find an excellent campground complete with hookups for recreational vehicles.

On the park grounds there stands a log house more than two centuries old. The park office is on one side and a small museum occupies the remainder of the old building. The park telephone number is (606) 654-3531.

Another old log house is in the middle of Falmouth. This one has been restored and is occupied. Nine miles north of Falmouth, on Hwy. 27 at the Butler exit, there is a solidly built stone house, locally known as one of the county's early residences.

"Northern" Kentucky

Across the Ohio River from Cincinnati are three counties known collectively in this part of the valley as "Northern" Kentucky. The Licking River glides northward through these Ken-

tucky hills to empty into the Ohio directly opposite Cincinnati
and in its final reaches separates two Kentucky cities. Newport
lies on its east and Covington, Kentucky's second largest city
famed for its German heritage and classic old homes, lies to the
west of the Licking.

Northern Kentucky and Cincinnati share, in addition to the
Ohio River and the prevailing weather, shopping centers, musical
attractions, restaurants, newspaper publishers, radio and television programs, colleges and universities, places of employment,
and the Reds and Bengals. Covington and Newport's restaurants
and night clubs add glitter and variety to the Cincinnati scene.

Covington and Cincinnati are also linked by the famous Suspension Bridge. As early as 1839 there was talk of a bridge to
connect these Ohio and Kentucky cities. A bridge supplementing
the ferryboats would be a boon to commerce as well as a convenience to citizens. But there was also the anti-bridge group, most
of them speaking for the steamboat owners and captains who
wanted nothing in the river that might impede the progress of
their boats or knock off their towering smokestacks In fighting a

*This historic suspension bridge connects Covington, Kentucky,
with Cincinnati.*

bridge the steamboaters had support from the ferry operators, and arguments raged on for years.

One solution, according to some enterprising engineers, would be to suspend the bridge all the way across the Ohio without putting a single pier in the water. This idea frightened a lot of people who doubted that a suspended bridge could withstand the weight of pedestrians and loaded wagons.

Charles Ellet thought the suspension bridge idea would work, and so did German-born engineer John A. Roebling. Ellet attempted to prove his point by building a suspension bridge across the Licking River between Covington and Newport. Ellet finished this bridge in 1854 and scarcely had time to stand back and admire his work when, a month after its completion, it fell into the Licking. Roebling, however, was still convinced that it was feasible to suspend a bridge from steel-wire cables, but he was delayed by the panic of 1857 and then by the Civil War. Not until 1866 did Roebling complete his bridge, and for the first time people, thousands of them, walked back and forth across the Ohio between Covington and Cincinnati. Roebling's bridge has stood there ever since, its 1,000-foot span suspended 100 feet above the Ohio with massive 230-foot-high stone towers on either shore.

Roebling went on to even greater glory. The bridge between Cincinnati and Covington was the prototype for the Brooklyn Bridge built by Roebling and his son.

The Kentucky end of the Suspension Bridge is an excellent place to start a walking tour of Covington. Just upstream is the historic point of land formed where the Licking empties into the Ohio. The first white man to stand here was Christopher Gist, an exceptionally well-educated and literate explorer who was sent to the Valley in 1751 by the Ohio Land Company, organized by Virginians. The Point was later a convenient location for launching military campaigns. George Rogers Clark mustered his troops here before crossing the river in pursuit of the Shawnees. With him went superscouts Daniel Boone and Simon Kenton. Later still, Civil War troops marched south from this place.

The first white man to own the land where Covington now stands must have had an overwhelming thirst. After he received the tract from the government in payment for military services, he traded it for a keg of whiskey. The new owner then traded the parcel of land for a quarter of fresh buffalo meat. The land changed hands a few more times until it became the property of James Welch, who hired a surveyor and determined that he owned 200 acres bounded on the north by the Ohio River and the east by the Licking. Welch sold the land to Thomas Kennedy who flatboated down the Ohio with his family. Kennedy built a fine stone house and made his living by operating a tavern and a ferry across the Ohio. Kennedy sold 150 acres and the town founded there was named for General Leonard Covington from Maryland, who died of wounds suffered in the War of 1812.

Visitors at the Point are entering Covington's famous Riverside District, the oldest and most historic section of the city. The Riverside District extends from the Ohio River on the north, south to Fourth Street, and from the Licking on the east, westward to the alley between Garrard and Greenup streets. This entire four-square-block area has been placed on the National Register of Historic Places.

Although the old homes of this area are still private residences and not open to the public, their exteriors are of sufficient interest to attract visitors. The best way to see them is to take a walking tour of the Riverside area.

1. We began our tour at the *George Rogers Clark Park*. The little quiet, shaded park is where Thomas Kennedy built his cabin and inn. There are benches from which to view the river and the Cincinnati skyline. There is also a fountain and a plaque relating the history of the Point.

2. *Skiff House,* 320 Riverside Dr. This house, immediately east of the Park, is an ivy-covered Victorian home with cast- and wrought-iron trim.

3. *Riverside House,* 321 Riverside Dr. Built in 1916 by prominent artist Charles McLaughlin, it was inspired by mansion architecture of the South.

4. *Fallis Lovell House,* 412 Second St., is reached by turning right on Shelby and right again on Second St. Built in the 1850s in the Italianate style—note columns and cornices. Also ornate ironwork.

5. *Carneal House,* 405 Second St., was built about 1815 and is considered the oldest brick structure in the city. It is in the Geor-

The Carneal House, 1815, had a tunnel linking it with the Licking River providing an escape route for runaway slaves.

Daniel Carter Beard, founder of the Boy Scouts of America, lived in this Covington, Kentucky, home.

gian style with Palladian influence. The house is said to have been connected to the Licking River by a tunnel built for the safety of runaway slaves.

6. *Laidley House,* 404 Second St., built around 1865, is a stately French Victorian house. It was the residence of the owner of the White Packet Line of steamboats.

7. *Graziani House,* 326 Second St., is a large French Victorian house.

8. *Shinkle Row,* northwest corner of Second and Garrard streets, built in the 1880s, followed an English row-house pattern common in Covington in the nineteenth century.

9. *Ranson House,* southwest corner of Second and Garrard streets, was built in 1852. This town house with its iron porch was built by the first president of the Covington and Cincinnati Bridge Company.

10. *Eaton House,* 213 Garrard St., is a very fine Greek Revival Mansion.

11. *Daniel Carter Beard Home.* Turn left on Third St. and follow it until it dead-ends. The Beard Home is the last house on the north side. Built in 1821, it was the boyhood home of the founder of the Boy Scouts of America. A Registered National Landmark.

This walking tour will take one to two hours. Those who want additional information on other Covington walking tours or other points of interest in the city should visit or call the Northern Kentucky Convention and Visitors' Bureau at 605 Philadelphia St., Covington. Phone: (606) 261-4677. Other buildings visitors often want to see here include the following:

Basilica of the Assumption (St. Mary's), 9 E. Twelfth St. The exterior is medieval French Gothic based on the Cathedral of Notre Dame, and the interior is patterned after the Abbey Church of St. Denis in Paris. The largest stained-glass window in the United States is found here. There are also four large murals by the internationally famous artist Frank Duveneck.

Mother of God Church, 119 Sixth St. The cornerstone of the building was laid in 1870. It is a Renaissance basilica-style building with twin towers and dome, murals, stained-glass windows, statuary, and an 1876 pipe organ.

Duveneck House, 1226 Greenup St., was the early home of the artist Frank Duveneck. It is now a framing gallery. Open Tues.–Sat. 9–4:30.

Frank Duveneck Gallery is housed in the old Carnegie Library at Robbins and Scott streets. Several Duveneck works are displayed.

Mainstrasse

Some years ago Covington's leaders, determined to attract more people to the city's business district, seized on its German background as a theme and began to restore a German village in the heart of the city. A 30-square-block section of Covington became the Mainstrasse. Its focal point is the 100-foot-high Carroll Bell Tower, housing a 43-bell carillon from which tunes ring forth hourly through much of the day. The tower, true to the Rhineland theme, has a Bavarian look. In addition to the clock, high in the tower, and its bells (forged in Holland), the tower houses a company of mechanical figures, *jaquemarts,* that emerge hourly, as the bells toll, enacting the story of *The Pied Piper of Hamelin.* The area around the tower is a pleasant parklike mall, the heart of the Mainstrasse with its hundred or so shops.

The Carroll Bell Tower is at Sixth and Philadelphia streets near I-75, Exit 192.

Dining Out

Northern Kentucky has many restaurants, and one of the finest is the Conservatory at 650 W. Third St. near the river and the I-75 bridge in Covington. Entering the Conservatory you find the more sedate dining area on the left and the disco dancing on the right. This popular place is decorated with green plants which give it its name. The food is good, so don't be put off by the disco image. Diners often find their way to the disco area after dinner.

On Sixth St. across from the Mother of God Church is Mick

Among Northern Kentucky's impressive structures is the Mother of God Church.

Noll's Covington Haus, a German-style restaurant in a renovated and tastefully decorated old firehouse. Upstairs, where firemen once slept, there are weekend live-music sessions.

Another favorite local restaurant, this one with a riverboat atmosphere, is the Mike Fink, located at the foot of Greenup St., literally on the river. The Mike Fink is a converted sternwheeler that once towed oil and coal barges on the Ohio. When we stopped there for lunch, we found the prices reasonable and service excellent. And the view is free.

Or if you want to have dinner on a boat that leaves the dock,

Carroll Chimes Tower is the focal point of Covington's Main-strasse with its small shops and festivals.

Resembling Notre Dame, the Basilica of the Assumption, which has the world's second-largest stained-glass window, is of French Gothic design.

there is the *Betty Blake*. Operated, in season, by BB Riverboats, Inc., the *Betty Blake* cruises the river for two to three hours in the evening while diners enjoy food, drink, and live entertainment. She departs from the dock in Covington just downstream from the Suspension Bridge. Reservations are required. Phone: (606) 261-8500.

The Airport

Visitors arriving in Cincinnati by air often think they are landing in Ohio, but the Greater Cincinnati International Airport lies 12.8 miles south of the Ohio River in Boone County, Kentucky.

Mid-America's Gateway to the World, as airport officials sometimes call it, is a complete city with its own shops, restaurants, hotels, fire department, and police force. The airport is also an attraction for tourists. The nearby circle freeway, I-275 which completely encircles the Greater Cincinnati area, passes within a mile of the airport.

Once inside the terminal, visitors should not miss the giant murals that decorate the terminal walls. There are 14 of these murals, each 20 feet square. They were created in the 1930s, not for the airport but for the Cincinnati Union Railroad Terminal. The murals depict important Cincinnati industries ranging from printing to the manufacture of machine tools. Each mural is a mosaic created from thousands of small pieces of colored glass. When the trains stopped running and the terminal was closed its owners talked of tearing the structure down. Local citizens organized and began raising money to rescue the murals.

Each mural was taken down and crated in a huge box, then loaded by cranes onto a special flatbed truck and gently driven the 15 miles to its new home. The first of the murals was five hours making the trip. The moving of the murals cost more than half a million dollars, but once again hundreds of thousands of travelers can see them every year.

Guided tours through the Greater Cincinnati International Airport are led by ex-flight attendants three times a day. These tours are for groups of 15 to 50 people. A call to the airport will tell you when space is available for these tours. Phone: (606) 283-3144.

There is also an observation tower where visitors can watch arrivals and departures of the numerous daily flights.

Big Bone Lick State Park

A dozen miles south of the airport, and in the same county, is Kentucky's northernmost state park, Big Bone Lick, a memorable place for overnight camping families on their way through the valley. Big Bone Lick State Park is near Walton on Hwy. 338. Signs on I-75 pointed us toward it.

On the top of a hill in this 512-acre park is a modern campground with plumbing, showers, dumping station, laundry facilities, grills, and electricity. Campers enjoy a pool and playground, and nearby is a 7-acre lake that offers bass, bluegill, and catfish. There is a mile-long trail around the lake for hikers.

Tennis, shuffleboard, volleyball, basketball, and horseshoes are all available with equipment provided free of charge. Superintendent Dennis Glacken tells us that several hundred thousand visitors come here every year, most of them from Ohio, Michigan, and Canada. The park is closed in winter.

The special story of the park, however, is suggested by the name. The drama of Big Bone Lick is traced in the small museum behind the park's gift shop.

During the Ice Age when great sheets of ice, sometimes 6,000 feet thick, inched down over the northeastern part of the continent, herds of animals advanced before the ice. These animals were drawn to the salt marshes at Big Bone Lick, and many of them became mired in the bogs, were unable to pull themselves out, and died there.

Early white explorers told of giant bones and huge tusks covering the ground. This attracted the attention of scientists and scholars, among them Benjamin Franklin and Thomas Jefferson. In 1807, President Jefferson sent William Clark and a party of ten men, apparently the first paleontological expedition in the New World, to Big Bone Lick, and three hundred bones were collected and shipped to the White House. Many of these bones are preserved now in museums in Philadelphia and in Paris, France.

The next professional excavation at Big Bone Lick was between 1962 and 1966 by scientists from the University of Nebraska. Remains were found of woolly mammoths, giant bison, mastodons, peccaries, tapirs, massive ground sloths, Arctic bear, musk oxen, elk, horses, and foxes. The tons of bones exhumed yielded new discoveries that excited paleontologists everywhere.

Today's visitors may hike the mile-long walkway through the original swampland. Along the way are plaques telling the story of the Ice Age creatures that lived in the Ohio Valley. There are also awesome, life-size models of the prehistoric mastodon and bison beside the last remaining salt-sulphur spring, as well as a model "dig" showing bone samples and replicas.

Big Bone Lick State Park is 20 miles southwest of Covington. Access is easiest, especially if you are driving a motorhome or pulling a trailer, if you exit I-75 at Hwy. 42 and drive southwest to Hwy. 338. Road signs point the way to Big Bone Lick. Phone: (606) 384-3522.

Visit Rabbit Hash

In winter the traffic through Rabbit Hash slows down until only the local folks are out and about. We stopped there one January day when skies were gray and there was the promise of more snow before evening. "The General Store," we had been told, "is about all there is, but it's a genuine old general store." That seemed reason enough to go.

Past Big Bone Lick State Park we drove toward the Ohio River and after 9 miles or so of narrow twisting road, sometimes within view of the river, we came to the junction of highways 388 and 536, and the Rabbit Hash General Store. Inside there would surely be an aged storekeeper, bent and bewhiskered. But there wasn't. Instead, there was pretty Pattie Purnell.

Pattie is the most recent in a long list of operators of the general store. When the store opened in 1831, the first proprietor of the business was James Wilson who specialized in selling livestock feed. The general store has filled a local need ever since.

Tiers of shelves covered the store's long walls, and counters held an assortment of goods, some of it displayed in old glass cases. On one wall in a back corner was the old Rabbit Hash Post Office with a pigeonhole for each family. But the post office has not functioned for many years. A wood-burning stove, built at the Rabbit Hash Stove Works across the road, warmed the big store room. Country hams hung from a rack above and canned goods lined the shelves. Souvenirs and pottery were for sale in the back room.

Pattie Purnell said a lot of curious tourists come in summer. There are different local stories, she said, to explain how Rabbit Hash got its name, but all agree that it was named for a once common method of cooking rabbit. It is said that there once was such an abundance of wild rabbits here that hunters sold them for meat to passing riverboats.

Part of the fun of a trip to Rabbit Hash is traveling the maze of back country roads that lead to it by way of the hollows and ridges of Boone County.

Gallatin County:
New Fishing Water

Downriver from Boone County lies Gallatin, the sparsely populated county whose seat of government is the river town of Warsaw, population 1,200.

The courthouse, built in 1838, is a tall white structure in the middle of town, and grouped around the courthouse on nearby streets are numerous historic homes still occupied. One of these, and the oldest building in Warsaw is the house that Henry Yates, one of the town's founders, built on High Street opposite the courthouse in 1809. One part of it was built of logs, and the log section still stands. Another notable house nearby is the house built by John Payne in 1825, a fine old brick structure resembling those built in the Tidewater section of Virginia.

There is a furniture factory in Warsaw, and other than this little by the way of industry. "This is just a nice, quiet river town," we were told by Dr. Carl Bogardus. "Of course, I'm prejudiced. I was born here and practiced medicine forty years in Indiana. Then, I came back here to retire. That's what I think of it." Dr. Bogardus as well as other Gallatin County citizens, told us about Craig Lake.

Markland Dam lifted the level of the Ohio River and backed water up into the mouths of tributary streams to create new lakes where these creeks enter the Ohio. One of these, Craigs Creek, covers 275 acres. Another, Paint Lick, forms a 90-acre backwater lake at the Ohio, while nearby Sugar Creek contains 70 acres. All of these fishing spots are within a few miles of Warsaw and two of them, Craig and Sugar, have public launching ramps easily reached from Hwy. 42. There are local bait shops and boat-rental businesses. Fishermen on Craigs Creek sometimes find this area heavily used by (fishermen say "infested with") water skiers. Bass fishing is popular in these waters, but crappie fishing is also productive, especially in Sugar Creek in spring and early summer.

Carroll County:
A Most Popular Park

Even if citizens of Ghent, Kentucky, the next town downstream, tried, they would be unable to forget that Henry Clay once visited here. He arrived in 1815, when the settlement was still called McCool's Creek, and local leaders dreamed that their town would become a major center of river commerce. But how in the world could anyone expect a place named "McCool's Creek" to grow in size and importance? What did Mr. Clay think would make a suitable new name?

Clay carried memories of his service on the Peace Commission that settled the War of 1812. He suggested that the tiny Kentucky town on the Ohio River adopt the name of the Belgian city where the Peace Commission had met. In this manner, McCool's Creek was given a new name few local people could pronounce and fewer yet had ever heard before. And Ghent it remains.

Among the old buildings still standing in Ghent is the First Baptist Church completed in 1844 at an outlay of $1,250, in gifts of cash, wool, hay, and a few barrels of whiskey.

The county seat of Carroll County is Carrollton, a major burley tobacco market. Going downriver on U.S. 42 toward Carrollton, the traveler passes the Richard Masterson House, the oldest two-story brick house anywhere on the Ohio River from Pittsburgh to Louisville. Slaves built this house in 1790 of bricks fired on the site. The Masterson House has recently been completely renovated and opened to the public by the Port William (the early name for Carrollton) Historical Society.

The main hall of the General Butler State Resort Lodge near Carrollton. (Photo by George Laycock)

This courthouse is the seat of government for Carroll County where the Kentucky River joins the Ohio. (Photo by George Laycock)

Carrollton has many fine old homes including the 1825 home of General William O. Butler, built in the Georgian Colonial style. The Carrollton Nursing Home, one of Port William's finest homes, was built in 1810 by Nicholas Blair.

In the center of town stands the attractive brick courthouse, built in 1884. During the devastating flood of 1937, Coast Guard boats negotiated the lower hall until water rose so high that boats could no longer clear the top of the front door to get inside the courthouse.

In the courthouse yard stands the old county jail, a gray fortress surrounded by a high fence. This century-old structure, replaced by a more modern jail, is maintained today for its historic value and as a convenient storage place for lawn mowers.

The Butler Mansion, in General Butler State Resort Park, is now a museum. (Photo by George Laycock)

The best-known name in the history of Carroll County is Butler, a family of fighting warriors. General Percival Butler, who
was at Valley Forge, was one of five brothers, all officers in the
Revolution. General Percival Butler and his wife came to Kentucky following the war. The mansion built by his eldest son,
Major Thomas Butler, remains in excellent condition and is today
a completely furnished museum open to the public.

The road leading up the hill past the mansion is the back entrance to the General Butler State Resort Park, another of Kentucky's fine vacation centers. Most visitors approach the park,
however, by its main entrance on Hwy. 227 which connects Carrollton with I-71.

This 809-acre state park, convenient to Cincinnati, Indianapolis, and Louisville, is one of the most popular in the Kentucky park system. Buford Rice, park superintendent, told us that
the lodge fills up much of the year. The dining room and lodge
are open throughout the year.

The lodge has 33 guest rooms plus dining hall and swimming
pool. There is the opportunity for visitors to go horseback riding,
hiking, and golfing.

Carrollton is bordered on its west side by the Kentucky River,
which flows down from the hills past Frankfort, the Kentucky
capital. This narrow meandering river runs deep enough to be a
favorite with pleasure boaters. Our first trip up the Kentucky
River some years ago was aboard a houseboat that we locked
through the dams. Boaters and fishermen still enjoy the Kentucky
River's secluded waters.

Before we left Carrollton we stopped at the new library across
from the courthouse, seeking leads about the next county
downriver. "What do you want to know about Trimble County?"
The librarian said she came originally from Trimble County.

"Is there anything there tourists should go to see?"

"I can't think of a thing," she said.

"Nothing?"

"Nothing at all. Save your time. But if you do go, there is a
terrific view from the cemetery."

Trimble: Bypassed

This Kentucky county, halfway between Louisville and Cincinnati, leads a mighty quiet life since I-71 to the east began speeding traffic through the county.

But driving south along the river from Carrollton toward Bedford offers an opportunity for those who like a leisurely hill-country drive along uncrowded roads. On one trip we passed this way in the autumn when fall colors were at their peak of brilliance, and instead of following I-71, we crossed the Kentucky River where it enters the Ohio at Carrollton and followed Hwy. 42. A couple of miles to the west, Hwy. 36 splits off and runs along the Ohio River toward Milton, while Hwy. 42 continues toward Bedford, Kentucky. Either route is a scenic drive, and an opportunity to explore parts of Kentucky seldom really seen by passengers in all those vehicles scurrying along the Interstate Highway.

We followed Hwy. 36 which ends at Milton, where Hwy. 421 goes either south toward Frankfort or crosses the Ohio on the bridge into Madison, Indiana. Our route on this day lay south toward Bedford, the Trimble County seat. At the top of the hill, as we worked our way up from the river, we came upon a spectacular view of southern Indiana's hills and the city of Madison across the river. At the brow of the hill there are coin-operated telescopes and parking spaces marked off for visitors' cars.

Then we came to a sign pointing to the Moffett Cemetery, and with the words of the librarian fresh in our minds, turned into the narrow lane to come eventually to the community burial grounds and its fine, sweeping upriver view of the Ohio. Following Hwy. 421 a dozen miles through prosperous-looking ridgetop farm country, we came into Bedford. As for Bedford, the lady was right.

Oldham County:
Shadow of the City

For 18 miles the waters of the Ohio slip quietly along the shores of Oldham County, Kentucky, which in recent years has become a major bedroom community for the big city a few miles downstream. Oldham County people like their combination of rural living with the nearby amenities of Louisville.

The old red-brick courthouse at LaGrange has stood among the towering trees in the center of the Public Square since 1875, and before that an earlier courthouse housed the local government. The county, dating back to 1824, was named to honor Colonel William Oldham who was killed by Indians in 1791. In those early days, Oldham County was farming country, and it remains so where estates and housing developments have not taken the land. There are large Thoroughbred horse farms, among them Hardscuffle Farm, scene of the annual Hardscuffle Steeplechase on the fourth Saturday of every May.

Among the famous citizens LaGrange likes to remember is Dr. Rob Morris, the noted Mason whose home at 110 Washington St. is a shrine honoring Morris who founded the Order of the Eastern Star. From this community also came a famous movie director, David Wark Griffith best remembered for directing *The Birth of a Nation*.

Oldham has its festivals and at least one of these, "Oldham County Days," on the third Saturday in July, brings hundreds of natives back for a colorful annual homecoming.

But much of the time, life around Oldham County is quietly prosperous. There is time for a family picnic out at Oldham County Park at Bruckner, which also offers tennis and fishing. Visitors can enjoy golf at any of the 4 major 18-hole courses. These courses, which are open to the public, include: Green Valley Country Club, Oldham County Country Club, Harmony Landing Country Club, and Sleepy Hollow Golf Course.

Louisville

Travelers compare one place with the other and look especially for the similarities. "It reminds me of Circleville." Larger cities are likened to St. Louis or Chicago or, if they have the beautiful hills for it, Cincinnati or San Francisco. Louisville, however, is not fitted for this game. This sparkling and busy city halfway down the Ohio River, resembles only Louisville, and this is a matter of local pride.

Those living here admit that their city is content and conservative. "Let a leader so much as whisper 'recession' and people in Louisville just stop spending," one youthful merchant told us. "This is one of the facts we have to face." Another said, "Louisville is a 'laid back' community. But we like it this way. Some of the younger people think that nothing ever happens here, but as they get older they begin to appreciate the stability."

If asked to associate their city with a geographic region of the country, Louisville citizens usually characterize it as southern, but it is not southern in the sense that Memphis or New Orleans or Birmingham is southern. Louisville is a crossroads, taking its character from North, South, East, and West, with just enough added emphasis on the South to give it a somewhat slower pace than cities to the north and east.

Local people like Louisville because, "It is a nice place to live. People visit a lot. Everyone is friendly. Strangers speak to you on the street." This comes through for visitors as well. Clerks are generally helpful, taxi drivers courteous, and hotel employees friendly. Being friendly and helpful is good business because Louisville makes a major industry of its tourism. Half a million convention visitors come to this city annually, along with hundreds of thousands more who arrive for the Kentucky Derby or pass through in their vacation travels.

Louisville's population is around 350,000 persons, and this, say Louisvillians, is neither too small nor too large but about right.

The population of the Greater Louisville area, including the adjacent Indiana counties across the river is about 931,600.

The people feel a closeness with the river that gives Louisville its river-city character and links it with distant places. The river helps account for the vitality of Louisville and the prosperity that industry, large and small, has brought.

Louisville claims its share of firsts, several of them edible. Burgoo is a speciality in some Louisville restaurants. This thick soup or stew has numerous ingredients including beef, chicken, and assorted vegetables, although the recipes vary from kitchen to kitchen.

Did you ever hear of a hot brown? You will in Louisville. This is a treat first created at the old Brown Hotel from which it took its name. The hot brown is an open-faced sandwich offering turkey smothered with a rich cream sauce and bacon.

Then, for dessert, there is Derby Pie, so distinctive that its recipe has been registered with the U. S. Patent Office. If it is listed on a menu, you are being offered the genuine article made of chocolate chips, walnuts, and various secret ingredients.

Downtown Louisville is noted for its modern buildings and the plaza on the waterfront.

The Riverfront Plaza/Belvedere is frequently the center of cultural activities and ethnic events.

Modjeska is another sweet first made in Louisville. Anton Busath created this carmel-coated marshmallow around the turn of the century and named it for a favorite actress.

Louisville even claims to be the home of the original cheeseburger. Carl Kaelin is said to have created the sandwich when he opened his restaurant here in 1934 and began adding a slice of cheese to his hamburgers.

The city had its origins on the banks of the Ohio more than two centuries ago when a gutsy young leader chose the site, not as a fitting place to build a city, but as the logical location for a military base that would play an important role in the American Revolution.

This leader was George Rogers Clark, a newly appointed twenty-six-year-old Lieutenant Colonel in the Virginia Militia. Clark arrived with secret orders not even known to the 150 soldiers or the few dozen uninvited settlers tagging along as the soldiers floated down the quiet waters of the Ohio River. There was a stretch of the river midway between Pittsburgh and the Mississippi called the Falls of the Ohio. At the Falls, really a series of rapids, the Ohio dropped twenty-two feet in two miles, and only after heavy rains could flatboats pass over the rocks.

When George Rogers Clark reached the Falls of the Ohio, he surveyed the broad river and the various islands studding it, and chose one seven-acre island as the base of his operations. Here he built a fort, and that first year the settlers planted corn, giving the

The Galt House is a major hotel in the heart of downtown Louisville. (Photo by George Laycock)

place its name—"Corn Island." But do not go searching today for Corn Island because the site has been covered by the rising river.

The young leader prepared to launch a bold plan. Clark reasoned that the frontier would be safe from attack only if there was an offensive action against the British in the northwest. His plan carried the approval of Virginia's Governor, Patrick Henry.

In a series of secret marches and surprise attacks Clark's little force took Kaskaskia and Cahokia, and Vincennes in Indiana. The British recaptured Vincennes, after which Clark, in a brilliant maneuver, attacked and recaptured the fort along with Henry Hamilton, Commander of the British forces in the West. By this defeat of the British forces Clark helped move the border of the United States north of the Ohio River.

In 1779 Clark moved his fortification from Corn Island to the mainland and built a new fort where Twelfth St. meets the Ohio River today. New settlers, comforted by Clark's successful campaigns in the Northwest, were soon flatboating down the river toward the new town of Louisville. Louisville, named in honor of France's King Louis XVI who had sided with the American revolutionary forces in the struggle against the British, was laid out in April 1779.

The nature of this stretch of the Ohio River had made it a logical place for a settlement. The falls at Louisville effectively halted boat traffic except in times of high water. Goods were unloaded from flatboats, hauled around the barrier, and reloaded on other boats. A lusty community of roustabouts grew up beside the river.

In October 1811 there came from the river a sound unlike anything the residents of Louisville had heard before. The *Orleans,* first steamboat on western waters, chugged and puffed its way into the harbor. Parties were held on board and ashore while leading citizens of the community took rides on the side-wheeler.

Then, in December, the rains came and the river rose. The *Orleans* eased away from her harbor, passed easily over the falls and was on her way to New Orleans. Her voyage down the river ushered in a new age of steam to the valley. Within a few years Louisville was building steamboats.

The need to unload and reload boats at the Falls of the Ohio was a costly barrier to commerce. What was needed was a canal that would take boats around the rapids. Promoters on both sides of the river wanted the canal. Finally, in 1830 the Portland Canal was completed, assuring Louisville renewed economic health. The town was on its way to becoming a bustling center of commerce and manufacturing.

In recent years Louisville has rejuvenated her downtown area. New buildings have risen on the skyline, and special attention has been devoted to making the waterfront attractive. Downtown on the river is Riverfront Plaza and Belvedere with parking garages below the streets and a park with green plants and fountains flowing into pools used in winter for ice skating. The plaza is a good place for brown baggers on warm days, strollers, even weddings, square dances, and ethnic festivals.

Beside the Belvedere stands the Galt House, a new hotel with an old Louisville name, 29 stories high with not one, but two, revolving restaurants on top, giving diners a superb view of downtown Louisville, the Ohio, and the Indiana cities on the other side.

Louisville's new Kentucky Center for the Arts downtown at Sixth and Main streets by the riverside is the city's bid to bring more people back to the heart of town. Auditoriums here seat 2,400 people in the large hall; 620 in the smaller hall. This is the new center for theater, dance, and music in Louisville as well as conventions, Broadway shows, closed-circuit sports events, and major country-music productions.

Driving in Louisville

This is the easiest of the large Ohio Valley cities in which to drive. Major thoroughfares lead toward the center of town like spokes in a wheel, while Interstate highways lead traffic into or around the city. The I-64 runs east and west through the city; I-65 runs north and south; and I-71 leads into the city from the northeast and Cincinnati. The big loop freeway is I-264, also called the Watterson Expressway, around the east, south, and west sides of Louisville.

Other major streets leading toward the center of town are Hwy. 42, Brownsboro Road; highways 60 and 460, Shelbyville Road;

Hwy. 31E, Bardstown Road; and Hwy. 31W, the Dixie Highway.
A surprising number of the major attractions in Louisville are
easily reached because they are either on or close to these important highways.

The Louisville Visitors' Bureau, Founders Sq., Louisville, KY
40202, phone: (502) 582-3377 can either send you, or hand
you, copies of an excellent city map with the attractions marked,
and on the back, lists of hotels, museums, distillers, restored
areas, and other attractions.

The River Approach

Modern visitors arrive by automobile, bus, and aircraft. But
our favorite approach to Louisville is coming downstream on the
Ohio River, late of a June evening with the river breeze in our
faces, the city skyline taking shape ahead of us, and a full moon
rising above the trees on the port side. The *Belle of Louisville,*
one of the last of the real river steamboats, churns smoothly
along beneath us. The captain sends a salute from the steam
whistle to the captain of a big diesel-powered boat plowing its
way upstream with a tow of barges. Shades of Mark Twain!

The steam-driven Belle of Louisville, *owned by the city, makes*
public excursions up and down the Ohio.

On the lower deck we find the youthful, burly first mate and stop to talk. He has been on the river since he came out of high school not many years ago. What about the Captain? Aging and gray? An ancient boatman with river water for blood, steeped in the lore of long-ago steamboats? "He's twenty-four," we're told.

The *Belle of Louisville* was built in 1914 and traveled under two other names before the city bought her at auction in 1962. Louisville still owns this river steamer and operates her in the Louisville vicinity so successfully that groups apply months in advance to charter her. The *Belle* is one of only five steamboats still in service on the inland rivers. "If they're not steam, I don't count 'em," explains the first mate.

We saw from the top deck the pair of gilded elk antlers the *Belle* wears proudly on the front of her wheelhouse. Elk antlers on a steamboat? These are more than antlers; they are a trophy awarded to the winner of an annual race.

Once a year, during Derby Week, the *Belle of Louisville* races the *Delta Queen* to determine which of the two venerable river steamboats is the faster. They start beneath the Clark Memorial Bridge, the *Belle* on the Indiana side, the *Delta Queen* on the Kentucky side, headed upstream. Crowds on board both boats pay premium prices for this special ride and stand at the rails while thousands of others line the riverbanks, both in Kentucky and Indiana, to watch the racing steamers push upstream to Six Mile Island, go around the island, and return to the finish line. There are moments when the speed of these racing monsters approaches 12 miles an hour on the downstream run.

We asked the first mate on the *Belle* why he thinks his boat beat the *Delta Queen* the previous year. "When the *Delta Queen* came upstream to Louisville she was just finishing a regular trip. She had to be fueled and made ready and take on a load of passengers. We were ready and waiting. Then, when the race started, the *Delta Queen*'s paddle sat lower in the water, and it takes more power to get her moving this way so we could make a faster start and we could maneuver better." The *Belle* wears her elk antlers proudly, the clear winner in the only big steamboat race left on the inland waters.

Steamboat racing has a long history. "Two red hot steam boats raging along neck and neck," wrote Mark Twain, "quaking and straining from stem to stern, spouting white steam from the pipes, pouring black smoke from the chimneys, raining down sparks, parting the river into long streams of hissing foam, this is sport that makes a body's very liver curl."

From the top deck of the *Belle,* I recalled again the words of the late Captain Ellis C. Mace, as he told me of the contest between the *Fleetwood* and the *New South* on these very waters. The race began in the summer of 1890 and lasted three months after the *New South* had come north to capture a share of the lucrative river shipping market between Cincinnati and Louisville. When the *New South* arrived, the *Fleetwood* was ready and waiting for what Captain Mace said, with a shake of his wrinkled

Belle of Louisville *passengers have a river-level view of the hills flanking the Ohio.*

head, was "the greatest river-boat race of all time," even including the famous tilt between the *Natchez* and the *Robert E. Lee*.

Day after day the *New South* and the *Fleetwood* raced up and down the Ohio between the two river cities with neither one able to gain a clear lead. Captain Mace was then first mate on the *Fleetwood*. As the race continued, the crowds grew. Both boats carried passengers cheering their boat on.

During the three months the *Fleetwood* carried 144,000 paying passengers and netted a $36,000 profit. "She was a faster boat," said Captain Mace. "But she was always so heavily loaded with passengers we couldn't keep ahead." In the three months these boats raced, they covered 26,000 miles on the Ohio River.

The fall of 1890 was dry and the river ran low. There was the ever-present hazard of running aground on a sandbar with a full load of passengers, so the two captains finally discontinued their racing by mutual consent. Neither had won. That winter the *New South* slipped away downstream to work out of Memphis. "Otherwise," said Captain Mace, "that race might have started up again in the spring. And nobody knows how long it might have gone on."

Old Louisville

On a bright afternoon in June we went searching for the Louisville that was. Old Louisville began in the 1830s and flourished after the Civil War when Old Louisville was New Louisville. This was the southern edge of the spreading city. Not until the 1970s, when the area was on the skids, did this section become known as Old Louisville. It was then that local citizens organized to preserve the splendid old section with its fine Victorian homes fashioned from red brick and Bedford limestone hauled from across the river in Indiana.

For twenty years, from 1950 to 1970, commercial interests were advancing on this historic section of the city. During those years, 3,000 of the fine old homes fell before the wrecking ball. Then, with formation of the Old Louisville Preservation District, the tide slowed, then turned. All Louisville is proud of the district

Historic homes along the quiet shaded streets of Old Louisville are being restored to their former grandeur. (Photo by George Laycock)

where 17,000 people now live in houses that have served people for a century and more.

The best way to see Old Louisville is to walk. Travel on foot gives one time to think about the homes and the pace of living along these wide streets in years past. For us, the favorite walk is along St. James Court between Magnolia at the edge of Central Park and Hill St. Here are some of the grandest of the Victorian homes, and through the center of the boulevard there is a wide median parkway with grass, towering shade trees, and a fountain. Along this street, and the courtyards that branch from it, some of Louisville's best-remembered poets and authors have lived, but today the homes are occupied by owners from a wide variety of occupations.

The Rosa Anna Hughes Home, now a home for the elderly,

St. James Court is a favorite street with tourists who visit Old Louisville.

stands at the entrance to St. James Court. The house at 1424 St. James Court is noted for its Victorian Gothic facade. Louisville poet, Madison Cawein, lived in the house at 1436 St. James Court. And down the block at 1444 is the Alice Hegan Rice Home where the author of *Mrs. Wiggs of the Cabbage Patch* lived. The entire section is on the National Register of Historic Places, one of the country's largest National Register Districts.

Even if you are not into old buildings and the study of the architecture of the late nineteenth and early twentieth centuries, you will enjoy a visit to Old Louisville, a reminder of a more gracious era.

Butchertown

Another famous old section of Louisville is Butchertown, so named because it was once the center of the meat industry. Today there are many small shops as well as renovated old homes in Butchertown. Bakery Square at the corner of Webster and Washington streets, is a three-story building where the rich odors of baking bread once wafted from the ovens. Some of the ovens are still there, but the old buildings have been converted to a community of boutiques and specialty shops offering everything from pulled taffy to antique dolls or fine-quality crafts. There is a restaurant in the courtyard.

Set off on a walking tour through Butchertown and see the renovations that are bringing the old structures back to their former glory. Of special interest are the St. Joseph's Catholic Church, in Gothic Revival style, at 1406 E. Washington St.; Dulaney Advertising, a restored Italianate building at 129 Adams St.; and along Story Ave. the renovated neighborhood cafes, homes, and taverns of which Min's Cafe at 1605 Story Ave. is probably the best known. The Hadley Pottery at 1570 Story Ave. has a factory outlet where you may find some bargains.

Once a year Butchertown stages the biggest party it can arrange and models it after an old Bavarian tradition. The Oktoberfest idea was born more than a century and a half ago in Bavaria where the celebration became a party of such proportions that everyone wanted to perpetuate the idea.

From this the Oktoberfest grew, and far away in Louisville, on the banks of the Ohio, the folk of Butchertown have for many years held their own celebration on the first weekend in October. This is one of the major community parties of the year in the Ohio Valley.

Funds raised help restore more of the historic old Butchertown buildings. Visitors find music and dancing in the street, with beer and food stands serving kartoffel salad, bratwurst, bohnen suppe, and other foods whose popularity has survived more than a century in the Ohio Valley. The site for Oktoberfest is 1332 Story Ave.

Heritage Weekends on the Plaza/Belvedere preserve the cultures of Louisville's numerous ethnic groups.

More Festivals

Louisville has its share of annual festivals where visitors are always welcome. Various "heritage weekend celebrations" are staged by ethnic groups on the Riverfront Plaza/Belvedere where there is food, music and dancing. For information, call the Heritage Corporation, (502) 582-2421.

In the Iroquois Park Amphitheatre, in August, The Kentucky Music Weekend, brings mountain music along with music workshops and workshops in instrument making.

The Kentucky State Fair comes to the fairgrounds, on Crittenden Dr., late in August.

The first weekend in June, downtown on the Riverfront Plaza/Belvedere, the Bluegrass Music Festival of the U.S. offers what

The annual Bluegrass Music Festival draws large crowds to Louisville.

is billed as the largest of the bluegrass music festivals, with big-name entertainers.

The St. James Art Fair is held in St. James Court the first weekend in October. Artwork and crafts are exhibited and sold. Tours of Old Louisville residences are included in the festivities.

Museums

The Filson Club was founded in 1884 to collect and display items of historic interest from in and around Louisville. This little museum is open to the public free of charge from 9 A.M. to 5 P.M. at 118 W. Breckinridge St.

We saw a number of paintings by noted regional artists, a collection of arrowheads, old guns, and hand tools.

Most famous of all the exhibits however, is a 3-foot-high section cut from a 300-year-old beech tree. The giant gray tree once stood in Iroquois Park beside the trail that led from the Falls of the Ohio to Green River. Once a message is carved on the trunk of a beech tree the letters last as long as the tree. The tree trunk in the Filson Club was cut in the spring of 1936. We peered into the case tracing the barely legible letters on the section of log.

> D BOONE
> KILL A BAR
> ZOIS 1803

"Zois"? Perhaps an abbreviation for the Louisiana Purchase. Nearby hangs a buckskin hunting jacket believed to have been worn by D. Boone.

In a little museum off I-264 (the Watterson Expressway) every exhibit honors one of Kentucky's all-time best-known colonels. Displayed in a prominent location is the small pressure cooker in which Colonel Harland Sanders prepared the first orders of the Kentucky Fried Chicken that was to make him famous and wealthy. Sanders, a sixth-grade dropout, lived to see his restaurants flourish in forty-eight countries. Fried chicken fanciers can find his remarkable career traced here. The museum at 1441 Gardiner Lane is off I-264 at Newburg Rd. exit.

On exhibit in the Filson Club's library and museum is the tree on which "D Boone kill a bar Zois 1803." (Photo by George Laycock)

Locust Grove, once the home of George Rogers Clark, "Father of the West," is a museum. (Photo by Kentucky Dept. of Public Information)

Also reached easily from the Watterson Expressway are two early homes that have been restored and opened as museums. They give thousands of visitors annually a better understanding of life in and around Louisville in the early nineteenth century. Farmington near the intersection of I-264 and Bardstown Rd. and off Wendell St., was the heart of a 1,500-acre plantation owned by John and Lucy Fry Speed. The 14-room house, designed by Thomas Jefferson, was begun in 1808 and stands as an excellent example of Federal architecture.

A pleasant volunteer lady with upswept white hair guides us through the house explaining details found in each room. The house is in excellent condition, and the rooms are fully furnished with pieces that were in use when the house was built and occupied. This is truly a look at the graceful life of wealthy people in Louisville's early times. The grounds are pleasant, and the giant trees shaded the lawn when Farmington was built. Admission is charged and Farmington is open every day but Thanksgiving, Christmas, and New Year's Day.

Where Hwy. 42 crosses the Watterson Expressway there are signs pointing to the Zachary Taylor Cemetery and Locust Grove.

Farmington, a historic home designed by Thomas Jefferson, is now a museum. (Photo by Kentucky Dept. of Public Information)

The burial grounds of Zachary Taylor, twelfth President of the United States, and thousands of other military people who served their country, is just off the Watterson Expressway. There is a monument to the ex-President.

Signs beyond the cemetery gate lead to Farmington, a large two-story brick plantation home set in 55 acres of quiet shaded

Zachary Taylor, twelfth President of the United States, is buried in the Zachary Taylor National Cemetery. (Photo by George Laycock)

lawns and fields at 561 Blankenbaker Lane. Farmington was the home of Major William Croghan, who came here in 1790. George Rogers Clark, Croghan's brother-in-law, lived here the last several years of his life, cared for by his sister Lucy Clark Croghan. In this home also the Croghans entertained a long list of noted visitors including: John James Audubon, Aaron Burr, and three Presidents of the United States. It was here that General George Rogers Clark's youngest brother, William, and Meriwether Lewis once told stories to eager listeners of their adventures blazing new trails to the Pacific.

The Museum of History and Science, home of a mummified Egyptian princess, in downtown Louisville, is one of the restored buildings on West Main Street.

Locust Grove is furnished from the ballroom to the summer kitchen. Admission is charged for the house tour. Closed Thanksgiving, Christmas, and New Year's Day.

In the heart of Louisville, at 727 W. Main St., is the Louisville Museum of History and Science where visitors can immerse themselves in river lore and natural history of the Valley. But exhibits displayed here reach far beyond the shores of the Ohio and range from an actual Apollo training capsule to a 2,000-year-old mummified Egyptian princess, named Then-Hotep, who has seen rough times since she arrived in Louisville. When the famous flood of 1937 lifted the Ohio River over its banks into the downtown flood plain, Then-Hotep floated. Mummy and case drifted freely about the museum premises for days until the water went down again.

As the flood waters receded the mummy seemed at first to be a total loss. But a museum does not abandon its mummy lightly. The linen cloth, 2,000 yards of it, was gently unwrapped from around the leathery mummy and taken to a laundry for drying. Then-Hotep was oven dried for fifteen hours, then kept in a vacuum tank for twenty-four hours. The remains were lovingly rewrapped, and the mummified Egyptian princess returned to her case where she lies in state. "Today," says an official museum report, "the condition of Then-Hotep is stable."

"She is not a mint specimen," admits a museum staff person, "but the case is on display because the mummy is such a popular exhibit locally."

Across the street from the Museum of History and Science, at 730 West Main St., is the American Saddle Horse Museum. The history of the saddle horse is traced here, and paintings and equipment related to the breed are displayed. For horse fanciers, this museum is an important stop because this is widely considered the finest collection of saddle horse materials in one place. Admission charged.

Perhaps the best-known museum in Louisville is the J. B. Speed Art Museum on the campus of the University of Louisville, at 2035 S. Third St. In all of Kentucky there is not an art museum older or larger. This nationally recognized art museum has paintings by Rembrandt, Peter Paul Rubens, and others, as well as noted collections of sculpture and tapestries.

The J. B. Speed Art Museum, Kentucky's oldest and largest art museum, is near the University of Louisville.

The Kentucky Railway Museum at the corner of LaGrange Rd. and Dorsey Lane, displays 60 pieces of railroad equipment including steam locomotives and assorted rail cars, some of them more than a century old. This museum is open weekend and holiday afternoons from Memorial Day to October and there is admission charged. Phone: (502) 245-9902.

The Kentucky Derby Museum is located at 700 Central Ave. It's just inside the main entrance to Churchill Downs, and exhibits here trace the complete history of the Derby. No admission charged. Open 9:30 to 4:30, except weekdays during meets when it is open only from 9 to 11 A.M.

Music and Drama

Louisville has outstanding cultural events and institutions. As a repertory theater, the award winning Actors Theatre of Louisville, often said to be the best of regional theaters, has become widely known. Its performances, at 316 W. Main St., are generally staged every evening except Mondays from October through May. Phone: (502) 584-1205.

Performances of the Louisville Ballet are at Memorial Auditorium, 970 S. Fourth St. There are five programs per season. Phone: (502) 582-1132.

The Louisville Orchestra performs at Macauley Theatre, 315 W. Broadway, and offers a variety of programs, including pop concerts and famous guest soloists and conductors. Phone: (502) 587-8681.

Macauley Theatre is also the setting for Broadway shows brought to town by the Louisville Theatrical Association. Phone: (502) 584-0180.

The Kentucky Opera Association also presents its performances here. There are four programs each season presented with leading national guest artists. This is among the country's oldest opera companies. Phone: (502) 584-4500.

The Louisville Bach Society offers four programs per season both in orchestral and choral music. Phone: (502) 893-5355.

Stage One, Louisville Children's Theatre, 2117 Payne St., offers professional productions almost the year around for audiences ranging through the high school level. Phone: (502) 895-9486.

Churchill Downs and the Derby

Horse racing belongs in Kentucky. It began with spirited dashes along country lanes and grew until raising and racing horses became a major Kentucky enterprise, making the bluegrass country and Louisville world famous.

The Kentucky Derby, the world's most famous horse race, is held at Churchill Downs on the first Saturday of May.

Following the Civil War the racing of Thoroughbreds slid into the doldrums and the breeders of Thoroughbreds across the bluegrass country faced less demand for their fine horses. The plantation owners no longer had the wealth that permitted them to indulge heavily in horse racing.

Instead of folding their tents and vanishing from the American scene, however, the horse breeders began searching for an answer, and this led to taking a note from the racing world in England. The Thoroughbred industry in Kentucky decided that it should have races with much larger purses than were being offered, that the horses should be matched by age, and that this would bring in big crowds to the race tracks.

South of Louisville, in what was then rural countryside, the
Louisville Jockey Club began to build a splendid new race track
in 1874. It was named Churchill Downs, and the new track
opened on May 17, 1875 when 10,000 fans flocked to Churchill
Downs to witness the first Kentucky Derby. That day Aristides
pulled out in front of the favorites to set a new record, and earn a
purse of $1,000. The Kentucky Derby was established immedi-
ately on the American sports scene.

No natural disaster so far has stopped the running of the Kentucky Derby. Following the famous flood of 1937, when water
and mud swamped 30 square miles of Louisville, including Churchill Downs, workmen moved in on the cleaning job. On the first
Saturday in May, War Admiral swept to victory on the famous
oval where six feet of water and mud stood three months earlier.
The Derby was right on schedule.

After more than a century, the Derby has grown from a two-
minute horse race to a 10-day-long "Derby Week" celebration
during which Louisville erupts with its own distinctive madness.
Each spring when the warm sun brings out the redbud and dogwood and the colts are frisking in the paddocks, the finest three-
year-old Thoroughbreds anywhere are being groomed for the
most famous of horse races.

As the community, joined by hundreds of thousands of visitors
from all over, prepares for the annual Derby on the first Saturday
in May, there is entertainment of all kinds. Parties, parades, din-
ners, dances, and picnics. Louisville claims its Derby Festival is
the northern equivalent of the Mardi Gras. Derby week begins
with a giant ball and the choosing of a queen.

The three-year-old Thoroughbreds are not the only ones com-
peting at Derby time. During the days of the Derby Festival there
is time for nearly everything raceable to get into the competition.
Balloonists race their colorful hot-air sacks in the Great Balloon
Race billed as one of the premier balloon races anywhere.

There is also a "Mini-Marathon" for runners who chase each
other along Louisville streets, following a 13.1-mile course from
Iroquois Park to the Plaza/Belvedere on the riverfront. Four
thousand runners, grouped by sex and ranging in age from 10 and
below to 60 and above, pursue their trophies.

Meanwhile, Louisville's waitresses and waiters have their own official race, not a marathon, but a brisk trot down the three-block-long River City Mall on Fourth St., each of them carrying, as delicately as possible, a tray of filled wine glasses. Those first to reach the finish line with the least wine spilled are winners, and contestants then drain the glasses on the spot.

Out on the Ohio River, the *Belle of Louisville,* the steamboating pride of the city, prepares for its biggest race of the year, against Cincinnati's *Delta Queen.* In 1982 the steamboat *Natchez* came upriver from New Orleans and finished ahead of both Ohio River boats.

Meanwhile, through the week, the horses race at Churchill Downs, all of these events leading inevitably to the grand old race that started the whole thing; the Kentucky Derby on the first Saturday of May. In two minutes the big race is over.

Nobody knows how many mint juleps are consumed through this frenetic week of joyous celebration in River City, or how many times they must listen to the mellow strains of "My Old Kentucky Home." For ten days Louisville forgets her reputation as a rather conservative, quiet city and lets her hair down. Everyone, native and visitor alike, loves it and business flourishes. At night, when the sun no longer shines bright on my old Kentucky home, the parties continue as Louisville celebrates the world's most famous horse race and whatever else there is to celebrate.

Horse Farms

This is horse country the year around, however, and visitors to central Kentucky often ask about touring the famous horse farms. Many of the best known are up the road around Lexington, but in the Louisville area there are eight important Thoroughbred farms and another dozen farms that raise saddle horses. Although many are open to visitors, nearly all require advance arrangements. Those open may change from time to time and the best plan is to ask the Louisville Visitors' Bureau for a rundown of horse farms that can be visited currently.

Whether you get beyond the gates or not, a drive through the bluegrass country is a pleasant outing, especially in spring and

The world's finest horses graze on bluegrass farms around Louisville. (Photo by Kentucky Dept. of Public Information)

summer, when the horses can be seen behind the wooden fences that divide the bluegrass pastures.

The Zoo

The Louisville Zoological Garden, which is also the Kentucky State Zoo, is open the year around. It is situated on 58 acres north of the Watterson Expressway between the Newburg and Poplar Level Road exits. The variety of creatures is wide here; everything from bald eagles to polar bears living in the 60 exhibits. The zoo also conducts special events during the year. Visitors reach the zoo easily; it is a 10-minute drive from downtown, and public transportation provides direct bus service. To check bus schedules, call (502) 585-1234.

From polar bears to friendly goats, there are favorite animals for all ages at Louisville's zoo.

Bike Trails

Louisville, which is relatively level, is rapidly becoming a bicycle town. There are more than a hundred miles of bike routes marked through the city. These are not free of all hazards, but they are chosen by bicyclists and traffic experts because they are relatively safe as well as convenient, and they offer a direct route between important points of interest.

There are three kinds of bike routes in the city. One is the roadway which the cyclists share with the motor vehicle drivers with no special bicycle path set apart. Another is the bicycle lane, an exclusive bicycle lane set apart from the rest of the street by a painted line. The third is a bike trail used only by bicycles. Louisville has a long-range plan to bring its bike routes up to 550 miles and encourage riders to enjoy their bicycles and use them increasingly for commuting. All the bike routes are marked with green signs.

In addition, Louisville provides bicycle parking racks and lockers in 12 downtown locations.

Louisville Sluggers

Baseball players everywhere know Louisville as home of the Louisville Slugger bats used not only by 90 percent of professional ballplayers, but also by millions of amateurs. Louisville might not be famous at all among baseball people if Pete Browning had not broken his bat.

Pete "The Old Gladiator" Browning was the favorite slugger of the Louisville Eclipse. One day in 1884 he went to the local woodworking shop of J. Fred Hillerich. Browning was scheduled to play the following day and needed a new bat. Hillerich, however, specialized in making butter churns and porch railings and wanted nothing to do with baseball.

On the other hand, his son, Bud Hillerich, was a serious baseball fan, so that evening Bud turned out a new bat for Browning, and the slugger went forth with it the following day and racked up three hits for three times at bat. Word spread among players that Hillerich knew how to make good bats.

This marked the birth of the Louisville Slugger bats. Today the company is Hillerich and Bradsby, and although the corporate offices are still in Louisville, the plant has been moved across the Ohio River to Jeffersonville, Indiana.

H&B has a vault containing hundreds of special bats that served as patterns for bats used by major league players. When a club orders new bats for one of its players, the master bat is taken from the vault, placed on a lathe, and duplicates are turned to exact specifications.

An H&B official told us they have some 50,000 visitors a year through the plant to see both baseball bats and golf clubs in production. Visitors can also see the company's baseball museum.

There are 2 half-hour tours daily, Monday through Friday. No reservations are needed. The tour director can be reached by calling (812) 288-6611.

From this factory come two million wooden ball bats annually. But in recent years aluminum has been replacing wood on the ball diamonds, and H&B has shifted with the demand. The company now turns out half a million aluminum bats a year in addition to those shaped from wood billets.

There is always talk around H&B about whether or not aluminum bats will be used in the big leagues. Tradition favors wood strongly. "Can you imagine," asks one baseball fan, "anybody saying, 'He really laid the aluminum to that one'?"

Kentucky Bourbon

In Louisville you have arrived at the home of Bourbon, the sippin' whiskey sometimes called our national drink. Half the world's supply of Bourbon is distilled in and around Louisville. It is said here, perhaps seriously, that the state candy is a Bourbon-filled chocolate.

Early farmers, up and down the Ohio, cleared their acres and grew corn, then faced the problem of how to ship their crop to market. The best answer was to convert it to a distilled beverage.

Quality varied, but word spread that the farmers of Bourbon County were producing a whiskey that was smoother and tastier than that from any other region. The grain they used was predominantly corn, and the water was pure limestone water from Kentucky's famous underground sources. The whiskey took the name of the county where it was first recognized as having special quality, and Bourbon became a product of major importance in Kentucky.

Louisville Bourbon had its origins in 1783 when Evan Williams opened a small distillery at the corner of Fifth and Water streets. After the Whiskey Rebellion in 1794, some of the distillers of Pennsylvania moved west. They came down the Ohio to the falls and set up business in 1816 in Louisville at the foot of Main Street. They knew of the growing reputation of Bourbon and invested their fortunes in the world's largest distillery. Louisville was now on its way to becoming the center of the Bourbon industry.

Today, when you are in Louisville, you can tour the distilleries to see how Bourbon is made. Brown Forman Distillery has tours on weekdays. Old Fitzgerald Distillery also conducts tours. Joseph E. Seagram & Sons, Inc. has two tours daily Monday through Friday. No children under 11 permitted.

The Federal Government keeps a firm hand on the whiskey industry and has decreed that Bourbon meet certain rigid specifications. It must, by law, be made from a grain mixture at least 51 percent corn, although usually the percentage is 65 to 70 percent corn. It must also be at least 80 proof (proof is two times the percentage of alcohol), be free of additives including coloring agents and flavoring, be distilled at temperatures below 160° F., and be aged for at least two years (a more common aging time is four years) in new white oak barrels charred on the inside. The charred wood is credited with giving the Bourbon its rich brown color.

During storage and aging the keys to the warehouses are kept by the Federal Government which has a major interest in the whole process because of the tax collected from whiskey sales.

The highest purpose to which Louisville produced Bourbon can rise is to be used in the production of a genuine mint julep during Kentucky Derby week.

The Official Drink

The mint julep, sometimes called "a depth charge with a drawl," mixes the freshness of spring and the mellowness of Kentucky Bourbon. Tradition surrounds this noted drink. The recipe may vary from one place to the next, but here is a widely accepted one.

In a tumbler, preferably silver, dissolve one teaspoon of granulated sugar in a teaspoon of water. Add three bruised mint leaves, then fill the tumbler three-quarters full of crushed ice and add two jiggers of Bourbon. Stand a fresh mint sprig in the ice and set the tumbler in the refrigerator to chill until frost forms on the tumbler.

Camping

If you are equipped with tent or trailer and plan to live outdoors, there are 8 parks with campgrounds. These include Chenoweth, Fisherman's, Forest View, Long Run, McNeely, Sun Valley, Tom Wallace, and Waverly. Only Sun Valley is open to trailer camping, however. Camping in these parks is free, but you will need a permit from the Metropolitan Park and Recreation Board. The campgrounds in the parks are on the primitive order. Across the river at Clarksville, Indiana, there's a plush KOA Campground at the Marriott Inn.

Louisville does not simply ignore the thousands who visit its parks but follows up to see that they have full opportunities to enjoy the experience. The family on a picnic in Creason Park can check out equipment for playing baseball, basketball, volleyball, or even tug-o-war. Meanwhile, Louisville's parks offer special programs of drama and music. In Central Park, at Fourth St. and Magnolia, in Old Louisville, there is Shakespeare in the Park in July and August. Iroquois Park offers free concerts, films, plays, and ballet in its amphitheater 40 nights during the summer.

The Parks

One hundred years ago Louisville leaders sensed the growing need for parks where people could relax. They decided on three large parks, all connected by a system of parkways, and this marked the birth of Cherokee, Shawnee, and Iroquois Parks.

Since then the roster of parks has continued to grow. There are 166 parks scattered around the city and county. The biggest of them is Jefferson County Memorial Forest—2,200 acres. Nearly any outdoor activity you might enjoy is available in these parks and, for the most part, they are free.

Tennis players flock to the parks because there are 190 outdoor courts. The only one for which there is a charge is the Louisville Tennis Center which has a tennis pro and pro shop. Reservations are required here at least forty-eight hours in advance. Elsewhere, the courts are open without reservations.

There is a reasonable fee charged at the 9 public golf courses on the park areas. These courses are open seven days a week. Each has its own pro and pro shop, and all have highly maintained greens.

If you want to go horseback riding, check in at Iroquois Riding Stable in Iroquois Park, where horses are rented by the hour. If you have your own horse, there are bridle paths ranging from 3 to 10 miles long at 5 metro parks.

E. P. "Tom" Sawyer State Park, 319 acres in southeastern Jefferson County offers tennis, swimming, picnic and playground, and an archery range.

Five parks in the metro system have access to the Ohio River for boaters and fishermen. But anglers who want to fish smaller waters can find fishing lakes at 7 parks where the fishing is free. All that is required is a Kentucky fishing license.

Dining Out

Ask about the best place to eat out and Louisville people no longer give you directions to Cincinnati. The growth of convention and tourist business in Louisville has spawned the rise of a wide range of excellent eating places offering varied ethnic dishes as well as standard menus.

The Louisville restaurant most likely to be labeled "the best" is Casa Grisanti, 100 E. Liberty St. This restaurant, rated four stars by the Mobile Guide, features northern Italian cuisine served in an elegant atmosphere. Reservations are advised. Open for dinner only. Closed Sunday.

Another Grisanti restaurant in Louisville, less expensive and less formal, is Mama Grisanti's at 3938 Dupont Circle. Mama's is the place for homemade pasta. Open evenings for dinner and on Sundays for brunch and dinner.

Kunz's The Dutchman, 526 River City Mall, was established in 1892 and claims to be the oldest restaurant in Louisville. It is open for lunch and dinner and is famous for its steaks and mint juleps. Park in The Dutchman's parking lot at Fifth and Chestnut streets.

Bill Boland's Dining Room, at 3708 Bardstown Rd., is a popular restaurant. Open for dinner only, and closed Monday.

The Old House at 432 S. Fifth St., a charming restaurant in a 150-year-old antebellum home, offers a varied menu for lunch and dinner.

For good seafood at reasonable prices, try one of the four Kingfish Restaurants. You'll find them at Sixth St. and River Rd., at 3401 Bardstown Rd., at 3021 Upper River Rd., and 7483 Dixie Hwy. They look like packet boats painted bright red and white. Dine in or carry out.

Other popular family dining places are the Bob Evans Farms Restaurants at Newburg Rd. and I-264, and also on Hurstbourne Lane at I-64. Open 7 days a week.

Bauer's, 3612 Brownsboro Rd., 2 miles west of the junction of Hwy. 42 and I-264, is famous for its steaks and German dishes. Bauer's is open for breakfast, lunch, and dinner and offers a children's menu.

The New Orleans House, 412 W. Chestnut St., just off Fourth Ave., and the New Orleans East, 9424 Shelbyville Rd., are for the seafood lover with a big appetite. Fairly expensive, but one price covers everything—if you can face a whole Maine lobster plus dessert, after feasting on the buffet of appetizers and side dishes.

Claiming the best Mexican food in town are the Tumbleweed Restaurants, 1900 Mellwood, off I-71 at the Zorn Ave. exit, or 3985 Dutchman Lane in Dupont Sq.

We like The Flagship, with its two revolving dining areas for a special treat. This is a posh, four-star restaurant at the top of the Galt House, Fourth Ave. and River Rd. Gourmet food, fine service, and a splendid ever-changing view of the Ohio River. Prices are on the high side.

Hasenour's is a well-known Louisville dining place, at Barret Ave. and Oak St. Open for lunch and dinner. Sunday, dinner only. Prime rib and sauerbraten.

Hardin County:
Mr. Lincoln and Gen. Patton

The courthouse in Elizabethtown is a hub, and streets radiate out from it like the spokes in a wheel, carrying traffic to the center of town and around the courthouse in a pattern that keeps pedestrians guessing about which way to jump. But Elizabethtown was designed in an age when there were no speeding automobiles or trucks. In 1780 Samuel Haycraft, Thomas Helm, and Andrew Hynes founded the town and named it in honor of Andrew's wife.

Also recalled as an early resident was Thomas Lincoln, father of Abraham, arriving sometime before 1804. The senior Lincoln stayed here after he married Nancy Hanks, and their first child, Sarah, was born here.

Before you have been long in Elizabethtown a local citizen will ask if you have seen the cannonball. During the Civil War, probably when John Hunt Morgan shelled the town, a cannonball imbedded itself in the middle of a brick building across from the courthouse. It is still there.

A block up the street is the Brown-Pusey House, dating back to 1825, once a stagecoach inn and boardinghouse. Then it was given to Elizabethtown for a community house in 1923 and now houses meeting rooms and a library. Weddings are frequently held in the reception room.

In a smaller stone house attached to the Brown-Pusey House, General George Armstrong Custer lived for two years during which he wrote *My Life on the Plains*. The Brown-Pusey House is on the National Register of Historic Places, and visitors are welcome here.

The Kentucky Fiddlers Contest and Convention is held in E'town each year the last weekend in May. More than $5,000 is given away as prizes for excellence in playing bluegrass banjo, mandolin, guitar, harmonica, and fiddle, while bluegrass bands and dancers also compete.

Visitors will find motels and restaurants located on highways 31W and 62. From I-65 take either exit 91 or 94. A short distance north of Elizabethtown on Hwy. 31W is the Coca-Cola Bottling Company and it is worth a stop whether thirsty or not. Visitors tour the plant to see bottles and cans filled at 300 a minute.

Bill Schmidt, president of the company, and his wife began some years ago collecting Coca-Cola memorabilia and now have the world's largest collection. "There is an association of people who collect Coke things," Schmidt told us, "called the Cola Clan of America. There are two thousand or more members, and they are scattered all over the country." As the Schmidt collection continued to grow, the Schmidts planned a special museum for it on the second floor of the bottling works.

One of the first exhibits in Schmidts' Marvelous Museum is an 1890 ice-cream parlor with its cut marble walls and counters. Cases display dozens of bottles designed for Coca-Cola. Over the years since the soft drink was first introduced in 1886, the com-

The world's finest collection of Coca-Cola memorabilia is housed in a special museum in Elizabethtown, where hundreds of visitors see the collection every week. (Photo by George Laycock)

pany has put its famous name on dozens of items ranging from calendars to pocketknives, and the Schmidts have brought these materials together in one place. Schmidt is especially proud of their collection of calendars and trays. "Some items," he says, "are worth thousands of dollars. It is getting harder to find them, but they still turn up in flea markets and sales when people clean out their attics."

The collection has grown to 3,000 pieces and is so large that Schmidt plans to move it to a separate building.

Behind the bottling works is Freeman Lake Park, and in it is the Lincoln Heritage House, which is on the National Register of Historic Places. It was built in 1789 and 1805 in two parts for a local pioneer, Hardin Thomas. One of the workmen building the larger section of the house was Thomas Lincoln, family friend, who did much of the interior woodwork. It is a handsome log house, a good place to take a picture for your album or enjoy a picnic lunch beside the lake.

Farther north on Hwy. 31W, on the edge of Fort Knox, is another famous museum. This sprawling military reservation is the Army's tank-training center. Easily seen from the highway, near the Chafee Ave. entrance, the Patton Museum of Cavalry and Armor houses the Patton Gallery with the World War II possessions of General George S. Patton, Jr. Those who might have seen Patton's famous jeep in Europe during WW II can see it here again, permanently retired and complete with its four stars.

Nearby are the famous pearl-handled pistols as well as General Patton's truck that served as field headquarters and the collection of medals presented him from both his own and foreign nations, along with countless other items by which the general is remembered.

In other galleries visitors trace the complete history of cavalry and armor, while outside on the grounds there are still more historic rows of armored vehicles. No admission charged and the museum is open the year around. Phone: (502) 624-3812.

Fort Knox is also famous for gold. In 1937 the massive vault in which the U. S. Government stores its gold bullion was new. The gold began arriving by rail. Bricks of it are stored today in the vault built with steel I beams and steel cylinders encased in con-

The General Patton Museum at Fort Knox traces the life and career of the famous WW II general. (Photo by George Laycock)

crete. The door, weighing more than 30 tons, can be opened only by various staff people each operating separate dials with combinations not known to anyone else.

If you have wondered about the size of these gold bricks, each is 7 × 3⅝ × 1¾ inches, roughly the size of a standard building brick. Each gold brick weighs about 27½ pounds.

The vault is inside a building made of 16,500 cubic feet of granite, lined with concrete and steel. It has its own water and emergency power supplies. The building is surrounded with high steel fences, guard towers, and assorted burglar alarms. Visitors allowed? Hardly.

Up the Road

Bardstown

By driving 25 miles east of Elizabethtown on the Bluegrass Parkway, one comes to the historic city of Bardstown. Near this central Kentucky city is the mansion where Stephen Foster came in 1852 to visit his cousins and was so inspired by the setting that he wrote "My Old Kentucky Home." The mansion, a stately three-story brick structure, stands in My Old Kentucky Home State Park, known as Federal Hill, and is open the year around. Visitors are led through the rooms by guides in antebellum costumes. Judge John Rowan completed the mansion in 1818. The popular *Stephen Foster Story,* an outdoor drama, is presented from mid-June through Labor Day, nightly except Monday. Phone: (502) 348-5971.

My Old Kentucky Home State Park has campsites with electrical hookup and water. Visitors will also find a 9-hole golf course, picnic area, and gift shop.

St. Joseph's Cathedral, first Catholic cathedral west of the Allegheny Mountains, is in Bardstown. It was completed in 1819 and is open to visitors. Displayed here are many paintings that have been given to the cathedral.

On Barton Rd., a quarter of a mile off Hwy. 62 west of Court Square, is the Barton Museum of Whiskey History, with displays that trace the history of the distilling industry in America back for 170 years. This is the place to learn about distiller E. C. Booz whose name became a slang generic term for alcoholic drink, and you can even see an 1854 Booz bottle. There are displays tracing the events of the Prohibition years, as well as exhibits telling of the Whiskey Rebellion and of the sales of liquor by both George Washington and Abraham Lincoln. There are daily tours and admission is free. This is also the place to see the daily operation of a major distillery where Kentucky Bourbon is distilled, aged, and bottled.

Lincoln's Birthplace

The Abraham Lincoln story begins, as we always heard, in a little log cabin 3 miles south of Hodgenville, Kentucky, which is 13 miles from Elizabethtown. Hodgenville, the county seat of Larue County, is the town Lincoln remembered from his early boyhood. For many visitors the best time to go to Hodgenville for fun, food, and music is on the second weekend in October when the community is paying honor to its famous son during the Lincoln Days Celebration. There are contests for Lincoln look-alikes, rail splitters, and beard growers, plus art shows, band contests, and pioneer games.

The Abraham Lincoln Birthplace National Historic Site is on highways 31E and 61, and this site has been operated by the National Park Service since 1916. Situated here is a simple log cabin, built from what are believed to be the original logs from the Lincoln cabin. It is housed in a stone memorial building, and the park is open every day but Christmas. There is an information center plus a picnic area.

The Lincolns lived here until Abe was about two and a half years old, then moved ten miles to the northeast to the Knob Creek Farm known as Lincoln's Boyhood Home, where they lived until he was nearly eight and the family departed for Indiana. It was on the toll road passing the Knob Creek Farm house that Lincoln first saw slaves being driven along the highway by dealers to be sold in the South. The Knob Creek Farm, 7 miles northeast of Hodgenville on Hwy. 31E, is open to visitors from April 1 through October. The cabin here was rebuilt of logs from a cabin owned by a Lincoln neighbor. There is a museum with gift shop and picnic area.

Bullitt County: Famous for Salt

Due south of Louisville on I-65 and Hwy. 44 is Shepherdsville, county seat of Bullitt County and one of Kentucky's oldest towns. When Shepherdsville was begun about 1778, Louisville was not yet established. There was a reason that early people came to Shepherdsville. Salt. This commodity was scarce and costly in the wilderness. Ancient animals and Indians, too, knew where salt deposits were. This was believed to be the earliest salt works west of the Alleghenies. At one time 3,000 people worked here refining salt.

There are two major Bullitt County attractions. One is Bernheim Forest. In this famous wildlife and plant sanctuary, covering 10,000 acres, there are lakes, forest, hiking trails, nature trails, and bridle trails. Visitors are welcome to picnic here, but there is no camping. To reach this nature center take I-65 or Hwy. 61 south a short drive from Shepherdsville and turn east on Hwy. 245.

Nearby is the famed James B. Beam Distilling Company which has been manufacturing Jim Beam whiskey for nearly two hundred years. Visitors are welcome here, and the plant offers tours Monday through Friday. The distillery is off Hwy. 245 beyond Bernheim Forest.

There is a KOA Campground off Hwy. 44 east of Shepherdsville.

Mead County: A Famous Inn

After one of our Elizabethtown visits we planned to have lunch at a famous country inn in the next county downriver. Finding Doe Run Inn was easy. We spotted a sign directing us off Hwy.

31W, onto Hwy. 1638. But we had gone only a short distance when we were short-stopped by Otter Creek Park, owned by the City of Louisville, which lies 30 miles upriver.

Otter Creek Park is heavily used, especially in summer and on autumn weekends. People come to picnic. And they walk the trails which wind for 10 miles through 3,000 wooded acres. They come with tents and recreational vehicles and stay in the campgrounds where there are hookups and a spectacular view of the Ohio River. Or they stay in the cabins and group lodges.

This park has 4 pools for swimmers, a nature center, boat ramp, and miniature golf course. In summer, there are horses available for riding the bridle trails. "The effort here," says a staff member, "is to keep the place wild, and we think this is what appeals to people."

The view from Van Buren Point, within the park, is famous, but stay well back from the edge of the cliffs because it is possible to fall hundreds of feet to the rocks below. It has happened.

A few miles to the west and south on Hwy. 448, there is a beautiful little creek that ripples down over limestone ledges, through hardwood forests, past grassy meadows and foot trails. In 1778, Squire Boone (Daniel's brother) and John McKinney dis-

Doe Run Inn is today the home of a favorite country inn and dining room. (Photo by George Laycock)

covered this stream. Later, Squire claimed a tract of land on the creek, and the deed was signed by Patrick Henry, then Virginia's Governor. When Boone first found the scenic little stream, the area had abundant wildlife, especially deer, and for this reason was named Doe Run.

As we drove into Doe Run Inn, two deer stood near the road as if they formed a welcoming committee. They lifted their heads to look at the car, then flipped their white tails straight up and bounded in a few leaps into the brush and out of sight.

Doe Run Inn is a tall stone structure with walls as much as 2 feet thick. It was begun in 1800, and Thomas Lincoln was one of the stonemasons who worked on the job. It was not originally built for an inn, but was used as a mill with water power from Doe Run.

Today if you arrive in summer or even in Indian summer, as we did, you may dine in the screened dining room, looking out over the creek, and listen to the sound of rippling waterfalls as you eat.

The Inn offers lodging as well as meals. Guests here enjoy the peaceful and picturesque countryside. They eat good food, stroll over the trails along the creek, and relax in rooms furnished with antiques. Phone: (502) 422-9982.

The county seat of Mead County is Brandenburg. This was the place selected as an Ohio River crossing by John Hunt Morgan when he invaded Indiana and Ohio. He used captured steamers to ferry his Confederate troops across the river. During the time Morgan was preparing for the crossing, his command post was a large, frame house on top of the hill on Lawrence Street. The house still stands and commands a view of the river in both directions. It is now the residence of a Brandenburg attorney and is on the National Register of Historic Places.

Breckinridge: The Rough River

The earliest structure erected here by white people was a fort built in 1780 by a frontiersman the Indians called "Big Bill," and whose name was William Hardin. When the county was organized in 1799, its founders named it for John Breckinridge, a United States Senator and U. S. Attorney General.

Talented local women in and around Hardinsburg create and sew beautiful quilts, robes, appliqued skirts, pillows, and other handmade gift items, and two wholesale companies sell these to retail shops throughout the country. One, the Eleanor Beard Gallery has a local outlet. You are welcome to visit this shop "just down from the Post Office" in Hardinsburg.

Out of Hardinsburg, Hwy. 60 is an exceptionally scenic route to Cloverport, which is a river town. A spot just west of Cloverport is believed to have been where Thomas Lincoln crossed the Ohio when he moved his family to Indiana.

On the southern side of Breckinridge County the Army Corps of Engineers built a dam across the Rough River to create one more of its flood-control structures. The lake, backed up behind the dam, is partly in Breckinridge County and partly in adjoining Grayson County. Kentucky built a state resort park here, 68 miles southwest of Louisville. The Rough River State Resort Park offers about anything this type of vacation destination might have.

The lake finds its way into lonely hollows where fishermen cast forested shorelines for bass or catch crappie by the hundreds. There are also monstrous catfish in this lake.

Rooms at the lodge overlook the lake. There is also a modern campground located beside the Rough River below the dam where the state frequently stocks trout. For campers who choose tennis instead of fishing, there are courts beside the campground. You will also find a 9-hole golf course plus an archery range.

There are motels nearby and, especially in summer, they all do a brisk business. There is even an airstrip for those flying in with their own planes.

There are picnic areas and playgrounds, and in the lodge a restaurant offers good meals at reasonable rates.

Kentucky maintains a central reservation service for all of its 16
resort parks. From Kentucky, call (800) 372-2961. From adjoining states, call (800) 626-8000.

Country Hams and
Red-Eye Gravy

All who travel the Bluegrass State will see whole hams hanging
in crossroads stores and fancy gift shops. Time was when every
home had its own smokehouse, and every family its favorite recipe for preparing and cooking ham. This gave rise to contests at
the Kentucky State Fair in Louisville where folks exhibit their
prize hams.

Picking a good country ham is not as simple as thumping a ripe
watermelon. The buyer is at the mercy of the merchant and the
supplier, but a real connoisseur chooses on the basis of aroma
and appearance. The ham must be lean, have flavor, and not be
too salty. (Smelling an ice pick stuck to the bone will reveal
flavors.)

Here is a cooking plan for country ham recommended by a
bluegrass hostess. Weigh the ham and remove the hock. Scrub
the ham with a brush, then soak it in water for 24 hours. Change
the water and cover the pot, then simmer the ham for 15 minutes
to the pound. When the ham is half cooked, change the water
again and continue to cook with the pot covered. Leave the ham
to cool overnight in the cooking water.

The following day pour off the water and skin off most of the
fat. Mix a cup of bread crumbs or cracker meal with 2 cups of
brown sugar and spread this over the ham. Bake at 350 degrees
until top of the ham is brown. Once the ham has cooled it can be
sliced very thin for serving.

For those who like country ham fried, first soak the slices in
milk for one to two hours.

Save the fat that fries out and add to these drippings a little water and a dash of black pepper. Allow it to boil and bubble while scraping the bottom of the pan continuously and you have red-eye gravy all ready for the biscuits.

Hancock County: History and Scenery

If you come into Hancock County, Kentucky, following Hwy. 60 from the east, and we recommend it, there are views of the valley that deserve a stop. On the hilltop east of Hawesville, the county seat, there are two scenic overlooks with parking space where even local people stop frequently to look out on the river far below.

Hawesville's history is closely linked with the river and its boats, and in July the community celebrates the relationship with the annual Hawesville Steamboat Festival.

Following a recent Steamboat Festival, the Hancock County *Clarion,* which has been published weekly in Hawesville for almost a century, reported, "The crowds paraded, danced, strolled and bicycled through the city streets to join the fun."

The courthouse square, where there are seldom more than half a dozen people relaxing at one time on any other weekend, was crowded to capacity for evening style shows, music, and especially the beauty pageant naming the "Belle of the River."

Social Note: Carl Reno of Central City won first place in the Checker Tournament during the Steamboat Festival, while first place in Arm Wrestling in the 200- to 225-pound class went to Jim Riley. William Flamion took first honors in Horseshoe Pitching, and in Water Skiing, Jack Brown won the Men's Division with 1,021 points.

Before the new bridge was built to carry highway traffic across the Ohio River to Cannelton, Indiana, the river was crossed by ferry service. There have been ferryboats operating here since before Hawesville was a town or Hancock a county, and the bridge ended a colorful segment of local history, including the story of Captain W. D. Crammond's heroic efforts to save his steam-operated ferryboat, the *K&I* during the devastating river freeze-up in January 1918.

Crammond decided to move his boat downstream ahead of the ice rather than see her crushed. According to a *Clarion* story by Bert Fenn, Crammond provisioned the boat for a trip all the way down the Mississippi if need be and rounded up his crew. All went aboard except one who said he had seen too many years on the river to take part in such a damn fool stunt.

They rode the angry Ohio current, pushed and buffeted by the ice floes from 5:30 Sunday evening until 9 o'clock the following morning with the river still rising and the current gaining speed all the time. Finally, when the current carried the *K&I* close to land, the men jumped off onto some planks that had been shoved out toward them and made it safely to the Indiana shore while the *K&I* bobbed on down the Ohio and out of sight around the first bend.

Captain Crammond borrowed an automobile and followed his boat as best he could, until eventually he found it resting in a corn field, and after the flood he recovered it. Not until later did the crew understand why Jim Bates had volunteered to be hull inspector for the entire voyage. He was the only one with foresight enough to take aboard a jug, which he had hidden belowdecks.

An earlier ferry story is one about Abraham Lincoln's first courtroom experience. At the age of eighteen the gangly Lincoln was operating a ferryboat owned by John and Lin Dill downstream from Hawesville. Two traveling salesmen asked Lincoln to take them out to a steamboat that could come no closer to shore than midstream because of a sandbar. Lincoln took them on his own raft which was easier to manage than the ferry, and each salesman gave him fifty cents.

His employers charged him with infringing on their ferry rights, and a date was set for his trial. Lincoln, who requested and received permission to defend himself, read the law over and over. His defense was that, while the law forbade one to transport persons "across" or "over" the river for reward or money, he had not broken the law because he only went halfway across the

Ohio. Charges were dismissed. Lincoln had won his first court case.

The Squire Pate House, where the trial occurred, still stands on Hwy. 334 two miles east of Lewisport.

Owensboro: Barbecue

Owensboro, a city of 61,000 lying 116 miles downriver from Louisville, is barbecue country and proud of it. This favorite food, which gained its popularity in backyard cookouts, spawned a gigantic festival that wafts aromas of cooking meat and pungent sauces over the river and surrounding neighborhoods drawing in 30,000 visitors.

Contestants, carrying carefully guarded secret recipes in their heads, set the meat to cooking in open pits along the riverfront. In one recent year, the International Bar-B-Q Festival fielded 11 teams of cooks who whipped up a feast consisting of 10 tons of mutton (the local favorite) 2,000 chickens, and 1,200 gallons of

These local chefs are creating barbecue ribs during the International Bar-B-Q Festival in Owensboro, Kentucky. (Photo by Will Lott)

burgoo over their outdoor fires. While these delicacies simmered, visitors assembled to hear bluegrass music and barbershop quartets and engage in square dances and country-style contests. This combination street festival and country church picnic returns to Owensboro on a May weekend every year to reconfirm Owensboro's claim that it is the "barbecue capital of the world."

In this city, however, one can have barbecue every day. Numerous restaurants around the city serve it regularly and proudly. Best known of them is the Moonlight Bar-B-Que Inn on Parrish Ave., a family operation noted for its smorgasbord-style feasts at reasonable prices. Also well known is the Ole Hickory Pit Bar-B-Q, Twenty-fifth and Frederica streets.

Not every restaurant in Owensboro, however, lets barbecue dominate its menu. There are many excellent eating places, and any list would include the Briarpatch, known for its steaks, 2760 Veach Rd.; Gabe's Restaurant at 1816 Triplett St.; Olive Tree, 1926 Triplett St.; and the Executive Inn Rivermont which has a gourmet restaurant, at One Executive Blvd.

In this city the riverfront is very much a part of the good life. The banks of the Ohio are not lined with shabby factories and railroad tracks but are instead open, pleasant approaches to the waterfront where people can stroll or watch the passing boats in pleasant surroundings such as Bill Smothers Park. Little wonder that the largest of the new attractions, the Executive Inn Rivermont, has a riverside location. Most of the rooms offer river views, and the Showroom Lounge, where performers from the Las Vegas circuit entertain, is built on piers over the edge of the Ohio. The Executive Inn includes shops and boutiques, swimming pools, racquetball courts, sauna, exercise rooms, and restaurants, as well as meeting rooms and convention facilities.

Outside, on the riverfront, there are spaces for guests who arrive by boat, and a giant parking lot for those coming by car, while courtesy cars shuttle visitors to and from the airport. The Rivermont is designed especially for the convention trade, but there is room for the average couple or the family seeking an unusual resort.

Around this city there are other lodging places including the Holiday Inn, Days Inn, Downtown Motor Inn, Motel 6, Imperial Inn, Towne Motel, and more.

KENTUCKY 189

Many of the city's attractions are away from the downtown area. The Owensboro Museum of Fine Art, however, is within a few blocks of the riverfront at 901 Frederica St. This museum features an eighteenth-century drawing room among its permanent exhibits and brings in monthly traveling exhibits.

A museum that includes natural science and history among its exhibits is the Owensboro Area Museum, 2829 S. Griffith Ave. at College Dr. Housed in this modern building is a special model railway display whose trains are started up for visitors on Sunday afternoons. There is also the opportunity to browse through a completely equipped country store from the turn of the century. There are a planetarium and natural history exhibits including small live animals.

When driving on South Frederica Street, a major thoroughfare, any tree lover will spot the biggest sassafras tree he ever saw, and those who stop to read the plaque learn that this tree, already famous a century ago, is considered the largest of its kind in the world. Legend tells us that this famous tree, threatened when the street was widened, was defended by a local lady with her double-barreled shotgun in hand. The giant sassafras, to widespread approval, was granted a reprieve.

Owensboro has its own symphony orchestra, arts commission, theater group, and ballet. There are two colleges and a business college.

The nearest state park is off Hwy. 60 west of town, the Ben Hawes State Park and Golf Course. In addition to the 18-hole golf course, there are archery ranges, ball diamond, picnic area, and playgrounds.

There is Thoroughbred racing at James C. Ellis Park, which although operated by an Owensboro club, is located 5 miles north of Henderson on Hwy. 41.

There is a sound industrial base in Daviess County, and many industries offer tours to visitors. The Colonial Bakery, 300 E. Twenty-fourth St.; Glenmore Distillery, Hwy. 60E; Medley Distillery, River Rd.; and Owensboro Grain Co., 923 E. Second St. are among those who welcome visitors. The Owensboro-Daviess County Tourist Commission can give you more information about these and others. Phone: (502) 926-1100.

Those who drive into the countryside around Owensboro will

discover another reason for the prosperity of the region. Daviess County is farming country, and Owensboro is the marketing center for corn and soybeans grown in western Kentucky, southern Indiana, and southern Illinois. Owensboro has the only soybean processing plant in western Kentucky. From the riverport at Owensboro, Ohio River barges haul these farm products off to market or to distant plants. Livestock is another major source of income for the area. There is even a catfish farm, producing 200,000 pounds of catfish annually for markets and restaurants. This farm has its own restaurant and recreation area for visitors, Diamond Lake Resort Campground. Diamond Lake is west of Owensboro near the village of St. Joseph on Hwy. 54.

Henderson: Audubon Country

Around the pleasant and attractive city of Henderson, Kentucky, dry cleaners, quick-printing establishments, and restaurants bear the name of the patron saint of bird watchers, John James Audubon, by all counts, the most famous, and perhaps the most talented wildlife artist ever to pick up a brush. Audubon, who came to Henderson in 1810, had engaged in various business enterprises, including the operation of a store and mill in Henderson. But most of his business ventures failed, perhaps because of Audubon's passion for birds. He was forever wandering the forests and fields to discover more of them. He found the Ohio Valley an untapped treasure of new species that flew through the sky above him and filled his world with exciting songs he had never heard before.

Audubon did many of his important paintings during the nine years he lived in Henderson. His specialty was painting birds, life size, in their natural settings, and during his lifetime he painted 1,065 birds of at least 489 species. Of these, 20 or more species were his own discoveries. A complete set of Audubon's Double Elephant Folios, containing 435 giant prints would demand hundreds of thousands of dollars on today's market, a fact that would have stunned the perpetually impoverished Audubon.

Understandably, this city is the home of one of the nation's oldest active chapters of the National Audubon Society. Local citizens organized this Audubon group in 1898, to honor the artist who left his imprint on the community. Almost at once they planned for a suitable memorial to Audubon. The artist's old mill still stood, and there was talk of converting it to a museum. But, in 1913, Audubon's mill burned to the ground, and the city turned that small area into a riverside park.

In the mid-1930s local people donated land that became the Audubon Memorial State Park. This unique park is found on the northeast edge of Henderson off Hwy. 41. The park has grown to 692 acres, laced with secluded trails leading the park visitors to locations where Audubon is believed to have studied birds. Bird watchers come to these woods from distant places. One couple comes from Los Angeles every spring when the warblers are migrating.

There are 5 cottages for rent and a campground with water, electricity, hot showers, and flush toilets. There is a lake offering fishing, swimming, and boating. Phone: (502) 826-2247.

Near the entrance to the park, on a wooded hill, stands the John James Audubon Museum, which resembles a French

This museum in Audubon State Park at Henderson, houses works of John J. Audubon who lived here for ten years.

Audubon's most famous prints were included in the Double Elephant Folios shown here in the glass cases of the museum. (Photo by George Laycock)

château. Visitors are shown one of the finest collections of Audubon's work anywhere. The Museum galleries display 126 of his original prints.

On the first weekend in October each year, the park becomes the scene of the Big River Arts and Crafts Festival, which draws an estimated 65,000 people. For 2 days 250 crafts people from 7 states offer paintings, handmade baskets, pottery, wildlife photographs, and other creative works. Local people insist this is one of the largest festivals in the state. Another is Henderson's Carrousel of Arts held in late May or early June. Then, there are continuous performances by musicians, storytellers, mimes, and vocalists.

Henderson Flatboat Days is a festival held each August in conjunction with the Greater Ohio River Flatboat Race. Flatboat crews build their own boats and race from Owensboro downriver to the finish line at Henderson. Meanwhile, on shore, enthusiastic festival goers watch frog-jumping contests, bed races, and evening fireworks.

Henderson was the birthplace of the blues. W. C. Handy lived here for ten years, married a Henderson girl, and told the late Joe Creason, columnist for the Louisville *Courier-Journal,* that Henderson was where he changed from a hobo to a professional musician.

Handy told of singing in the church choir in Alabama as a boy, and of later beginning to understand how notes could be given a special blues rhythm. He traced the birth of the blues to the days when he played trumpet in a Henderson band.

Later, Handy wrote more than a hundred blues and spirituals including "St. Louis Blues," and "Steal Away."

Golfers enjoy the Henderson Municipal Golf Course, and the 9-hole course at Audubon State Park, while race fans have their choice of harness racing at the Audubon Raceway with harness racing in spring and fall meets, or Thoroughbred events at Ellis Park from June to Labor Day.

Hunters and fishermen will find both state-operated and privately managed areas. One of the most popular locations is the Henderson Sloughs Wildlife Area, covering 6,500 acres bordering the Ohio River northwest of Henderson. In season, there is duck and goose shooting here, as well as quail and dove hunting.

Henderson, the county seat of Henderson County, is an old town. It was founded in 1797. We admired its wide tree-lined streets and were told that the founding fathers laid out the streets 100 feet across so fires wouldn't jump them. The wide streets, clean waterfront, and prosperous downtown area help give Henderson its appeal today. We found it a pleasant place to visit, rich in history, yet progressive, one of the most attractive towns along the river.

Most restaurants and motels are found out on "the strip" on Hwy. 41. Our favorite restaurant is the Hunan, on Hwy. 41S. The menu offers a variety in Chinese cuisine, well prepared.

Three Quiet Counties

Union County, Kentucky, is tucked away against the south shore of the Ohio River in a remote location that caused one historian to write in 1886, "It is somewhat out of the world to a considerable degree." But people have found here two major resources. First is the soil. Union County still ranks as an important general farming area. Later, coal became an important product, helping to ensure the prosperity of this peaceful, thriving county.

One major coal mine here transports its product from mine to the Ohio River barges, 12 miles away, on what was once the longest conveyor belt anywhere. The honor was lost when a company in Utah constructed a conveyor belt one mile longer.

Union County was founded in 1811 and once had three of its communities under consideration to become the county seat. A delegation from the legislature came to investigate the three places, however, and the first stop was at Morganfield. Legend has it that Jeremiah Riddle, who came here in 1802 and was the earliest settler, opened enough jugs of corn whiskey that the officials never went on to the other two locations. Morganfield remains the county seat. Another event of historical significance occurred in 1840. That year Abraham Lincoln came here and delivered the only political speech he ever made in Kentucky.

"This is a good place to live," says newspaperman John N. Munford, publisher of the family-owned *Union County Advocate.* "We have only a three percent unemployment rate."

John J. Crittenden, lawyer, legislator, and once the youngest U. S. Senator, had already made his reputation by 1842 when the next downriver county was formed, so the county fathers named the county Crittenden. Marion, the county seat, was named for General Francis Marion, the famous Revolutionary War leader known as "the Swamp Fox."

It was a quiet little village, and still is. But Marion is also pleasant and prosperous looking with neatly kept houses and lawns.

In Marion, the local historical society has brought together its accumulated treasures and set up the Bob Wheeler Museum. The museum collection of early farm hand tools is especially noteworthy. The library at the corner of Court and Carlisle streets has genealogical shelves for those seeking their roots in this part of the world.

Eleven miles north of Marion, at the terminus of Hwy. 91, is the Ohio River Ferry connecting Crittenden County with Cave-in-Rock, Illinois.

Livingston County is general farming country. Big rivers dominate this county. Along its northern and western boundaries runs the broad Ohio. The Tennessee, including a corner of Kentucky Lake, forms Livingston County's southern border. Then, right through the heart of the county flows the Cumberland River entering the Ohio at the little county-seat town of Smithland, which sits on a bluff above the Ohio. Smithland Locks and Dam lie just upstream.

The busiest corner of the county is around Lake City near which Hwy. 62, from Eddyville to Paducah, crosses the Kentucky Dam. Fishermen frequently stop in Lake City to stock up on bait and other necessities on their way to fishing spots on Kentucky Lake and Lake Barkley.

Paducah: A Favorite Chief

"I would rather be born a homeless orphan in Paducah, Kentucky, than duly certified twins anywhere else on earth." These were the words of author, journalist, and humorist Irvin S. Cobb, one of Paducah's most famous citizens. If the rotund, cigar chomping, "Duke of Paducah" were still strolling the streets of his native river city, he would still like the place. Paducah, as Cobb insisted, is a clean, friendly, and appealing city—among the most pleasant anywhere along the Ohio's shores.

The best way to get a look at Paducah, both the old central part and the outlying areas, is to watch the streets for the red lines. In the 1960s the city's promoters decided they could make it easy for visitors to guide themselves through the historic and interesting parts of town. They painted bright red lines at intervals right down the middle of the streets, and the best thing about this plan is that it works. Paducah calls this its Red Line Tour. A good place to begin the 12-mile drive is in front of the Tourist and Convention Commission across from City Hall at 417 Washington St. or at Fourth and Broadway, the heart of Paducah. Stop in the Tourist Commission office and pick up a free copy of the map that tells you the high points along the route.

Near the river on Second St. is old Market House Square, where farmers from out in McCracken County once brought their produce for sale. The Market House, no longer a fresh-food

Paducah's unusual City Hall is a tourist attraction. (Photo by George Laycock)

market, has become a cultural center. It houses a public art gallery, a community theater, and a museum.

The best way for most visitors to see the center of downtown Paducah is to take a walking tour. There is perhaps a greater concentration of historic plaques marking points of interest in downtown Paducah than we saw in a like area anywhere else in the Ohio Valley. Broadway, in the vicinity of the old Market House, abounds in little shops, and the friendly local people are eager to talk and visit.

Land between the Tennessee and Mississippi rivers was originally granted to George Rogers Clark as partial payment for his brilliant leadership in securing the Northwest for the United

Irvin S. Cobb, a Paducah favorite son, included the people and places of his hometown in many of his writings. (Photo by George Laycock)

In Paducah, the Red Line Tour leads to historic buildings including the Old Market, now home of art gallery, museum, and theater. (Photo by George Laycock)

States. But the title was clouded since the Chickasaws still occupied the territory, and Clark died impoverished. After the Indians were moved to Mississippi, the land, however, went to Clark's younger brother, William, who had explored the wilderness all the way to the Pacific with Meriwether Lewis.

General William Clark founded the town in 1827, laying out the site on the banks of the Ohio. He named the town for his good friend, Paduke, chief of the Chickasaws, and immortalized the chief, at least in the city of Paducah. At stop No. 19 on the Red Line Tour, in the broad median strip of Jefferson St., stands the Lorado Taft statue of Paduke who, according to popular legend, was "tall, massive, perfect in physique and generous in spirit."

Along this trail, with its red line, the Paducah explorer finds more than 40 points of interest significant enough to deserve mention. Downtown there are the public buildings. The unusual and beautiful city hall, designed by Edward Durell Stone and the McCracken County Court House sit between Washington and

Clark streets with the fountain and Civic Mall between them. Nearby is the Federal building with its fine mural, and the St. Francis de Sales Church, dating back to 1889. On the riverfront is the boat works, a major local industry. Here the Ohio is joined by the big waters of its tributary, the Tennessee River, which at this point ends its long journey from the Great Smoky Mountains.

Stop No. 15, Barkley Park, introduces the visitor to another name once recognized throughout the nation. Alben W. Barkley was a member of Congress, Senate majority leader, and Vice-President of the United States during the presidency of Harry S Truman. There is a monument to the former Vice-President in the median on Jefferson St., and the Alben W. Barkley Museum at Sixth and Madison.

Out at Oak Grove Cemetery, still on the Red Line Tour, is the grave of Irvin S. Cobb, marked by a huge boulder of Kentucky native stone, located and moved to the cemetery with great effort because Cobb said that, after he went, he did not want anything fancy that would demand much work—just a native stone.

This statue honors the Chickasaw Chief Paduke, for whom the city was named. (Photo by George Laycock)

Paducah is a friendly, busy city where there are community activities that bring people together. The season's outdoor activities begin when the dogwood blooms in April. The whole town looks forward to this harbinger of spring and the annual Paducah Dogwood Trail Celebration. At night, the blooming dogwood trees are lighted all over town and the festival spirit includes musical programs and home tours.

The last weekend in July the Paducah Summer Festival begins and continues through the following weekend. The action centers on the waterfront but includes other parts of the city, with large crowds coming out for the music and good times.

Paducah also holds an autumn celebration. October Days comes the first weekend in October. Meanwhile, in season, there are programs of the Paducah Symphony Orchestra, productions at the community theater in the Market House, and country music concerts on the riverfront. For a guide to current events of interest, pick up a copy of *Paducah Happenings* at the Tourist Commission.

The Market House Museum in downtown Paducah houses many displays out of the city's past, including this complete antique drugstore. (Photo by George Laycock)

Thousands of visitors come to Paducah during the annual Dog-wood Festival in spring.

The largest park is the Bob Noble Park where there is swimming as well as a wide range of other activities including tennis, pony rides, playgrounds, an amusement park, picnic areas, ball fields, and shaded hiking trails.

Paducah has an 18-hole golf course open to the public, Paxton Park, site of numerous golf tournaments.

This city at the lower end of the Ohio River is an increasingly important convention center, and this is due, in part, to the coming of the new Executive Inn complex. The Inn, with more than 400 rooms, is built on the edge of the Ohio River near the downtown. Those staying here are surrounded with fine restaurants, shops, and lounges. There is big-name entertainment. Outside, on the riverfront the *Executive Belle,* the hotel's own river-going party boat, is docked.

Elsewhere, Paducah has a wide choice of restaurants. The visitor to this river city soon hears about going to Skinhead's for breakfast. Enough local folk go to Skinhead's Restaurant, 1020 S. Twenty-first St., to make this one of the busiest places in town in the early morning. Not big on atmosphere, but food is good, plentiful, and reasonable.

At the other end of the scale is the Ninth Street House, 323 N. Ninth St., said by many to be Paducah's finest restaurant, and perhaps its most expensive.

There is also the Old Towne Tavern, 701 Park Ave., a good place for lunch and dinner; the Bank, 225 Broadway; and Stacey's, 1300 Broadway. Adrian's, 2910 Lone Oak Rd., is a favorite for those wanting vegetables and fried chicken. The Whaler's Catch, 306 N. Thirteenth St., opens for dinner and offers seafood. And there are others. Bogy's, 128 Broadway, is popular. For Chinese food try China Boy at 2000 Broadway, or Chong's on Hwy. 62E. The Farmer's Market Cafeteria, 3333 Clarks River Rd., is a local favorite, and so is Harned's, 4421 Clarks River Rd. At the Holiday Inn, 727 Joe Clifton Dr., there is the Front Porch, while The Embers, 2701 Park Ave., is in the Diplomat Inn, offering three meals a day. For those who like barbecue—and Paducah is famous for it—there are Starnes, at 2854 Lone Oak Rd.; Slim's at N. Eleventh St.; and Price's, 3001 Broadway. Paducah is a good place to eat out.

Land Between the Lakes

Paducah is the nearest major city to an outdoor vacation area that was fathered by the Tennessee Valley Authority and nourished by enough federal funds to give it special appeal for just about everyone who likes the outdoors. The region is known as the "Land Between the Lakes," and it is one of America's major recreation areas, drawing thousands of visitors from hundreds of miles around.

The Land Between the Lakes is made possible by the geography. Here, in western Kentucky, two major rivers flow northward parallel to each other on their way to join the Ohio. Between these rivers, the Cumberland and the Tennessee, lies a strip of rugged wooded country from 5 to 8 miles wide.

Before there were lakes, this land was known as the "Land Twixt the Rivers," and the people living here were independent and openly suspicious of outsiders. Their lack of trust in strangers may have grown from the government's occasional efforts to break up bootlegging operations that flourished in these wooded hills. There was a sense of cooperation among the neighbors. Let a stranger board the ferryboat to cross to the region between the rivers, and his motives were at once suspect. There were no telephones, but there were dinner bells, and their doleful clanging was picked up and repeated by other dinner bells on adjoining

The Land Between the Lakes in western Kentucky is a major midcontinent recreation area visited by hundreds of thousands of vacationers annually.

farms. Men banked their woodland fires, slipped away from their stills, and went home to sit on the porch until they heard three shotgun blasts, a signal that the stranger had departed.

With the birth of the TVA, big changes began to take place. A series of dams turned the long Tennessee River into lakes, and the biggest of them all was Kentucky Lake backed up behind the dam nearest the Ohio. Kentucky Dam was completed in 1944 with a major highway running across the top of it. Kentucky Lake has 2,380 miles of shoreline that reaches fingers of water back into remote hollows for 184 miles.

Then, in 1966, Barkley Lake, on the Cumberland, added another lake of 62,000 acres. The two are connected by a canal used by boaters. Between these two giant impoundments lies the Land Between the Lakes, 170,000 acres maintained by the TVA for recreation and environmental education. The land, once worn thin by poor agricultural practices, has gone back to forests, and in these woodlands are herds of deer and flocks of wild turkeys, which, along with other wild creatures, may be spotted anytime by those driving the back roads. There are miles of these back-country roads leading through a rolling landscape uncluttered by gas stations, billboards, shopping centers, traffic jams, or other reminders of the crowded world beyond the rivers.

These roads lead to fine campgrounds with hundreds of campsites overlooking the lakes. There are also quiet backcountry trails leading to remote primitive campgrounds for those wanting to escape.

Three of Kentucky's state resort parks are in this area. Kentucky Dam Village State Resort Park is at Gilbertsville, KY 42044, phone: (502) 362-4271. This one has a dining room and lodge with 72 rooms in addition to cottages and a mammoth campground. There is a lighted airstrip here, and rental cars are available. Kenlake State Resort, Hardin, KY 42048, phone: (502) 474-2211 is 25 miles to the south. This resort park also has lodge, cottages, campground, and dining room. Lake Barkley State Resort Park, with a 120-room lodge plus cottages and campgrounds, is at Cadiz, KY 42211, phone: (502) 924-1171. It is reached by Hwy. 68 off the Western Kentucky Parkway.

Fishing and boating are major interests of many who vacation in the Land Between the Lakes. There are many launching areas.

This is excellent fishing country for largemouth bass. It is also noted for large crappies. In the spring, fishermen come from as far away as Chicago to catch these panfish. Big catfish also live in these waters. The best known spot for catching monster catfish is in the tail waters below Kentucky Lake Dam. One catfish taken there some years ago weighed an even 100 pounds.

Vacationers also have the opportunity to rent houseboats from

Map of Land Between the Lakes.

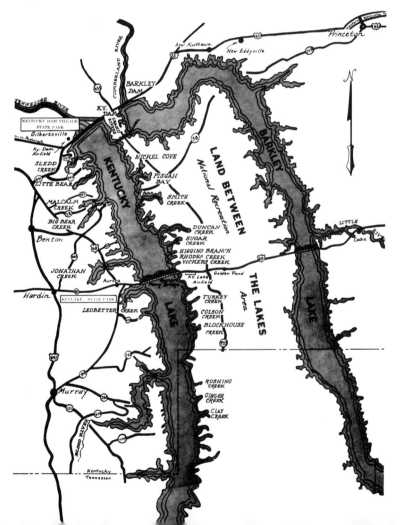

Buffalo graze in fenced pasture in Land Between the Lakes.
(Photo by George Laycock)

the various private marinas and cruise the lakes, fishing, swimming, and tying up for the night in remote wooded coves on the
islands.

For hikers there are 125 miles of developed trails, including a
60-mile trail planned especially for backpackers.

Those who come with horses find special trails and Wrangler's
Camp.

For a touch of history, there is a 250-acre working farm—
Homeplace 1850. Visitors see workers engaged in rural home and
field tasks as they were performed in the middle of the nineteenth
century.

Near here you can see what remains of an aging pyramidlike
structure made of large blocks of stone, the Center Furnace,
where once the sad story of William Kelly unfolded. Kelly was an
Irishman from Pittsburgh who came here to work in the flourish-
ing iron industry in the mid-1800s. Kelly was a man of ideas. He
believed that air was fuel and could be injected into molten iron
to make steel. Furthermore, he perfected the process, and this
should have been the founding of a vast fortune for Kelly. Also

working there at the time, however, was an Englishman who saw promise in what Kelly was doing. It is said that the Englishman left so quickly that he neither collected his pay nor picked up his clothes. He obtained a patent on the idea, said to be Kelly's, made a fortune and to this day is credited with discovering the process. His name was Bessemer.

Wildlife is an attraction in the Land Between the Lakes. There is a herd of buffalo that can be observed from the roadside, and this is the best place in the Ohio Valley to see the bald eagle, our majestic national bird. In winter eagles drift south to spend the cold months around these open waters where they can find food. The best time to see them is from November 1 to April 1. The numbers peak in February, when there may be fifty or more eagles perching on tall trees in the coves and soaring above the lakes. Watch the sky and scan the tops of the trees; there is an excellent possibility of seeing an eagle, a thrill that most modern Americans never experience.

Ballard County:
Geese Over the Ohio

The last Kentucky county on the Ohio River is Ballard. At this point, where the Ohio joins the Mississippi, there are two attractions that bring in visitors. One of these is waterfowl, especially geese, that descend on the valley in the fall. The story of Kentucky's success with the management of Canada geese in Ballard County began in the 1950s, when the Kentucky Department of Fish and Wildlife Resources created a special wildlife production area in Ballard County.

Land purchases began in 1954 on a section of bottomland 7 miles west of Bandana, Kentucky, using money that came from sportsmen, through their taxes and license purchases. Three years later the state opened the 8,000-acre Ballard County Waterfowl

Management Area, including both a refuge and public hunting area, with buffer zones between them.

From the beginning, this area proved successful for sportsmen as well as many kinds of wildlife, and there are several reasons. First, waterfowl biologists designed nineteen new lakes and ponds, and lake areas increased from 150 to 786 acres in less than ten years. Bridges and roads were built to make it easier for people to get around on the area.

As the refuge staff labored to create new lakes with bulldozer and scraper, a family of beavers moved in to help. The manager of the Ballard County area, first noticed the beavers when they plugged up a drain tile and flooded an area the manager planned not to flood. The plug was removed but the next night the beavers were back, busier than ever, and not only did they plug the tile, but they also built a new dam above it. When the refuge men returned, they had to blow the dam out with dynamite. This was repeated several times with the beavers working at night and the men working during the daytime.

Finally, the manager changed his plans to accommodate the beavers, who rewarded him with a 39-acre lake, cost free. The new beaver pond provided the beavers with a home and also created living conditions for more waterfowl, herons, songbirds, kingfishers, and turtles, as well as fish, which brought in appreciative bass and crappie fishermen. The new impoundment was named Castor Lake, to honor its builders whose scientific name is *Castor canadensis.*

The Ballard County area is designed not alone for hunters and fishermen. There are camping areas, trails for hiking, and places for families to have picnics, as well as good opportunities for studying and photographing wildlife.

The goose-hunting season comes with the cold weather, and the number of hunters is limited. Those wanting to hunt here should write to the Kentucky Department of Fish and Wildlife Resources, Arnold L. Mitchell Building, 1 Game Farm Rd., Frankfort, KY 40601, for current information on reservations. There is a fee for goose shooting.

The other Ballard County attraction for visitors is the Ancient Buried City. This is a partly excavated village built by ancient people more than one thousand years ago. Visitors walk the paths that lead to temples, council house, and burial grounds. This village is on a high bluff, the only high ground at the confluence of the Ohio and Mississippi rivers. Ancient Buried City is on highways 60 and 62 on the north edge of Wickliffe. It is privately owned and there is an admission charge.

Wickliffe, on the Mississippi River, is the county seat of Ballard County. The county was named for Captain Bland Ballard who came to Kentucky in 1779. He was a scout for George Rogers Clark, fought in many battles against the British and the Indians, and served five terms in the Kentucky Legislature.

Part III

The North Shore

Ohio

Columbiana: Into Ohio

Our trail led along the winding Ohio River northward, then southwest as we crossed out of Pennsylvania into Ohio and Columbiana County. We came first to the river city of East Liverpool, the town that is proud to be known as "Crockery City." By 1890 East Liverpool had become the largest pottery center in the United States. One major pottery still operates a plant here and maintains a sales outlet where both tourists and local people search for bargains.

The eastern Ohio pottery industry began with the arrival here of James Bennett. He sent back to England for his three brothers, and other English potters followed. East Liverpool, with its nearby sources of clay, grew into a thriving single-industry town.

The whole story was spread before us when we visited East Liverpool's old post office building. This imposing stone structure at Fifth St. and Broadway has recently been converted by the Ohio Historical Society into a permanent Museum of Ceramics, perhaps the finest of its kind in the country.

Exhibits and dioramas, old photographs, and extensive collections of valuable antique ceramics trace the pottery industry's growth. Life-sized figures bend to their tasks, molding, glazing, and decorating East Liverpool ware. Our verdict? An excellent museum, worth a visit by anyone touring the Upper Ohio Valley.

As you drive north along Hwy. 11, you will see signs pointing toward the historical monument at West Point on Hwy. 518. At this spot, as the monument tells us, General John Hunt Morgan, a Confederate raider, was finally captured, at the northernmost point reached by Confederate troops during the Civil War.

Next, we drove north toward the historic old town of Lisbon, the county seat where Rev. Lewis Kinney, who built the first cabin here in 1802, laid out and incorporated the town the following year. This is a pleasant village with fine old homes and wide shaded streets. Many of the older homes have plaques giving the dates of construction. We wondered who had gone to the trouble of making these signs and placing them, and the question led us to Clara McGee of the Lisbon Historical Society.

Clara McGee explained that they didn't have money enough for brass plaques. "I painted those signs myself," she said, "and I have to get busy and do some more." She offered to show us the Old Stone House Museum.

"This is my baby," she laughed as we stopped in front of the two-story stone structure. The house now serves as the Lisbon Museum, and inside are all manner of memorabilia and antiques gathered from families in the area. The Old Stone House has served in the past as tavern, courtroom, bank, residence, and church. People in Lisbon believe it to be Ohio's oldest stone house still standing; it dates from 1805.

At 335 N. Beaver St. stands a log cabin, covered now with clapboards. It was built in 1808, and here William D. Lepper published, in German, *Der Patriot Am Ohio,* the first newspaper in Columbiana County.

Much of the downtown area is included in the Lisbon National Historic District. Hamilton's Drug Store on the village square is the oldest brick building in Ohio (1806), and probably the oldest active store in the state. Morgan's Drug Store and the Arter Building were both built in 1810. Marcus A. Hanna, U. S. Senator and industrialist, was born in the Arter Building.

The house at 441 E. Washington St., 1830, was once the home of Dr. George McCook of the "fighting McCook" family. When the Civil War was declared, George's brother Daniel and his eight sons all volunteered. So did his brother John and his five sons. Among them there were four major generals, three brigadiers, one colonel, two majors, two lieutenants, a chaplain, one private, and one navy man. The Lisbon Historical Society says in its booklet, *A History of Lisbon, Ohio,* that Dr. George McCook also did his share although he didn't leave home. "The story is told that he actually fired the first shots of the war when he mounted a cannon at Wellsville and banged away at a Southern steamer headed upstream because he 'suspicioned something.' "

The Vallandigham Home, 431 W. Lincoln Way, built in 1811, was the home of Rev. Clement Vallandigham who came to Lisbon in 1807, founded the first Presbyterian Church, and was its pastor until 1839. His son, Clement L. Vallandigham, was born here, became a lawyer, a congressman, and leader of the "Copperheads," who opposed the War Between the States.

President William McKinley's parents were married in the Vallandigham house, and his mother, Nancy Allison, lived in Lisbon.

On the historic "Village Green" or town square, Lisbon's Appleseed Restaurant is the place the natives recommend. But the best restaurant in the county may be Lock 24, at Elkton. People drive in from Youngstown and elsewhere to dine at the Lock 24.

Salem, Columbiana's second-largest town, lies north of Lisbon on Hwy. 45. Salem was founded in 1806 by The Society of Friends. It was a center of abolitionist activities before the Civil War and sheltered many escaping slaves. Legend has it that Erastus Eells, Lisbon undertaker, hid slaves in coffins and shipped them to Salem.

In Salem you may want to visit the South Lincoln National Historic District. The Durand House is at 731 N. Ellsworth Ave. The Salem Historical Museum is located at 208 S. Broadway.

Columbiana has two state parks and a wild river. Guilford State Park, off State Rt. 172 west of Lisbon, was originally built as a reservoir for Ohio's system of canals. Vacationers swim, fish, and boat here. Rebecca Furnace, built in 1808 and one of the first iron furnaces west of the Appalachians, still stands on Furnace Rd., which is Township Rd. 868. President McKinley's parents lived for a time in the old house across the road from the furnace.

Beaver Creek State Park is 8 miles northwest of East Liverpool. Turn off Hwy. 7 between the Middle School and the High School and follow signs to the park entrance. This park offers primitive camping, picnicking in the pines along the creek, fishing, and hiking on the more than 15 miles of trails. In addition, there are bridle trails and camps for horsemen.

Near the park office stands a water-driven mill, log cabins, and an old school. The buildings, including the mill, are open on weekends.

The site of the ghost town, Sprucevale, is in the park on County Rd. 428 at the bridge over Little Beaver Creek. The only remnant of the town are three standing walls of Hambleton's grist mill. Speak softly so as not to disturb the ghost of Ester Hale who, it is said, returns on dark evenings to haunt the old mill.

Little Beaver Creek has been officially made part of the system of wild and scenic rivers. Canoeists interested in running these cool clear waters will find a livery on Hwy. 170 at Fredericktown. The livery rents canoes, paddles, and life jackets, and provides transportation back from the take-out point. Phone: (216) 385-8579.

Those interested in covered bridges can find six of these historic old structures still in their original locations in Columbiana County. One of these, the Church Hill Road Bridge, 3 miles out of Lisbon on Township Rd. 894, measures only 19 feet 2 inches long, making it the shortest covered bridge in the United States. Although it has been bypassed, it stands within easy camera range of the unimproved township road. Once a year there is a covered bridge tour of Columbiana County, and details are available from the Chamber of Commerce at the village hall in Lisbon.

Another annual event popular in this county is the Johnny Appleseed Festival in Lisbon from Thursday through Saturday the week after Labor Day.

Jefferson County:
Steubenville's Legacy

Color Steubenville gray. This factory town, 45 miles west of Pittsburgh on the Ohio side of the river, is not the kind of city that vacationers purposely seek out. Her citizens have found neither the will nor the means to clean up their town.

This river city, however, rose from auspicious beginnings, and imbedded in her past are the names of famous statesmen and artists. Among the noted early citizens of Steubenville was Edwin M. Stanton who served as U. S. Attorney General under President Buchanan and Secretary of War under President Lincoln. A youthful Andrew Carnegie once worked here as a telegraph operator. These names are often missed by modern observers who, nurtured on television, point to Steubenville proudly as the birthplace of Dino Crocetti who grew up, after stints as a steel-mill worker and a croupier, to become Dean Martin, singer and actor.

Historians know Steubenville as one of the earliest settlements in Ohio. In 1765 Jacob Walker arrived at this plain above the river, liked the place, and settled down in Indian country on 400 acres, which is now in the heart of town. It is recorded that Walker paid someone sixteen cents an acre for the land.

Two decades later government scouts, seeking the best locations for a fort on the Upper Ohio, saw the merits of this location, and on the site rose Fort Steuben, named to honor Baron Frederick von Steuben, the Prussian drillmaster who had been of service to the American colonies during the War of Independence. A Fort Steuben monument still reminds us of the city's origins. A little community of settlers sprang up in the shadow of the fort. The settlement, named La Belle, was later renamed Steubenville. The town was laid out in 1797 and is the seat of Jefferson County.

Over the years this city thrived on the production of glass, wool, steel, pottery, coal, and other products. It also became an important river port and center for riverboat building. Most famous of the boats built here was one of the earliest steamers on the Ohio, the *Bezaleel Wells* launched in 1819. The *Beelzebub,* as she was known locally, was ill-equipped with twin smokestacks fashioned from local bricks, all of which came tumbling down when the boat ran aground on her maiden voyage scarcely out of sight of Steubenville.

Northwest of Steubenville, off Hwy. 43 near Richmond, is Jefferson Lake State Park. This park, with its 25-acre lake, offers camping, hiking, boating, fishing, and hunting in season.

Another Jefferson County tourist attraction is the Friends Meeting House at Mt. Pleasant, operated by the Ohio Historical Society. This large brick structure, capacity 2,000, was built in 1814, the first yearly meeting house west of the Alleghenies, birthplace for all of Quakerdom west of Ohio. It is located on Hwy. 150 and to reach it exit Hwy. 7 at Rayland and drive west about 10 miles to Mt. Pleasant.

Belmont (French: "Beautiful Mountain")

Our earlier trips into this Ohio county across the Ohio River from Wheeling, West Virginia, had not done the place justice. Interstate 70 whisks traffic through the hills with little indication of what lies off the main road on either side. This time we left I-70 to explore the secondary roads and scenic hills and hollows.

At St. Clairsville, the county seat, we turned south on Hwy. 9 and drove through Centerville then on to Powhatan Point, the Ohio River village where, according to a roadside plaque, George Washington camped in 1770. On the narrow, twisting roads one watches for coal trucks, hauling fuel from the mines (Belmont is Ohio's leading county in coal production) to the power plants along the Ohio.

We turned northward to follow highways 148 and 800 to Barnesville, where travelers interested in history, old homes, and museums should allow some extra time. At the corner of Chestnut St. and Walton Ave. (on Hwy. 800), north of the center of town, stands the Belmont County Museum, an impressive old red-brick mansion out of the Gay 90s, a rare and perfect example of Romanesque architecture. The structure, after five years of construction, was completed in 1893 by banker J. W. Bradfield.

There are 26 rooms in this building, including ballroom, twin parlors, and 7 basement rooms. The building was rescued from demolition when the Belmont County Historical Society acquired it. Often small county museums are characterized by their collections of unrelated odds and ends salvaged from local attics and barns, but the Belmont County Museum is beautifully furnished with a wealth of exhibits of which much larger museums could be proud. Definitely one of the better small museums in the valley.

The problem is being in Barnesville when this museum is open —Thursday, Sunday, and holiday afternoons. We arrived on a day the building was not open, but found Charlie Moore, a member of the Society, directing work in the yard, and because he was already on the scene, he gave us a tour of the building. "Not many people come," he said. "Most of our visitors are tour groups from out of town because tour leaders know about us." Write: Belmont County Historical Society, P. O. Box 434, Barnesville, OH 43713, for special tours.

We followed Hwy. 800 back to I-70. This loop through the hills, however, has bypassed the attractions of Barkcamp State Park and the 117-acre Belmont Lake that is part of the park. The park is reached by leaving I-70 at Exit 208 and following Hwy. 149 south, then taking a left turn onto Township Rd. 92 and following the state park signs. The family campground in this park has 150 sites, a large number of them pleasantly shaded by large trees. There are Class-B campgrounds, meaning, primarily, that they have no modern plumbing. On major holidays the campground fills up as families flock into Barkcamp to swim, fish, boat, hike, and ride their horses on the bridle trails.

The best place in Belmont County to find food and lodging is off I-70 near St. Clairsville where there are several good motels and a large shopping mall.

Monroe County:
Switzerland of Ohio

At Clarington, Hwy. 556 beckons travelers into hills so steep and green they reminded early Swiss and German settlers of their native homelands. For hundreds of miles around, people know this as the "Switzerland of Ohio."

The roads follow the ridges, and the slopes fall away abruptly to deep, narrow hollows. Homes and barns perch on the ridges, often stuck out on points of land reached by country lanes. These hills, too steep for plowing, look prosperous anyhow because herds of dairy and beef cattle graze on the lush green pastures.

Drive slowly. On these roads, 40 miles an hour can be hazardous. Curves are sharp and roads are narrow. Besides, there are views to enjoy. We suggest the following scenic tour. Start at Clarington, traveling northwest on Hwy. 556, then Hwy. 145, to Malaga. Turn south on Hwy. 800 to Woodsfield, the county seat. Then follow Hwy. 78E. Turn right on Hwy. 536 to Hannibal.

In autumn, hundreds of people come to Monroe County, and especially Switzer Township in the northeast corner of Monroe County, to see the spectacular colors. The Monroe County Park District sponsors a different self-guiding tour each year, usually in late September, and furnishes a leaflet telling travelers of special stops where local people welcome them and sometimes demonstrate crafts. Address: Courthouse, Woodsfield, OH 43793.

The Park District also maintains Kiedaish Point, north off Hwy. 536, a towering hilltop overlook commanding a sweeping view of the Ohio River. This is an excellent place to make pictures of the Hannibal Locks and Dam, the sprawling industrial buildings in the riverbottom lands, and New Martinsville, West Virginia, across the river.

Also on the river, at the village of Fly, a ferry links the Ohio shore with Sistersville, West Virginia.

If you are asked in Monroe County if you have been to "the caves," the question refers to Piatt Park, where there is a deep gorge with waterfalls, rock shelters, and hidden natural gardens of northern plants. Piatt Park is east of Woodsfield on a county road north of Hwy. 78.

There is pride in these hills. In Monroe County's high country the picturesque farmsteads look neat and the roads are not flanked by signboards or discarded beer cans. "People know they have a good thing here," we were told by the county agricultural extension agent, Don Pollock, "and they don't want to see it change." This county is not geared for tourism, and there is little evidence that it wants to be. We made the mistake of thinking we would spend the night in the county seat. The single small motel had no vacancy, and seldom does. Like most visitors to Monroe County, we crossed the bridge at Hannibal to stay in New Martinsville, West Virginia. But Woodsfield does have a good restaurant, The Heritage House, down the street from the courthouse.

Washington County: Where the West Began

One does not visit Marietta and disregard its history. This neat and attractive town, with its museums, old houses, scenic drives, and showboat dramas in a vital college community, seems to offer something for everyone.

Marietta was the first lawfully organized, permanent settlement in Ohio. No other settlement in America had been so carefully prepared and planned. The Ordinance of 1787 provided for the sale of land and for the establishment of government in the Northwest Territories.

But even before 1787, a group of prominent men from New England had organized The Ohio Company to purchase and settle land on the Ohio River. General Rufus Putnam was elected chairman of The Ohio Company and was destined to become the

leader of the new settlement on the frontier. Most of the men had
been officers in the Revolutionary War. They sent the Reverend
Manasseh Cutler to lobby Congress for the Company, and it may
have been through his influence that the Ordinance of 1787 was
pushed through Congress at that early date. Next, Cutler made a
contract for the purchase of 1,500,000 acres of land on the Ohio
and Muskingum rivers, for The Ohio Company.

The travelers gathered at Sumrill's Ferry on the Youghiogheny
River, above Pittsburgh, and began building boats to carry them
down the Ohio. A flatboat, a barge, and three dugout canoes
brought them to their destination in five days, and they landed on
April 7, 1788, on the east side of the Muskingum River. Across
the Muskingum stood Fort Harmar, a military post, and the travelers rejoiced at the sight of the American flag flying above its log
walls.

They started at once to build houses near the river. On a rise a
short distance away, they built a log fort and called it Campus
Martius. They planted vegetable gardens and grain in preparation
for their families' arrival.

On July 2 they held a meeting and decided to name their settlement Marietta, in honor of Queen Marie Antoinette who had per-
suaded the French emperor to take the American side in the Revolution. Also at this meeting, they agreed on laws for the
community. Return Jonathan Meigs drew them up and on July 4
nailed the paper to a tree for all to read. Meigs later was Governor of Ohio, Judge of the Supreme Court of Ohio, U. S. Senator,
and Postmaster General.

When we entered Washington County, we were driving from
Athens on Hwy. 550, a scenic route winding through the hills,
where there are apple orchards and fruit stands along the road.
Some travelers prefer Hwy. 7, which follows the river closely with
river views of islands and occasionally a riverboat. Interstate 77
approaches Marietta from the north, then crosses the bridge into
West Virginia. Another scenic route is Hwy. 60 along the Muskingum River.

In town, the first stop for tourists should be the Marietta Tourist & Convention Bureau at 310 Front St. for a supply of brochures, including the Adventure Tour, a self-guided drive around
town, as well as a walking tour of historical sites. The walking

The Campus Martius, at Marietta, preserves the historic story of settling the Northwest Territories. (Photo by George Laycock)

The oldest building in the Northwest Territories is this Land Office, part of the Campus Martius Museum at Marietta. (Photo by George Laycock)

tour begins at Lafayette Park (Lafayette landed here on his American tour in 1825) and follows the Muskingum River upstream along Front St. past a marker showing where Rufus Putnam and his men came ashore.

The Return Jonathan Meigs House, 326 Front St., built in 1802 by Meigs, is of Federal design. The portico and balcony were added later, and in 1916 the house was moved back from the street 25 feet and north 10 feet from the original site, to center it on the property.

The Buckley House, 332 Front St., is also of Federal style with a two-tiered porch, showing a southern influence, built in 1879.

Both the Shipman House at 404 Front St. and the James Holden House at 408 Front St. are examples of Greek Revival architecture.

The Pratt-McGirr House, 430 Front St., was built by Azariah Pratt, one of the first settlers, in 1809. The hand-hewn beams are still held together with wooden pegs.

The Pardon Cook House, 524 Front St., was built around 1850; the style is Eclectic. Notice the scrolled brackets under the eaves.

The Merydith House, 610 Front St., and the Brockmeier House, 622 Front St., are both in the Greek Revival style.

These houses are close to Marietta's two famous museums. The Campus Martius Museum is located at the corner of Washington and Second streets, on the site of the original fort. Inside is the home of Rufus Putnam, on its original foundation. The back wall also served as the outer wall of the fort. The interior of the house is furnished with Putnam family pieces as well as other period furniture. Other exhibits include tools, crafts, paintings, furniture, and firearms.

One block down St. Clair St., at Washington and Front streets, is the Ohio River Museum with models, maps, and illustrations tracing the river through prehistoric and historic times. A 30-minute multi-media presentation using 16 projectors depicts "The River" from its earliest exploration through steamboat days to the present. Relics on display are from old legendary steamboats. Behind the buildings the *W. P. Snyder, Jr.,* one of the last steam-powered sternwheeled towboats to operate in America, is tied to the shore. Explore the boat. Climb to its pilothouse. Look out on the river and imagine what life was like in days gone by.

The Ohio River Museum, at Marietta, Ohio, traces the history of boating on this famous American river. (Photo by George Laycock)

This reproduction of a typical early Ohio River flatboat stands on the grounds of the Ohio River Museum. (Photo by George Laycock)

Nearby is a full-scale replica of one of the flatboats that the earliest settlers rode down the Ohio.

Both museums are closed Thanksgiving, Christmas, and New Years. The towboat and flatboat are closed from November through March.

Marietta College, one of the oldest in Ohio, was founded in 1835. During the summer the college drama department presents dinner theater on board the *Becky Thatcher Showboat*. The Marietta College Crafts National is held here each fall.

Marietta plays host to the Ohio River Sternwheel Festival in September with dances, music, free live shows, and fireworks.

Mound Cemetery contains the 30-foot-high "Conus," the burial place of an ancient chief. Also in the cemetery are graves of early settlers, including Rufus Putnam and Return Jonathan Meigs.

Children and their parents enjoy cruising on the *Valley Gem,* a replica of a sternwheeler. Departures are hourly on summer afternoons. There are fall foliage tours on weekends in October. Phone: (614) 373-7862 for reservations. Or write Captain James E. Sands, 123 Strecker Hill, Marietta, OH 45750.

Most of Marietta's motels are along Hwy. 7, east of the city. The Lafayette Motor Hotel is downtown at Front and Green streets, opposite Lafayette Park, and the Gun Room here is one of Marietta's nicer dining rooms.

From May 1 through the season of fall color in October the Lafayette offers package weekends, with various combinations of meals, lodging, river trips, museum visits, and showboat dramas for special prices. Write: Lafayette Motor Hotel, 101 Front St., Marietta, OH 45750. Or call: (614) 373-5522.

Campers coming to the Marietta area will find accommodations at three campgrounds. At the north end of the city is Civitan Park on the fairgrounds. Address: Box 2, Civitan Park, Marietta, OH 45750. Near the county fairgrounds is Marietta R/V Park, 819 Front St., Marietta, OH 45750. Another is The Landings, P. O. Box 376, Reno, OH 45773, three miles east of Hwy. 77 on Hwy. 7N.

Athens of the West

The university town of Athens had its origins in the Bunch of Grapes Tavern in Boston, Massachusetts, nearly two centuries ago. Founders of The Ohio Company met there and agreed that there should be centers of education on the frontier, and just as Athens had become the center of Greek learning and culture, Athens, Ohio, given the same name, might become an academic center in the wilds of the Ohio Valley. In 1808 Ohio University opened its doors in Athens with one building, one professor, and three students. The student body has since grown to 14,000, and Athens has fulfilled its purpose by developing into a cultural center not only of Athens County but for all of southeastern Ohio.

All year there are musical programs, dramas, lectures, and conferences underway on the campus and open to the public. Visitors can learn of current attractions at the Information Desk in Baker Center at the corner of College and Union streets, or by calling (614) 594-6704. There are daily guided tours of the campus the year around, beginning at 10 A.M. weekdays, 2 P.M. weekends.

One favorite stop on the campus is the Trisolini Gallery, 48 E. Union St., housing both permanent and traveling art exhibits and a gift shop offering the handiworks of local artists and craftsmen.

Home industries have sprung up in the hills and valleys around Athens in recent times, making this Ohio's leading center for craftsmen and artists who create jewelry, paintings, pottery, wooden furniture, toys, quilts, and many other items. Finding these studios is not always easy, and also visitors are often asked to make appointments in advance. The best place to see local crafts is an old dairy barn on former state property on the edge of Athens.

After the herd was sold and the dairy closed, the dairy barn was threatened with demolition. The wrecking crew was only three weeks away when retired banker Ora Anderson and his wife, Harriett, backed by local citizens, earned it a reprieve. The Southeastern Ohio Cultural Arts Center, Inc., bought the barn and began turning the building into a center that brings in craftsmen, musicians, and tourists, not only from the nearby hills, but also from distant states.

The Dairy Barn has been cleaned, painted, and converted to an exhibition center. For three weeks in July, during odd-numbered years, the Dairy Barn becomes the national center for contemporary quilting, and the finest contemporary quilts from around this country and several foreign countries are displayed during the Quilt National. The Annual Barn Raisin' Arts and Crafts Festival is also held here each Labor Day.

For current programs call or write Executive Director, Dairy Barn, P. O. Box 747, Athens, OH 45701. Phone: (614) 592-4981. To find the Dairy Barn turn into Dairy Rd. on the east side of the University Inn and drive until you see the big white barn on the left.

Although Athens is not noted for fine restaurants, one commendable eating place is the dining room at Ohio University Inn, 331 Richland Ave.

Nelsonville is northwest of Athens on Hwy. 33, and one reason thousands of people come here every summer is to ride the old-fashioned railroad cars on the Hocking Valley Scenic Railway. On weekends, from Memorial Day weekend until the first weekend in November, the steam engine chugs and puffs through the Hocking Valley on its hour-and-twenty-minute run. The depot is beside Hwy. 33, half a mile south of Nelsonville.

By driving another 20 miles or so north on Hwy. 33, then south on Hwy. 664, the traveler reaches the famous Hocking Hills State Park with its scenic rugged sandstone gorges, caves, waterfalls, and rock shelters, easily one of the most popular attractions in central Ohio. This park includes a cluster of scenic areas: Old Man's Cave, Cantwell Cliffs, Rock House, Ash Cave, Cedar Falls, and Conkles Hollow, with hiking trails through deep cool forests, pleasant drives, and fine picnic areas.

If you come to the Athens area equipped to camp, a good bet is Stroud's Run State Park a few miles east of the city. There are 13 miles of hiking trails marked through rugged forests, plus a

161-acre fishing lake with a sand beach for swimmers. Besides, the ride out to Stroud's Run is another of southeastern Ohio's unforgettable ridgetop trips. Our favorite way to get to Stroud's Run, but not the easiest, is to go east from Athens on Hwy. 50, then north on Hwy. 690, and turn left at the sign on Scatter Ridge Road.

Another state park in the northern part of Athens County is Burr Oak State Park, with not only a lake and campground, but also housekeeping cabins, a lodge, and dining room.

Northeast of Athens on Hwy. 550, a most scenic drive between Marietta and Athens, is the hamlet of Amesville, famous only because the first library in Ohio was here. In 1795 local settlers, hungry for education, lamented the fact that they had no books and precious little money to buy them. They trapped furs and collected $73.50 which purchased 51 books brought in across the mountains from Boston by horseback. The Coonskin Library is no longer here, but the house in which it was lodged, now a private residence, still stands. A plaque attached to a rock beside the bank preserves the memory of this frontier library in which coonskins were exchanged for books.

Meigs County and Pomeroy

We entered Meigs County from the east following Hwy. 7, which leaves the Ohio River at Little Hocking to wind up and over the rolling hills. Pomeroy, the county seat, is built on a large bend in the river and, for the most part, extends one street wide for 7 miles. The business district is two streets wide.

Pomeroy traces its early history to a few lumps of coal picked up by Valentine B. Horton. Horton came out from the East at the request of Samuel Wyllys Pomeroy, who for twenty-six years had owned a large tract of Ohio land he had never seen. Horton carried the coal back to Boston, showed it to Pomeroy, and convinced him that he should make a journey out to Ohio.

After Pomeroy arrived, he was smitten with the place. He took special pleasure in the view from Nyes Tavern while feasting on wild turkey from the woods and fish from the waters. But most of all he was impressed with the coal in the surrounding hills. He bought even more land and then organized a company to mine the coal.

With this accomplished, Pomeroy moved on downstream to Cincinnati to establish his offices in more civilized surroundings. Then, he dispatched young Horton upstream to Meigs County to operate his coal company. Horton, who had just married Pomeroy's daughter, Clara, was now part of the family.

Horton's arrival ushered in a new era: He immediately advertised in the East for miners and workers, and hundreds of Welsh and Irish responded. The town grew rapidly. Horton pioneered conversion of steamboat fuel from wood to coal, and long lines of paddlewheelers began tying up at the Pomeroy docks. The coal mines flourished. Barges even carried Pomeroy coal downriver to New Orleans. Until the railroads came, Meigs County remained the only county in Ohio where coal was mined commercially. But the coming of the railroads brought Pomeroy's decline. Boats no longer stop at Pomeroy and haven't for years.

The town is quiet. We asked a shopkeeper what visitors might do if they found themselves in Pomeroy. "Sit and watch the river, I suppose," he answered. "We do have a regatta and frog jump— but I wouldn't advise you to come."

Upriver from Pomeroy is Forked Run State Park, which has trails, picnic area, nature programs, and a fishing lake. One local fisherman speaking of the lake at Forked Run said, "It's nice, but not as nice as some. I go to Rocky Fork instead."

Earlier visitors spoke more kindly of the area. George Washington camped near here in 1770 when he came to meet with the Iroquois Chief Kiashuta. Washington wrote of the beauty of the country and the bountiful game. Near the site of that camp, the Daughters of the American Revolution have installed a plaque to remind us that Valentine Horton was neither the first nor the only famous person here.

Travelers who take Hwy. 124, the river road through this country, come to a roadside park at Buffington Island and a sign with a history lesson. At this point General John Hunt Morgan attempted to escape back across the Ohio River with his rebel force of 2,500 cavalrymen. Morgan was either a swashbuckling hero or a scoundrel, depending on which side of the conflict you embraced. But all agreed that he was a daring leader.

He first crossed the Ohio into southern Indiana, then rode off at the head of his column, sweeping around north of Cincinnati while home guards were madly preparing for his invasion.

Morgan pushed east at a fast pace with fresh mounts taken at will from barnyards and fields. One family forty miles from the nearest point on Morgan's route brought its best horse into the parlor to spend the night.

Morgan, however, was soon on the run, trying to escape the pursuing Union forces. He saw his opportunity at Buffington Island, and many of his soldiers did make it safely back across the river here. Morgan and a few of his top aides, however, were captured in Columbiana County and sent off to prison at the Ohio State Penitentiary in Columbus, where Morgan languished for six months before escaping. He boarded a streetcar that carried him right past the prison on his way south. Legend has it that the person sitting beside him said, "That's where that General Morgan is being held."

Morgan smiled and answered, "And may he always be as securely held as he is at this moment."

Gallia County: We Do It Right

Gallipolis, county seat of Gallia County, was settled in 1790 by the French Five Hundred. The story of the French settlers is a sad story, beginning during the French Revolution. Amidst the anarchy and bloodshed in their native land, these French aristocrats and skilled artisans were easily convinced that a paradise was waiting for them in the New World. Land speculators representing the Scioto Company promised fertile land and wild game, rivers filled with fish, and a fine climate where the temperature seldom dropped below freezing. Artisans were told there was a ready market for their goods, and glassblowers, woodcarvers, gilders, coachmakers, watchmakers, and confectioners sold everything they had to buy deeds and pay passage for themselves and their families to America. They joined many wealthy families fleeing the revolution.

When the first shipload arrived in Alexandria, Virginia, in May 1790, the immigrants were quickly disillusioned. They learned not only that it would be necessary to travel for several months over the mountains and down the Ohio River through the wilderness to reach the land they had bought, but also that their handsomely printed deeds to it were worthless. The Scioto Company had obtained only preemptory rights and had not paid for the land.

Outraged, they appealed to President Washington and the government. The hospitable citizens of Alexandria, remembering the role of France in our war for independence, took in the French Five Hundred until they could receive help. They were given wagons and provisions and, with two expert woodsmen to guide them, set out for their new homes still without title to their land. A crew of men was recruited by General Rufus Putnam in Vermont and Massachusetts and sent to the site of the new village to clear land and build log cabins. In October 1790 the first flatboats reached Gallipolis, which means "town of the Gauls."

Plaque at Gallipolis. (Photo by George Laycock)

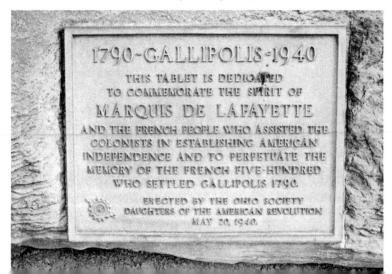

The new settlers found eighty cabins arranged in four rows, twenty to a row, with blockhouses at each corner, connected by a low breastwork to provide protection from the Indians. Stumps of the felled trees still stood around them, behind the place was a swamp, and beyond that the dense wilderness.

But these spirited people were French! They trooped up the hill to the cabins, unpacked, shook out silk gowns and powdered wigs, and celebrated their arrival with music and dancing in one of the blockhouses.

That kind of spirit deserves a story with a happier ending. In answer to their petition, two years later Congress awarded them 24,000 acres in Scioto County. A few of the French moved there, but more sold their shares to English settlers or speculators. Many had returned to eastern cities or gone on to the French towns on the lower Ohio and Mississippi. Some chose to remain in Gallipolis where they had to buy the land they had already settled and developed. In a few years they were engulfed in the wave of settlers from the East and were assimilated; after twenty or thirty years scarcely a trace of French influence remained.

Gallipolis today is a pleasant surprise, clean and prosperous in appearance, the kind of town you might expect to find on a list of best towns in which to live. Teenagers smile and speak to passersby. The heart of the town is the Gallipolis City Park, facing the river. This park is the site of the original settlement where the cabins of the French once stood. Boaters will find a public launching area down on the riverbank, and there are picnic tables and benches.

Stop in at the Chamber of Commerce on the east side of the square and pick up brochures that will help you locate several historic old houses of Gallipolis.

At 1 Court St. stands the house built in 1811 by Francis LeClercq, one of the French Five Hundred. One side of the house was used as a store and post office.

The house at 408 First Ave. dates from 1824. It was built by Robert Warth, once the wealthiest man in town.

John P. Romaine Bureau built the house at 2 State St. in 1811. He was a well-educated and prominent man who is said to have done more for the general welfare of the area than any other person.

The row houses at 413, 417, and 421 First Ave. were built in 1811 by Joseph De Vacht, a Dutch silversmith who arrived with the French Five Hundred and later married one of the French ladies.

The Eagle Tavern was built in 1809 by Henry Cushing at 433 First Ave. It is said that he walked across the street and down to the landing to meet new arrivals with a hearty "Come up to our house!" Soon the tavern was known to all as "Our House." Lafayette stayed there in 1825, and Jenny Lind in 1851. O. O. McIntyre, reared in Gallipolis, made Our House famous in his

Famous early travelers stopped at "Our House" in Gallipolis. (Photo by Ohio Dept. of Industrial and Economic Development)

syndicated newspaper column, "New York Day by Day." Our House, restored and furnished with authentic furniture, is a State Memorial, administered by the Ohio Historical Society.

Riverby, 530 First Ave., is the home of the French Art Colony. The house was built in 1856 and is the former home of Dr. and Mrs. Charles E. Holzer. Art classes are given here, as well as music recitals, antique seminars, and patio theater presentations. Featured exhibits change monthly. Riverby is open to the public.

Dining Out

There are several pleasant restaurants in Gallipolis. One day at noon we chose The Down Under, which is not easy to find the first time. This restaurant is located in the Lafayette Mall, an old brick building converted to a small chic shopping area at the corner of Second and Court streets. You may enter from Court, descending the stairs, or from the mall itself. Famous for its beef and ethnic dishes.

Oscar's, north on Court St., features seafood and steak and was also highly recommended to us, along with the Holiday Inn and the two Bob Evans establishments—The Bob Evans Steakhouse and The Sausage Shop.

Bob Evans, without doubt the best-known resident of Gallia County, is recognized throughout the Midwest and beyond for his Bob Evans Sausage and his chain of popular restaurants. The Evans Homestead is on Route 35 near Rio Grande, and the grounds are open to visitors from May 1 through October.

Evans grew up here, part of a large family with deep roots in Gallia County. He explained that as a young man he made a bucket of sausage from his own recipe and began selling his sausage to a local store. Word of the Evans product spread and the number of stores selling it grew. Evans built a restaurant, with a menu leaning heavily to sausages. This idea also caught on, and Bob Evans, the onetime Ohio farm boy, became a legend in his own time, and the Midwest's best-known farmer. On the big farm at Rio Grande there are many special events and weekend craft demonstrations, and admission to the farm is always free.

The Ohio Valley's largest festival is held in October on the Bob Evans farm at Rio Grande, Ohio. Buses and private cars bring people from several states for the weekend event. (Photo by George Laycock)

For information, stop at the restored log cabins where the highway crosses Raccoon Creek. Here too is the Raccoon Creek Canoe Livery where canoe trips originate. One of the trips takes you to the Daniel Boone Cave where that famed frontiersman is said to have spent two winters early in the 1790s.

Children enjoy the small animal barnyard where they can see chickens, goats, sheep, cattle, horses, pigs, and rabbits.

At the riding stables you can rent horses as well as gear for overnight trail rides.

The sorghum mill and grist mill may be in operation.

The Craft Barn opens early in May until late September. Stop by on summer weekends when various craftsmen are demonstrating their skills.

Bob Evans' extensive collection of farm tools and implements is displayed at the Farm Museum.

On the farm, and facing Hwy. 35, is the Bob Evans Restaurant and General Store, open all year.

Special May events include a canoe race and the Grandma Gatewood Spring Hike. The Annual International Chicken Flying Meet is held the third Saturday in May. Every year hundreds of contestants and thousands of spectators gather for this meet. Seeing is believing.

Each weekend in July the Bob Evans farm hosts a musical

Festival exhibitors dress in the costumes of their ancestors. (Photo by George Laycock)

drama called *Gallia Country,* a presentation that tells of early Welsh settlers in Gallia County. Admission is charged. This is a fun evening.

There may also be a Dulcimer Festival, an Antique Festival, a Bean Dinner, or a Horse Show, depending on when you arrive. Write to Bob Evans Farm, Box 330, Rt. 35, Rio Grande, OH 45674 for dates and details of these events and for information on the biggest festival of all: the annual Bob Evans Farm Festival, held in October. This is the largest free festival of its kind in the nation, and it features craft displays and demonstrations of everything from apple-butter making, quilting, weaving, and wood chopping to shingle making and sorghum grinding. Craftsmen covet invitations to exhibit their wares and skills at this festival, and there is a long waiting list.

During the festival weekend cars, buses, and recreational vehicles roll into Rio Grande from throughout the Midwest bringing an estimated 140,000 visitors.

There are refreshment stands and places to sit and rest while listening to visiting groups of bluegrass musicians or watching the square dancers. It's just the best-run festival we've seen.

Lawrence County:
A National Forest

In the river city of Ironton we stopped to visit with a friend, a local resident, who promptly asked, "What can you find around here that's interesting, except Vesuvius?" There was the challenge. We began talking with people and visiting points of interest and concluded that Ironton, and the surrounding countryside, for all its industrial image, does boast special events and even some outstanding vacation possibilities.

First, we drove north out of town on Hwy. 93 for 7 miles to the Vesuvius Recreation Area, part of Wayne National Forest. The heart of the area is Vesuvius, a long, narrow lake reaching deep into hidden coves and rocky forested glens. Fishing boats can be launched from the public ramp, but because power is limited to nearly silent electric motors, there are no loud outboards to disturb the quiet.

An 8-mile-long hiking trail winds around the lake and through scenery that is sometimes spectacular. Other trails in the forest penetrate hidden valleys and timbered ridges. Backpackers make good use of the 35 miles of trails in every season. Camping is permitted along much of the route. The U. S. Forest Service provides a trail map and encourages hiking, camping, and fishing. There is also hunting, in season and in keeping with state regulations, for grouse, deer, and wild turkeys.

There are in this Ironton section of Wayne National Forest two campgrounds with individual ridgetop sites that put the tent or trailer in the edge of the deep forest and give the camping family a sense of isolation.

The ranger's address is U. S. Forest Service, 710 Park Ave., Ironton, OH 45638. Phone: (614) 532-3223.

These hills grow quality trees, as the earliest settlers knew. Wood from the forests was cut and burned to provide charcoal for the numerous iron furnaces. Ironton was founded by John Campbell, one of the first ironmasters who moved here to process ore dug from the hills. Each of the old furnaces was named, and around each a community grew, often complete with school, church, and store. Some of these aging iron furnaces still stand, and one of the best remaining examples is the Vesuvius Furnace, a massive stone structure near the dam forming Lake Vesuvius.

This early iron making comes to life near Wellston in adjoining Jackson County where the reconstructed Buckeye Furnace State Memorial is open to the public. There simply is no better place to see how the early industrialists of the Hanging Rock region around Ironton converted the native ore to useful metal.

Ironton still has some of the large homes built by the early ironmasters, but the city has done little to attract attention to these aging mansions.

The most festive time of the year in and around Ironton comes during a week-long Tri-State Fair and Regatta every year in June when continuous events bring 300,000 people trooping into town from the surrounding hills of Ohio, Kentucky, and West Virginia.

There are races on the river, sales on the sidewalks, and music everywhere. There are championship contests for school bands, Frisbee throwers, horseshoe pitchers, horsemen, and outboard boat drivers. The big event is the annual Valvoline Cup Races, said to offer the second-largest purse in the country for outboard racing. During this week there are also festivities in other towns and cities on both sides of the Ohio. Write Tri-State Fair and Regatta, P. O. Box 1643, Ashland, KY 41101. Phone: (606) 329-8737.

As sure as Memorial Day comes around, Ironton turns out huge crowds for the town's oldest tradition, the Memorial Day Parade. The parade has gone down the streets of Ironton on this day for more than 112 years without missing a year. "The oldest Memorial Day parade in the country," say Ironton people, and nobody has disputed their claim.

Upriver 20 miles or so we stopped beside a small monument near the county fairgrounds at Proctorville to read about an apple. In 1816 a Rome township farmer, Joel Gillette, gave his son a little tree from a shipment of 100 apple seedlings shipped down from Marietta. This seedling, the runt of the lot, was set out with loving care and watched over during the early years of its life.

Once the tree began to bloom and bear fruit some 15 years later, the family discovered that its firm red apples offered a wonderful combination of flavor and tartness. Outstanding for apple pie. Or simply to eat as you walked along the country lane or rocked the evening away on the front porch.

This apple from Rome township gained popularity around the world as the Rome Beauty.

Scioto County: Forest Vistas

If we had not stopped in Wheelersburg to buy apples at the Nancy Rae Super-Valu store, we might have missed Pioneer Village. In this store there are the usual rows of canned goods and fresh fruits and vegetables. But the shelves above them are filled with antique tools. The old tools are Ray Litteral's idea, and he is free to display antiques along with his groceries if the idea pleases him because he owns the store.

We found Litteral at the back of the store putting pies out on the counter. "We have more antiques over in Pioneer Village," he said. "I'll be out front shortly and take you over."

He led us across the parking lot toward a row of three restored log houses. A brick walk connected them, and around them was a low picket fence. "I found the cabins out in the country," Litteral explained. "We took them down, numbered the parts, moved them here and put them back together just like they were.

"I started collecting antiques because my daughter got me a dinner bell for a present. But I didn't have any interest in old things then. Didn't even put the bell up for two years." After that, he began noticing old tools, and when he did begin collecting, Litteral found that the old farms back in the hollows and along the ridges on both sides of the river were a gold mine for antique hunters. He collected froes, broadaxes, candle molds, blacksmith tools, and enough other equipment from earlier times to turn his grocery store into a showplace.

The overflow sent Litteral out searching for the log buildings,

The Ohio River as towboat captains see it. (Photo by George Laycock)

and these were filled almost as fast as they were erected. In a dozen years he accumulated enough antiques to build as fine a privately operated museum as there is anywhere in the valley, and thousands of tourists and schoolchildren come every year to see how their ancestors lived and worked when the Ohio Valley was younger.

Litteral, who was born in a log house across the river in Magoffin County, Kentucky, first led us to the blacksmith shop he re-created. There was charcoal in the forge because this is a working shop; two local blacksmiths come here each afternoon to make fireplace tools and other iron goods they sell.

In the nearby washhouse were tubs and scrubbing boards, as well as washers powered by gasoline motors. The history of early American kitchens was here too. The kitchen of the pioneer woman, with its massive open fireplace where the cooking was done with kettles, contrasted with the later kitchen of the early 1900s and its familiar Home Comfort range that burned wood or coal.

Litteral was proud of the general store he had re-created in the Village, and especially of the little post office tucked into one corner of the old store. He found the post office, one of the last of its kind, while exploring the hills. "The Smithsonian Institution wants it," Litteral tells us. But he plans to keep the post office right here in Pioneer Village.

Once a year, on a weekend in October, Litteral hosts Frontier Days and thousands of people come to Pioneer Village from all around. They wander through the cabins and store, while Litteral happily brings out his ancient steam threshing machine, and starts up his sorghum mill, processing crops grown locally especially for this celebration of our past.

Those who are interested in covered bridges can travel north of Wheelersburg to the village of Minford and find the old covered bridge built in 1868 on Bennett Schoolhouse Rd. Another of these antique bridges still stands in Scioto County, west of the junction of highways 73 and 348 in Otway. This bridge, constructed of local timbers in 1874, is no longer used for vehicles, but local citizens have joined forces to preserve it.

Portsmouth

Down the road from Wheelersburg we approached the eastern outskirts of Portsmouth, which like its namesake in southern England is more a working city than a place of beauty. Since the days of its founding in 1803, the year Ohio became a state, Portsmouth has taken its wealth from the earth. Sandstone, clay, and iron once helped sustain the bustling center of manufacture.

Portsmouth is built at the mouth of the Scioto, a major tributary connecting Portsmouth with Columbus and the heart of Ohio. The first roads were mud, and the going difficult or impossible, but in 1832, the Ohio and Erie Canal was completed south to Portsmouth and mule-drawn cargo boats moved up and down the narrow canal, carrying produce north and south, and making Portsmouth a busy center for shipment of goods to southern states. Portsmouth was on the way!

In time its charcoal-fired iron furnaces were replaced by giant steel mills, and the smoke of prosperity fanned out over the surrounding valley. On the bustling riverfront steamers loaded and unloaded. In recent years the city's growth slowed then stopped, and the population slid somewhat from the peak years.

If you hurry through the city as we had done many times, you may never know of the places and events that give Portsmouth her sense of pride. This time we were determined to slow down and learn something of the community at the mouth of the Scioto.

Behind City Hall and along the edge of the Ohio River there is a little park with picnic tables, and one way to get there is to climb the steps up and over the giant floodwall that keeps the Ohio River out of town. Standing on the crest of the floodwall, we remembered stories of the famous flood of 1937 when the Ohio rose and buried the old floodwall under 12 feet of muddy water that washed out over two thirds of Greater Portsmouth. Damage ran into the millions of dollars, and this sent the citizens of Portsmouth back to the drawing boards to raise the floodwall to its present level of 77 feet. The wall and the connecting levees form 6 miles of river barrier against floods higher than anyone living can remember. There is a heavily used city campground on the river's edge with space for 50 families.

Among the early settlers to float down the Ohio to this site was Aaron Kinney, a veteran of the Revolution and a tanner by trade. Kinney took possession of some 700 acres of forested land, cleared the trees, and raised a dozen children in a big two-story house built of hand-hewn timbers and brick manufactured on the site. The house still stands, and we started out late one afternoon to find it.

Known today as "The 1810 House," Aaron Kinney's place is easily located on the hill at 1926 Waller St. It is a sturdy no-non-sense building with red-brick walls and tall white porch columns. The old Kinney place, owned now by the Scioto County Histori-cal Society, and listed on the National Register of Historic Places, is open to the public at regular hours. But we arrived late and the doors were locked. We had learned that Aaron Kinney's great-great-grandson lives around the corner and two houses down. So, we went looking for Don Porter.

Porter, genial and gray-haired, happily led us back to the 1810 House for one of his guided tours through the home of his pioneering ancestors. His enthusiasm mounted as we moved from room to room. While he described the contents piece by piece, we traveled back through the years trying to answer Porter's repeated question, "Know what this is?" He touched the old furniture lov-ingly and lingered over the extensive collection of clothing dating from the early 1800s up through the Roaring Twenties, plus noo-dle cutters, candle molds, flatirons, kettles, sauerkraut cutters, and old, old toys.

The 1810 House, among the finest small museums in the val-ley, gives assurance that the roots of Portsmouth are deep in the earth.

Around Portsmouth you hear of the Boneyfiddle District. Nobody we talked with knows where the name came from, but they do know where it is. Boneyfiddle is on the riverfront in the western section of town, and it was here that the riverboat cap-tains and crewmen lived when steamboats plied the Ohio River.

Visitors go to the Boneyfiddle District now to see the Civil War vintage homes and to visit small shops in the old brewery at 224 Second St., renovated to become the Brewery Arcade. The old brewery is on the National Register of Historic Places.

In the heart of Portsmouth, at 825 Gallia St., we found a bank building that is no longer a bank. One of the volunteer ladies working inside told us of the transformation of the bank into Portsmouth's center of culture. "For ten years or more we had dreamed of having a museum. But we never thought we might have a building like this, in this location, right in the middle of town."

Then the bank officers decided to move to a new building and gave their old fortresslike structure to the city which leased it, in turn, at $1.00 a year for 40 years, to a Portsmouth group struggling to start an art museum. Instead of "Security Central Na-

In Portsmouth, Ohio, an old bank building was converted into the Southern Ohio Museum & Cultural Center. (Photo by George Laycock)

tional Bank," the words above the entrance facing Gallia St. now say "Southern Ohio Museum & Cultural Center."

The group raised funds and hired professional help. The building was renovated with remarkably few changes and converted to a fine display center for the traveling art exhibits that come here throughout the year.

Meanwhile, there are classes for painters, and in the little Hopkins Theatre for the Performing Arts, housed in the basement where there once were bank vaults, there are dramas produced. Yellow school buses bringing classes from the surrounding districts wait in line in front of the museum while groups of children are exposed to the works and ideas of artists from around the country.

The cultural center brought a new dimension to life in Scioto County. One girl, who first visited the museum with her class, insisted that her daddy come and see what she had seen. The whole family returned, and the girl was their guide. "They may never have been in an art museum before," said the volunteer. "That means we are making an impression."

There is no charge for visiting this museum.

There is a season when Portsmouth becomes a carnival town. Locally they call it "River Days," and it seems to celebrate no historic event or commemorate anything other than a desire to have a rousing good time—and perhaps stimulate business. River Days Festival comes late in August and lasts for one week.

In our travels we once picked up a small booklet entitled rather ostentatiously, we thought then, *Dining in Portsmouth*. Portsmouth restaurants at first glance seemed limited to the usual fast-food franchises, plus some home cooking and a Chinese restaurant.

Then there is Harold's. We found this gourmet dining room and lounge at 1630 Gallia St., east of the center of Portsmouth. The menu changes frequently, reflecting the owner's current interests and latest ideas on fine dishes that will please his customers. Harold's claims to have Ohio's most varied menu.

The restaurant's owner, and its head chef, is Harold Micklethwait, a towering friendly man with a passion for serving fine food. Harold, who comes from a family of restaurant people, left Portsmouth temporarily to earn a degree in food management from Michigan State University. He followed that with advanced study in Paris and Munich, and what he learned he brought back to Gallia Street in this river city. We hope you enjoy eating at Harold's as much as we did.

Gary Shepard is a Portsmouth photographer who serves as the community's most active booster. "People don't really appreciate all we have around here," Shepard told us. "They don't appreciate the scenery." He mentioned one of his landscape photographs that was on display at a local restaurant. He was in the restaurant the day a visitor from Connecticut came in. "She argued with me for fifteen minutes, insisting that I had made the picture in Connecticut and tried to get me to tell her where in Connecticut's hills I had been with my camera."

Shepard had made the picture a long way from Connecticut. "I told her she could find the location twenty minutes from here." Then he gave us directions to the same vista he had photographed.

We drove west out of town on Hwy. 52 along the river. When we came to Hwy. 125, we turned northwest into the hills, and after driving some miles turned from the state highway to follow Forest Rd. ✗1 then Forest Rd. ✗9, narrow roads, leading through giant oaks and hickories always upward toward the highest ridges in what people around this part of southern Ohio like to call "The Little Smokies." This road led us to Picnic Point where Gary Shepard had stood with his camera.

Steep wooded slopes fell away from the ridges into deep narrow hollows. Farmlands lay far below us in the river bottoms, and beyond that we could see the broad Ohio winding along the Kentucky hills in the distance. A dozen miles upriver we could see the buildings of Portsmouth.

Strong November winds gusted across the ridge plucking brown leaves from the oaks and whirling them aloft on updrafts, up and away over the valley. Like Gary Shepard, we set up our cameras and made our own record of the view, and if Connecticut or Vermont or Tennessee want to claim the scene, we will understand.

Thirteen miles west of Portsmouth and 5 miles west of Friendship on Hwy. 125 is Shawnee State Park, which sits right in the middle of the much larger Shawnee State Forest, a major attraction for vacationers. The state park has a fine Class-A campground with 107 sites. For those preferring indoor living, there are 25 deluxe 2-bedroom housekeeping cabins, and a lodge with 50 guest rooms, restaurant, indoor and outdoor pools, putting green, and tennis courts. Shawnee State Park also has organized hikes and naturalist programs.

There are two lakes where fishermen catch bass, catfish, bluegills, and crappie. The surrounding state forest lands have high populations of deer, grouse, and wild turkey that attract hunters during the open seasons. There is also a special campground at Bear Lake for horsemen.

The Shawnee State Forest is well known to backpackers because Ohio maintains 42 miles of trails here along which hikers may camp. All of this hill country is rugged and heavily timbered, and part of the backpack trail runs through the Shawnee Wilderness Area, 8,000 acres of wild backcountry where there are no vehicles and no roads.

Shawnee State Forest has a new 18-hole golf course, one of the finest in this part of the country. The golf course is on the river side of Hwy. 52, downriver from Hwy. 125.

The address is Shawnee State Park, State Rt. 125, Portsmouth, OH 45662. Phone: (614) 858-4561. The number at the lodge is (614) 858-6621.

Adams County:
A Magnificent Serpent

In Manchester, the fourth-oldest town in Ohio, we discovered an official plaque revealing the rich history of this river village. Nathaniel Massey, a pioneering surveyor, organized settlers to cross the Ohio River, from the comparative safety of Kentucky, and settle here four years before the 1795 treaty with the Indians made the Ohio country comparatively safe for white settlers.

Massey (whose ancestry reached back to Manchester, England) encouraged his settlers with promises of land and the safety of a fort which they would construct by communal effort. The sturdy fort, which was never challenged by the Indians, is gone, but the town that descended from it lingers on, locally noted for having the only retail liquor store in an otherwise dry county.

Driving along the river on Hwy. 52, a few miles southwest of Manchester, we came to the attractive restaurant and winery operated by Ken and Mary Moyer, and were reminded that this valley was once famous for its wines. Nicholas Longworth started the industry in the Ohio Valley during the 1820s. His grapes flourished on the slopes above the river. More vineyards appeared and wine fanciers praised Ohio Valley vintages.

Then disease struck. The vineyards were destroyed and with them the dreams. The hills returned to growing corn and pasture. Then, after a century and a half, the Ohio Valley wine industry began to show evidence of new life. This reawakening began in the fields of the Ohio State University experimental farm, established to test new grape varieties and cultural practices, in the hills above the Ohio River near Ripley. What the scientists learned there helped a handful of vintners pick up where Nicholas Longworth left off. These modern wine producers manage family enterprises that started from modest beginnings. The Moyers still look back with wonder on their own entry into the wine business.

Ken, a soft-spoken and friendly man, is a ceramic engineer. He worked in different places in the United States, and for several years managed a plant in Mexico City. In his spare time, Ken grew grapes because he enjoyed making his own wine.

Then he learned that his company planned to send him to Morocco to manage a new factory. "We did not see this as a dream assignment," says Ken quietly, "and we decided it was time to see if my winemaking could become a full-time enterprise. We hoped it would support our family."

Ken and Mary visited seven states seeking regions suitable for growing grapes. They came eventually to southern Ohio, and outside Manchester Ken found the setting he wanted. A high hill protects the riverbottom lands from late spring frosts, providing a long growing season. The Moyers bought 64 acres lying in a nar-

Near Peebles, Ohio, is the world-famous Serpent Mound, a giant effigy mound created centuries ago by prehistoric people. (Ohio Office of Travel and Tourism photo)

row strip along the river. Their new property included a run-down roadside tavern. Ken set out his first 5,000 hybrid grape vines, and three years later began harvesting his first crop.

Early customers were served cheese. When they began requesting other foods, the Moyers were eased into the restaurant business. They remodeled their building and today they operate one of the most attractive and successful restaurants and wineries along the Ohio. Guests are welcome to visit the floor below the restaurant to see Ken Moyer's vats and presses at work. For fair weather, we recommend a table on the deck overlooking the river, a bottle of Moyer's fine wine, and watching the towboats pass as you dine.

West Union, the county seat of Adams County, is so quiet that some folks say not much exciting has happened here since the public hanging of David Beckett outside the courthouse in 1808. While in town, stop at the Olde Wayside Inn, just up the street from the courthouse. Built in 1804 as a stage stop, this old inn offers the best country food, and the biggest servings for the money, of any place around. And the guest rooms are furnished with antiques.

North out of West Union on Hwy. 41 (the famous Zane's Trace by which early congressmen rode horseback from Kentucky to the nation's capital) is Dunkinsville. If you drive west out of this tiny settlement, following Wheat Ridge Road, you enter a scattered community of Amish people who farm, make clocks and furniture, and bake goods for sale.

Serpent Mound

The Ohio Valley was long ago inhabited by people who built mounds of earth as burial places and centers of worship. Hundreds of these mounds were constructed in the valley. A few were elaborate effigies in the form of animals, and the largest of all the effigy mounds was built in the northern part of what is now Adams County. Lines of workers carried earth in baskets made of bark, and when the mound was completed it was a giant serpent twisting along a ridgetop for 1,335 feet. Its tail is coiled, as serpent tails often are, and the massive head displays a gaping mouth grasping a huge egg.

Once a year Peebles, Ohio, blocks off its main street for Old Timers Day, typical of many small-town festivals in the Ohio Valley. (Photo by George Laycock)

Early European explorers stumbling upon the giant serpent mound marveled at its size and perfect shape. Later scientists came to probe the mound and search out the secrets of its ancient builders.

Today the serpent, in perfect condition, lies quietly on its peaceful hilltop. To find Serpent Mound, take a scenic drive north from Peebles, Ohio, 3 miles on Hwy. 41 then west 4 miles on Hwy. 73 to Serpent Mound State Memorial.

In the eastern part of Adams County we discovered a lovely scenic drive through the rugged hill country. The drive begins where Hwy. 125 crosses Ohio Brush Creek, 5 miles east of West Union. Here Hwy. 348 leads northward, then swings east toward Scioto County. We arrived here on a splendid autumn day when the hills were at the peak of their seasonal brilliance. The road, blacktop all the way, winds up and over the hills, past sleepy settlements, through little valleys and deep forests. We've marked it on our map to help us remember it next year.

Brown County: The "Freedom Light"

On the Ohio side of the river, 9 miles downriver from Maysville, Kentucky, stands the old river town of Ripley, with the hills rising sharply in the background. The town was laid out by Colonel James Poage, a Virginian, and named for General Ripley, who distinguished himself in the War of 1812. Many of its old homes still stand, most of them facing the river, and brass plaques on them recall the little city's fading glory.

Ripley rose to its greatest heights during the Civil War, to which it contributed four admirals and four generals, including Ulysses Simpson Grant whom it proudly claims because he spent a year in school there. Ripley also became famous as a center of the abolitionist movement.

On the west side of town we found a sign pointing the way up a narrow and winding road to the Rankin House on the hill. From this hilltop there is a splendid view across the rooftops of Ripley and over the river to the green hills of Kentucky. This is the birthplace of a story that Abraham Lincoln once said helped start a war.

The story begins in the days of slavery when the Rev. John Rankin from Tennessee arrived in Ripley. Searching for a place to build his home, Rankin climbed the high hill behind the city and realized that, cleared of its brush, this place would serve his special need.

In the years that followed, escaping slaves came at night to the edge of the Ohio River and from the Kentucky shore could see a "freedom" light on the top of Rankin's hill, which they knew as Liberty Hill. Slaves who crossed the Ohio and climbed the steep hill were welcomed, fed, and secretly escorted, in defiance of Federal law, to the next station where other abolitionists waited to help.

The young Harriet Beecher first saw the Rankin House in October 1834, when she came to Ripley from Cincinnati with her father to attend meetings of the Presbyterian synod. The Beechers stayed at the Rankin home, and during that visit Harriet first heard Rankin's stories of slaves escaping across the Ohio River. One unforgettable story was of a young mother who came to the south shore of the river in the darkness of a bitter winter night clutching her infant to her breast. The melting ice threatened to break at any moment, but the young mother, pursued by slave catchers, waded onto the melting ice and made her way over the river, guided by the flickering yellow light on the hilltop. She made the long climb up the hill, and one of Rankin's sons (he had nine) led her northward toward freedom. Her pursuers, arriving at the river the following morning, found that the ice had broken. The facts seemed clear to them: The slave girl and her baby had drowned.

For thirty-five years the determined Rankin lived in Ripley, and it is said that during those years more than 2,000 slaves made their way to his home on Liberty Hill, the first station in the Underground Railroad.

Years later Harriet Beecher, living in the East and now the wife of Calvin Stowe, wrote that story and included it in *Uncle*

Tom's Cabin. Her book became an instant success, catapulted Harriet Beecher Stowe to fame, and helped fan the fires of the growing conflict between North and South.

Today the Rankin House still stands on the hill above Ripley, and the Ohio Historical Society maintains it. Visitors come to explore the house with its hidden closets under the eaves, and to look down on the river that the fleeing Eliza crossed on the ice.

If you should drive through Ripley in the Christmas season, or view it from across the river, you will see a light burning on top of Liberty Hill, a star placed there to keep alive memories of long ago.

As the Civil War approached, Ripley felt compelled to defend itself, and the town spent $1,000 for a new cannon which it pointed toward the hills of Kentucky. A century and a quarter later the Ripley cannon stands silent guard in the center of town on the library lawn. At least one published account told us that it is still pointed toward Kentucky. We went to see. The cannon is there, as reported, but the big gun, once trained on Kentucky, now takes a bead on a Pepsi-Cola sign across the street.

In early winter all the major tobacco companies send buyers to Ripley where there are four tobacco warehouses. A tobacco auctioneer arrives and from Thanksgiving week until late January his chant can be heard in the big metal sheds on the east edge of town. This is Ohio's only remaining tobacco auction, and visitors are welcome. The sales are held Monday, Tuesday, Wednesday, and Thursday from 10 A.M. to about 1 P.M.

In her early years Ripley lost a bid to become the county seat of Brown County. The honor went to the more centrally located community of Georgetown which, like Ripley, still retains much of the flavor of its nineteenth-century roots.

In the center of Georgetown stands her historic courthouse, still showing the ravages of the fire set in the late 1970s by vandals who tried to burn it down. That fire started a long and painful campaign to restore the historic building to its former glory. Mrs. John Markley, a spritely ninety-year-old Brown Countian, told us the story one day in her home.

"It was one of the buildings designed by Hubbard Baker," she explained. Baker was an early Georgetown builder, a skilled woodworker, with a world of ability. Baker's Georgetown buildings are noted for their colonial lines, and their feeling of space. They would have become classics anywhere. Baker came to Georgetown from Kentucky, and in 1849 the county commissioners gave him the contract for the new courthouse. "The building is pure Brown County," said Mrs. Markley. "There was not a thing used in it that didn't come from here except the metal roofing and the glazing. The bricks were made up the road. The subcontractor was in such a hurry for the last load that the bricks were still hot and they burned the bottom out of the wagon on the way to town."

When the courthouse was completed in 1851, admirers praised its beautiful simple lines, the high white columns standing at the front of the building, and the cupola that graced the roof. But when it was damaged by fire some citizens argued for replacing it with a new structure. "Some even said, 'Tear it down and put a swimming pool in its place,'" said Mrs. Markley. "Then all the drunks could go take a bath." But the restoration continues and the courthouse will stand again in her original glory in the center of Georgetown.

This covered bridge in Brown County, Ohio, is one of many still in use in the Ohio Valley. (Photo by George Laycock)

Take time for a walking tour. Many of the buildings around the old town square have been renovated, and other restorations are still in progress. Around the corner at 203 E. Grant St. is the Thompson House, built in 1836 by John Kay. If the door is unlocked, step inside because this is now a wildlife art gallery where visitors are welcome.

Many of the paintings offered here are those of internationally famous wildlife artist John Ruthven, Georgetown's best-known living citizen. Ruthven and his wife, Judy, have been a moving force behind the revitalization of Georgetown and the renovation of its buildings. They bought the Thompson House to serve as John's gallery. Then one day they learned that the next house down the street was also going on the market.

This tall white-brick structure at 219 E. Grant St. was the boyhood home of Ulysses S. Grant, and it was across the street from the family tannery operated by Jesse Grant, father of Ulysses. The family moved here when Ulysses was two, and it was from

The Ohio is one of the nation's busiest streams. (Photo by George Laycock)

here that young Grant left for West Point fifteen years later. John and Judy Ruthven were concerned about what new owners might do with this historic building. They made their own bid and, to their amazement, found themselves owners of the house where a past-President of the United States lived through his formative years.

The Grant House is open today to visitors because the Ruthvens believe it belongs to our national heritage. They have filled it with period furnishings that help tell the story of both General Grant and the town where he grew up.

In the yard stand two metal plaques. One tells of President Grant. The other memorializes General Thomas Lyon Hamer, another Brown County war hero, who died in the Mexican War.

A few blocks away is Grant's Schoolhouse, and this small building, where Grant studied, is maintained by the Ohio Historical Society.

Several of the old homes around town were designed and built by the talented Hubbard Baker. Perhaps the most impressive of all his designs is the Presbyterian Church. Another Baker structure worthy of attention is the Bullock House, southwest of Georgetown on Hwy. 221. Today this old home serves as an antique shop, one of the finest in the Ohio Valley.

Before leaving Georgetown, we suggest lunch at Annie's Loft. It's upstairs, on the west side of the square; an unusual restaurant.

Clermont County: East Fork Park

Clermont County lies on the eastern edge of Greater Cincinnati and lives in the cultural shadow of that city. Shopping centers, industrial plants, highways, and new housing complexes push steadily eastward. But Batavia, the seat of county government, resists change successfully enough to retain its character as a quiet, little town nestled in the hills that flank the East Fork of the Little Miami River. People here, and throughout the county, combine the pleasures of small-town or country living with the advantages of having a major city within easy driving distance.

Travelers following the Ohio River into this county from the east on Hwy. 52 soon arrive at Point Pleasant, noted as the birthplace of Ulysses S. Grant. The little white-frame house in which Grant was born still stands, and the Ohio Historical Society maintains it as a museum. We once took a visiting Chilian exchange student there, and he marveled that a President of the United States had come from such humble origins.

There is a little state park on the Ohio River side of Hwy. 52, west of the bridge over Big Indian Creek. If the weather is pleasant, this is a shady spot for a picnic lunch while watching the riverboats pass.

The East Fork State Park and Reservoir lie in the central part of Clermont County where the East Fork of the Little Miami River is backed up behind a huge dam to form a new lake 7 miles long and up to a mile wide. The reservoir covers more than 2,000 acres and is part of a major state park recreation complex, with outdoor attractions for everyone. The campground, with modern facilities and spaces for 416 families, draws vacationers bringing tents and recreational vehicles.

Horseback riders come with their trailers, mounts, and camping outfits. The park's trails have a combined length of 85 miles, some short for easy walking, others longer for backpackers and horseback riders. The trail around the perimeter of the park winds among the wooded hills above the lake for 40 miles.

When completed, this park will have vacation cabins as well as a lodge with restaurant and a golf course.

Fishing is excellent. At park headquarters we talked with George Rooks, assistant park manager, who worked in the area even before it became a state park. "The biggest largemouth bass I've heard of? Eight pounds," he says, "and as the lake grows older there should be bigger ones. We had a six-and-a-half-pound smallmouth too." Rooks told us of catching half a hundred crappie and bluegills in a few hours during one autumn evening.

Ohio River tributaries are favorites with canoeists. These canoeists are on the Little Miami River, a National Scenic and Recreational River flowing into the Ohio on the eastern edge of Cincinnati. (Photo by George Laycock)

No one has much doubt that this park will become heavily used because it is close to Cincinnati and easily reached from every direction. Follow the signs off Hwy. 32 near Williamsburg on the north, or from Hwy. 125 near Bantam on the south.

Another smaller lake and state park are hidden away in the rural countryside at the north edge of Clermont County near Edenton. Stonelick Lake offers only 181 acres of water and there are no motors larger than electric motors to disturb the peace. But the fishing is fair, the sand beach is a big attraction, and campers come, we are told, from all over the country. The campground, open the year around, is fully modern and space can be reserved. If you want to camp but have no equipment of your own, you can rent a camping outfit at any time from Memorial Day to Labor Day by reserving it ahead. For details write to Stonelick State Park, Rt. 1, Pleasant Plain, OH 45162. Phone: (513) 625-7544.

Downstream several miles, a barn-red, 140-feet-long covered bridge, built in 1878, crosses Stonelick Creek. Covered bridge enthusiasts call this structure an especially fine example of the bridge-builder's art. "It has been kept in repair," says Cincinnati photographer, Clarence W. Koch, an authority on covered bridges, "and that's why it has lasted so long." People come from all over the country to see it. This bridge is a favorite with photographers, and it promises to stand steadfastly year after year, resisting the combined forces of weather and vehicular traffic. "It's a good one," says Koch.

Cincinnati Nature Center

If your interests run to quiet trails, birds, and wild flowers, you will want to visit the Cincinnati Nature Center while you are in Clermont County. This nature center is among the finest of its kind anywhere. Visitors (non-members pay a small parking fee and are welcome Monday through Friday) walk miles of trails that wind through deep forests and beside gurgling little limestone creeks. Spring brings a carpet of wild flowers to the woodland as well as flocks of migrating warblers. We recall a visit here when we watched a mink search along the creekbank for food while we stood silently on a little bridge above.

And if you are one who can't resist gift shops, go forewarned: The shop at the Cincinnati Nature Center offers items ranging from jewelry to bird feeders and has perhaps the finest stock of nature books in the Ohio Valley. The Cincinnati Nature Center is off Hwy. 32, north of Glen Este, at 4949 Tealtown Rd.

Cincinnati

In December 1788 a little band of settlers pushed their boats away from the shore at Limestone, known to us today as Maysville, Kentucky, and headed downstream. Two days later, after traveling about 50 miles, they landed on the north shore of the river not far from where Riverfront Stadium stands today. But none of them dreamed of calling this place Cincinnati. Instead, the new settlement they built was given a name suggested by Kentucky school teacher John Filson who combined syllables of Greek, Latin, and French to compound a word translated as "the city opposite the mouth." Directly across the Ohio River was the mouth of the Licking River which flows northward into the Ohio. So the new settlement was called "Losantiville." But not for long.

When Losantiville was little more than a year old, General Arthur St. Clair, Governor of the Northwest Territories, arrived from Marietta. He had come down the river to dedicate officially the newly formed county of Hamilton and its seat of government, "the city opposite the mouth." As he floated down the Ohio he must have given the name of the budding village considerable thought because he decided to change it.

St. Clair had been a founder of The Society of Cincinnati, an organization of Revolutionary War officers. Determined to honor the officers of the Revolution, he eliminated by executive order the rather strange-sounding name, Losantiville. To this day all who must ask, "Is it spelled with one n or two?" can thank Governor St. Clair for substituting another strange-sounding name that would become known around the world. Cincinnati.

When the *Orleans,* the first steamboat on the Ohio, chugged down the river in 1811, life along the waterfront lost its leisurely pace for all time. Other steamboats were soon plowing up and down the Ohio, coughing the black smoke of prosperity into the valley air, and Cincinnati flourished. By 1825 the system of inland canals began opening up the heartland, and farmers could move their products to the river cities for shipping to southern markets. Along Cincinnati's bustling waterfront, steamboats were loaded with barrels of pork, flour, and whiskey.

By 1830 German immigrants, driven by the search for freedom and opportunity, began arriving in America in large numbers, and many of them headed for Cincinnati to join relatives who had already found work in the growing river city. Then came the Irish, escaping the potato famine of the 1840s. By 1859, 160,000 people lived here, and steamboats were tied up bow to stern along six miles of riverfront.

On occasion, early travelers found kind things to say about this city halfway down the Ohio. Henry Wadsworth Longfellow celebrated Cincinnati as the "Queen City of the West," thereby endearing himself to Cincinnatians who still call their city "The Queen City." Charles Dickens said that only Boston was prettier. Modern writers are more likely to compare Cincinnati and its hills to San Francisco.

Fountain Square is the heart of Cincinnati. (Greater Cincinnati Convention & Visitors' Bureau photo)

The century-old Tyler-Davidson Fountain dominates the modern Fountain Square in downtown Cincinnati. (Courtesy Greater Cincinnati Convention & Visitors' Bureau, Mayhew Photographers)

Polk Laffoon, a writer who lived in Cincinnati and worked on the Cincinnati *Post* in the 1970s, once wrote in *Cincinnati* magazine, "And how charming it is! The green hills in summer, the Ohio River, the sounds of the *Delta Queen,* who could blame anyone for loving it intensely? I think of the little things so often overlooked and that make life here sparkle; the triangles of

flowers planted by the Park Board, the corporate-sponsored concerts in the parks, the abundance of bakeries . . ."

Cincinnati, politically conservative, accepts change carefully.
Its people like their city as it is, with its hills, river views, parks,
and the fact there is always something to do, whether it is going
to the opera at the Music Hall or Graeters for an ice-cream cone
(Graeters ice cream is so famous, and justifiably so, that it is frequently packed in dry ice at Graeters stores and hand carried to
friends and relatives in other cities, both in and beyond the Ohio
Valley).

Cincinnati claims more trees per capita than any other city in
the country. It was once said that the city, like Rome, was
founded on seven hills. This may be true, but Cincinnati has since
spread over dozens of hills in every direction. Outside the center
of the city, in the sprawling residential communities, homes are
surrounded by spacious green yards. No resident is far from one
of the city or county parks.

The success of Cincinnati is found partly in the diversity of its
industries. From its early history as a shipping center for grain
and pork (it was once called "Porkopolis"), Cincinnati has be-

*This view of Cincinnati's skyline, including riverfront, is from
across the river in Covington, Kentucky.* (Photo by George
Laycock)

come a world-famous producer of machine tools, soap and detergents, cosmetics, jet engines, automobile parts, and playing cards. Visitors interested in seeing Cincinnati industries at work should get details about current industry tours from the Cincinnati Chamber of Commerce. Interesting possibilities include Procter & Gamble's Ivorydale plant, Meiers Winery, General Motors, Riverfront Stadium, and Wiedemann's Brewery, which is across the river.

For the best overall look at Cincinnati's downtown, and some of her famous hills, visitors go to the top of the tallest building, the Carew Tower, 441 Vine St. One afternoon we went aloft for the view. An elevator whisked us straight up 45 floors of offices in 32 seconds. We disembarked and boarded a slower elevator to be lifted 3 more floors. Finally, we climbed a few flights of stairs and came into a miniature welcoming center where a friendly lady sells souvenirs and collects the fifty-cent admission charged those who want to go outside to the open observation platform.

From here the visitor can see more of the city than is visible from any other land-based location. To the south, across the Ohio River, lie Kentucky's hills, and over these hills stretch I-75 and I-71 toward Lexington, Louisville, or Florida. From here you can also look down on Riverfront Stadium, home of the Cincinnati Reds and the Bengals.

To the east is Mt. Adams, and winding downstream from Pittsburgh is the Ohio River. To the north is a view of the old red-brick buildings of the basin and the section of Cincinnati that has, since canal days, been known as the "Over the Rhine." From this elevation you can see the home office buildings of such giant businesses as the Kroger Company, the world's second-largest food store chain which grew from a little neighborhood grocery opened in 1883 on Pearl Street by Barney Kroger, a twenty-three-year-old peddler. Also in view is the home office of Procter & Gamble, which started with the soap and candle factory opened by candlemaker William Procter and soapmaker James Gamble on Main Street in 1837 and became the biggest soapmaker in the world. To the west in the distance is the Union Terminal, called the best example of Art Deco architecture in the world, now a shopping center and tourist attraction.

In view also is the new public library covering a full block at Eighth and Vine streets. Cincinnati reads. The Cincinnati and

Hamilton County Public Library circulates six million books a year, more than the number circulated in much larger cities. This library, which first opened in 1853, now owns three and a quarter million volumes with especially fine collections on genealogy, heraldry, fine arts, science, and the inland rivers.

In addition to the main library downtown, the system includes 39 branches scattered over every part of the city and county. Each year the library staff answers a million and a half questions of those coming to the library, and another half million questions over the telephone.

An even older library is the Cincinnati Mercantile Library at 414 Walnut St. on the eleventh floor, with a history going back a century and a half to an age when libraries were financed by memberships. Mercantile Library members still cherish this quiet downtown refuge. And they have provided for the future with a 10,000-year lease. Renewable.

The heart of the downtown area is Fountain Square where, on a fair day, hundreds of pedestrians crisscross in all directions, rows of brown baggers eat their lunches, chat with their friends, and girl watch. In summer the Cincinnati Symphony Orchestra sometimes gives concerts on the Square at noon. The Square is named for the ornate Tyler-Davidson Fountain that, during the warm months, spouts water from various angles. The 38-foot-tall

Cincinnati's famous skywalks, some of them enclosed and air-conditioned, allow shoppers to walk above the traffic. (Photo by George Laycock)

bronze fountain, designed by August von Kreling of Nuremburg and cast (in 1871) in the Royal Bronze Foundry of Bavaria, is of another age. But it remains the heart of a dazzling downtown renewal project.

Out of sight, beneath Fountain Square is a public parking lot several layers deep. This, and other parking, encourages shoppers and visitors to come downtown to the stores, ball games, restaurants, and Convention Center because the heart of Cincinnati is alive and well. One of the reasons for her vitality is the maze of skywalks. These elevated sidewalks, the newer ones enclosed and air-conditioned, enable pedestrians to escape vehicle traffic, avoid the street crossings, and walk freely around the downtown to restaurants, stores, cinemas, and hotels that open directly onto the elevated walkways.

Finding Your Way in Cincinnati

Cincinnati is a collection of neighborhoods. Visitors in town need not learn all the subdivision names and their locations and characteristics. Street maps are available at bookstores and newsstands. And the people are helpful. "The zoo? Oh, that's way out on Vine Street, which runs north and south all the way through town."

"Kings Island? It's not right in town, you know. Get on I-71 headed north like you're going to Columbus, and just keep on going. It's about twenty miles from town. You'll know it when you get there."

The first-time Cincinnati visitor does well to learn a few major streets. Numbered streets, beginning with Second, run parallel to the river, while Vine Street divides the city east and west. Highway 50 east, Montgomery Road, Reading Road, Hamilton Avenue, and the River Road (Hwy. 50 west) are all major spokes radiating from the downtown hub of the city. The Interstate Highway system is excellent through Cincinnati, and the circle freeway, I-275, connects three states and circles the Greater Cincinnati area—all of it, intersecting I-74, I-71, I-75, and I-471. Four bridges carry the Interstate Highway system over the Ohio River.

The following major attractions are close to the downtown area: The Convention Center, Riverfront Stadium, Coliseum, Music Hall, Union Terminal, Cincinnati Art Museum, Taft Museum, Cincinnati Natural History Museum, and Playhouse in the Park.

Where to Stay

Seldom, even in the busiest summer season, is there difficulty finding a place to stay in Cincinnati. The city, according to one count, has 46 hotels and motels within 30 minutes of its downtown area. Some are easily spotted at major intersections of the Interstate highways leading into Cincinnati; others are located to accommodate downtown visitors, and there is a third group across the river in Northern Kentucky.

Facing Fountain Square in the middle of town is the new Westin Hotel, the only downtown hotel in Cincinnati with a year-around pool and health club. The Westin, which connects to the skywalks, has 460 guest rooms, 3 restaurants, 2 lounges, 18 shops, and ample parking. It also has a family plan. Phone: (513) 621-7700.

Other downtown hotels offer rooms with scenic views of the river. Rates vary, as might be anticipated, but the cost of lodging in Cincinnati is somewhat lower than it is in most other large cities around the country.

Dining Out

Cincinnati is renowned for its restaurants. Even New York, Chicago, and Los Angeles have fewer four- and five-star restaurants than Cincinnati does. Only San Francisco, with twice Cincinnati's population, outranks this Ohio River city for superior restaurants. And at the top of a superlative list is the Maisonette, 114 E. Sixth St. Dining in this five-star restaurant is expensive. French cuisine, served with style by a skilled staff. We suggest lunch or dinner at the Maisonette for special occasions.

Cincinnati has six restaurants which either are or recently have been four-star rated. Excellent French menus are offered by Pigalls, 127 W. Fourth St., charming and expensive, and the Gourmet Room, small and smart and with a stunning view from the top floor of the Terrace Hilton Hotel, Sixth St.

The others are outside the downtown area. LaRonde, in the Carrousel Inn at 8001 Reading Rd., serves both French and American food. Our personal all-time favorite is The Heritage, in an old inn at 7664 Wooster Pike, Hwy. 50, east of Mariemont. The Heritage offers distinctive American food plus the light nouvelle cuisine. Friendly and efficient service. The Mama Francesca Italian Restaurant, 5552 Colerain Ave., dates from the early 1800s. In addition there is Mechlenburg's Garden, 302 E. University.

If you want a table with a view, try the revolving Top of the Crown at Stouffer's downtown. The Riverview, at the top of the Quality Inn across the river, revolves too. Another with a spectacular view of river and city is the Sovereign in the Queen's Tower on Price Hill. Interesting menu, and early diners can watch the lights go on in the city below.

Grammer's, the oldest and best known of Cincinnati's remaining old German restaurants, is in a Bavarian-style building at Vine and Thirteenth streets. Offers weiner schnitzels, bratwurst, and other German fare. German food is also served at Zimmers, 3355 Madison Rd., and across the Ohio River at Mick Noll's, 100 W. Sixth St. in Covington.

Other fine restaurants include Charley's Crab and Chester's Roadhouse across from each other on Montgomery Rd., in Montgomery; Grand Finale, Sharon Rd. and Congress Ave., in Glendale; and Dante's in the Imperial House at I-74W and Rybolt Rd.

Cincinnatians often tell visitors that the best ribs served in town are found at the Montgomery Inn, 9440 Montgomery Rd. Bob Hope likes them too. This is a busy place, family-operated, and very successful.

There are good Italian restaurants here. Among them is Edward's at Fifth and Butler streets, downtown—a favorite among our friends.

Cincinnati has seen a recent proliferation of Chinese restaurants offering a wide variety of cuisine. Wong's, 216 E. Sixth St., has good Cantonese food, served by Chinese waiters. The Yum Yum, 909 Race St., was the first Szechuan Chinese restaurant in town. Cheng Tu on Reading Rd. has Hunan, Cantonese, Szechuan, and Mandarin cuisine. Emperor's Wok on Chester Rd. has magnificent decor; good food too. There are many more: We especially like the Kali Kai, 6202 Montgomery Rd. A family restaurant; not fancy but good food and reasonable.

Cincinnati is famous for its chili, and the best in town is said to be found at Skyline Chili. For pizza, we suggest any of the La Rosa's restaurants. And if you have a yen for hamburgers, those served at Rookwood Pottery on Mt. Adams are considered the best in town. This popular restaurant and lounge is in a remodeled building where Rookwood pottery was once made, and your table may be inside a kiln. At lunchtime, the busiest place in Cincinnati may be LaNormandie, lower level, 118 E. Sixth St. Known for its beef dishes.

Museums

Cincinnati is a bonanza for museum goers. There are seashells and Shawnee ornaments, Rembrandts and Gainsboroughs, fire trucks and playing cards, butterflies and polar bears, African masks and oriental vases. Even the casual visitor can spend a couple of days in the city's museums.

Art Museum

The largest art museum in the Ohio Valley, and one of the top twenty in the country, is the Cincinnati Art Museum on the hilltop in Eden Park. The museum was founded in 1881 and the massive stone building housing it was completed in 1886, making this the first general art museum housed in a building of its own west of the Alleghenies.

The permanent collections here are strong in American painters, especially Cincinnati painters, including Farney and Duveneck. In addition, the museum is known in museum circles for its fine collection of ancient musical instruments and for its Middle East collection.

Closed on Mondays and major holidays. Admission charged.

The Taft Museum

Within easy walking distance of Fountain Square in the center of downtown Cincinnati, the Taft Museum, 316 Pike St., faces Lytle Park and houses one of America's finest private art collections. The structure is considered an outstanding example of Federal architecture, and it stands in a carefully groomed formal garden.

The house, with its fabulous art collections, was donated to the city in 1927 to become a museum. Its rooms are furnished with Duncan Phyfe furniture and Regency and Empire fabrics and tapestries. On display are paintings by Rembrandt, Goya, Gainsborough, Van Dyck, Whistler, and Ruisdael. Its treasures also include Chinese porcelains and French Renaissance enamels.

Chamber music concerts are frequently held in the ballroom on

The Taft Museum in downtown Cincinnati houses a famous collection of artworks. (Photo by George Laycock)

Sunday afternoons. The Taft Museum, open weekdays 10 A.M. to 5 P.M., and Sundays 2 to 5 P.M., except Thanksgiving and Christmas, is free to the public, and there is parking space provided behind the museum.

Gallery of Jewish Art and Artifacts

The Hebrew Union College, which opened in 1875, is the largest Jewish theological seminary in the world. Hebrew Union now occupies 18 acres at 3101 Clifton Ave. across from the University of Cincinnati.

The Gallery of Jewish Art and Artifacts on this campus holds collections of cuneiform tablets, maps, charts, jewelry, coins, pottery, and other archaeological treasures arranged to make ancient history understandable. There are special exhibits and programs for children, and there is no charge for admission.

Fire, Fire!

As Cincinnati grew, so did its need for fire fighters. Private fire companies vied to answer fire calls. Each new fire started a headlong race to see which company reached the scene first. As the friction increased, fire-fighting companies taunted and insulted each other until the spirit of competition, often fanned by ethnic differences, led to fights that grew into brawls and near riots.

By 1873, however, Cincinnati had the country's first full-time professional fire department, and the story is told at 315 W. Court St. The old firehouse at this downtown address reopened its doors in 1980, not for the clanging fire engines, but to admit visitors to the new Cincinnati Fire Museum. Admission charged. Phone: (513) 621-5553. And the kids can ring the fire bell!

Old Homes

If you want to see how wealthy Cincinnatians lived a century ago, visit the Hauck House. Hauck was a German brewer who came to Cincinnati in the 1800s and became both wealthy and locally prominent. His home, 812 Dayton St., was part of the "millionaires row" of the 1890s. Today the house is open to visitors. The house is in Italianate style and has large rooms and high ceilings. Walls and ceilings are intricately decorated. Mantels are marble and the woodwork massive. The house has been restored and furnished with everything of the period from furniture to children's toys.

This museum home is in the Dayton Street Historic District covering two blocks of Cincinnati's West End, not far from downtown. The phone is (513) 721-4506. Admission charged.

The Miami Purchase Association, which maintains the Hauck House, has also established a restored village in the northern part of the county in Sharon Woods Park, twenty minutes from downtown. From I-275, exit at Hwy. 42 and turn south. Included are several historic buildings rescued from demolition and brought to the park to provide a link with the Ohio Valley of a century ago. There is a railroad station and a doctor's office in a Steamboat Gothic-style building. All furnished.

The houses include the Elk Lick House, a Carpenter Gothic; the John M. Hayner House, a grand Greek Revival building; and the brick Samuel Vorhes House, built in Federal style.

The barn complex houses a collection of nineteenth-century farm tools and machinery. Open May through October. Admission charged.

Harriet Beecher Stowe House

The Harriet Beecher Stowe House, which stands at 2950 Gilbert Ave., is on the National Register of Historic Places. This was the home of Harriet Beecher from 1832 to 1836 when she married Professor Calvin Ellis Stowe. While she lived here she gathered much of the material for *Uncle Tom's Cabin.*

The house is now owned by the Ohio Historical Society, and has been restored and renovated. It is open to the public on weekdays and by appointment on weekends.

A President's Home

The only person ever to serve both as President of the United States and Chief Justice of the U. S. Supreme Court was William Howard Taft of Cincinnati. Both his son and grandson followed

him to Washington to serve in the U. S. Senate, while another
son, Charles, became Cincinnati's long-time councilman and be-
loved elder statesman. Younger members of this noted Cincinnati
family are still in politics.

The dynasty began in 1838 when Alphonso Taft, a young Ver-
monter with a new degree in law, methodically surveyed a number of American cities seeking the best place to settle and go into
business. Cincinnati was his choice on every count. His son, the
future President, was born in the first-floor bedroom of a large
two-story home on one of Cincinnati's famous hills.

The Taft House, at 2038 Auburn Ave., is a National Historic
Site. Visitors may tour the home. This is the only property administered by the National Park Service in the Greater Cincinnati
area. Phone: (513) 684-3262.

Mammoth Country

In the summer of 1980 Cincinnatians driving to work along
Gilbert Avenue slowed down and occasionally blocked traffic.
Standing in front of the city's Museum of Natural History, on the
edge of Eden Park, was a whole family of woolly mammoths.
These extinct members of the elephant family once were native to
much of North America, including the Ohio Valley.

*The Cincinnati Museum of Natural History specializes in early
Ohio Valley people and the valley's natural features.* (Photo by
George Laycock)

A family of life-sized mammoths stands guard before the entrance of the Cincinnati Museum of Natural History. (Photo by George Laycock)

The ponderous herbivores were larger than modern African elephants. Their bodies were protected by three-inch layers of fat and blanketed by heavy wool, insulating them from the frigid Ice Age weather. They were neither very graceful nor nimble as they plodded age-old trails around the ancient Ohio Valley, and many fell into gravel pits or became mired in swamps where their bones remained intact for scientists of later days to unearth and reconstruct.

The idea for the mammoth display originated with Charles Oehler, and we went to talk with Oehler in his secluded laboratory in the depths of the museum. Oehler first came to the Museum of Natural History as a youthful part-time employee, when the museum occupied part of a downtown building and had only two other employees, including the director, Charles Dury.

The museum was a treasure house for Oehler. "I spent the first two years just looking in boxes," he said. Oehler, who had some training in art, began painting backgrounds for museum exhibits and eventually became one of the country's best-known creators of museum exhibits. His work is displayed today in almost every wing of the museum. One of his favorite exhibits is a complete limestone cave, the only exhibit of its kind in the world. Thousands of visitors climb through this multi-level cave every month to see the formations and the cave animals in their shadowy environment.

There is also a Wilderness Trail, leading visitors through the Ohio Valley seasons as they looked before the settlers came. The museum also has a planetarium with regular programs. There are collections of shells, fossils, birds, mammals, reptiles, and prehistoric artifacts.

Cincinnati has had a natural history museum for more than a century and a half, and among the early museum workers here was a bird artist, John James Audubon.

One day late in the 1970s, museum director DeVere Burt and Oehler went into a planning session. The museum had accepted a gift from a prominent Cincinnatian, and Burt wanted ideas on how best to spend the money. Oehler had a backlog of ideas, including one that had been incubating in his mind since he saw the unforgettable life-size models of dinosaurs at the Chicago World's Fair forty years earlier. He suggested that the Museum of Natural

The Serpentine Wall along Cincinnati's waterfront is a favorite place for music festivals, river watching, and holiday celebrations. (Photo by George Laycock)

History build a life-size model of the woolly mammoth and put it up outside the building permanently where everyone could see it. Burt added one suggestion Why not a family group of mammoths?

The mammoths were a year in the making. Oehler and his crew modeled mammoth parts in clay, made casts of them, then assembled and painted them. The largest of the models were made under Oehler's supervision by an outside firm. A towering crane finally lowered four mammoths into position on the lawn in front of the museum. The family of great, brown shaggy mammoths stands there surrounded by living arctic plants, species found in the Ohio Valley in the Ice Age.

The Cincinnati Museum of Natural History and Planetarium is located at 1720 Gilbert Ave. From I-71 downtown take Reading Rd. exit to Gilbert Ave. Admission charged. Closed Mondays. Phone: (513) 621-3889.

Mt. Adams and Eden Park

The hill most easily seen from downtown is Mt. Adams, and reaching the crest would seem simple enough. But visitors find few signs to guide them to Mt. Adams. Solving the puzzle is worth the effort because of the scenic view, the narrow streets with their quaint and colorful shops, and the cultural attractions in the adjoining Eden Park.

Legend tells us that the first human resident of Mt. Adams lived in a hollow sycamore tree. The size of the tree is not a matter of record, but the name of its occupant was Ida Martin, who dwelled there alone, presumably enjoying her splendid-view property. Ida Martin left her mark. In the vicinity you can still find Martin Drive and Ida Street.

On the slopes of Mt. Adams, Nicholas Longworth grew the first of his Ohio Valley grapes. Then, with the threat of civil war coming, Mt. Adams was fortified with cannon that pointed menacingly out upon the Ohio River, but were never fired. In the 1880s, the Rookwood Pottery, known as one of the five finest in the world, rose on Mt. Adams. The pottery building still stands and houses a popular restaurant.

The same ridgetop extends into Eden Park, the best-known park in and around Cincinnati. The city has 138 developed park areas ranging in size from Mt. Airy with 1,466 acres down to a vest-pocket park that covers .010 acre, providing just enough land to support a statue of an unknown Indian citizen. But Eden Park is the showplace.

The avenues twist through Eden Park past open grassy hillsides, groves of native trees, plantings of showy flowers, and a scenic Ohio River overlook. Within this park stand several of Cincinnati's most famous cultural attractions.

In addition to the city parks, Hamilton County has its own park district, and its parks are well known to local people who make excellent use of them for everything from horseback riding to flying model aircraft.

Krohn Conservatory—House of Plants

Jack Wilsey has the greenest thumb in town. For more than a quarter of a century he has watered, fertilized, nourished, and ad-

Spring brings acres of flowers to Cincinnati parks. (Photo by George Laycock)

The Conservatory in Eden Park is open, free, the year around.
(Photo by George Laycock)

This stone gateway at the entrance to Eden Park is among the landmark structures Cincinnati has preserved. (Photo by George Laycock)

mired the biggest collection of rare plants in the Ohio Valley. As superintendent of the Krohn Conservatory, he labors in a giant greenhouse covering more than a half acre of Eden Park. The main hall in this all-glass building has a ceiling 45 feet high.

The conservatory is open to the public, free, every day of the year, and in the course of the year half a million people visit this indoor garden. They show their children how bananas grow and that oranges really come from trees. They visit the cactus garden with its 300 varieties of succulents. "We have between 500 and 600 varieties of plants displayed at any time," says Wilsey. Included are hundreds of orchids.

The special Christmas and Easter exhibits attract the largest crowds, and people bring their cameras and photograph each other against backgrounds of hundreds of poinsettias or Easter lilies.

Wilsey is Cincinnati's resident plant doctor, and a fair portion of his workday is consumed in telephone consultations with distraught citizens asking what to do for a wilting plant or a geranium that refuses to bloom. Others go home from their jobs and water their plants. But Wilsey doesn't. "I don't have any house plants," he admits. "At home I get away from plants."

The Reds

If you meet an Ohio Valley native halfway around the world, the first question will be "How are the Reds doing?" People who may seldom get to Cincinnati still speak of the city's professional National League baseball team as "our Reds." The Reds have been in existence for more than a century.

Until 1869 all baseball teams were made up of amateurs. But that was the year that Harry Wright, a jeweler across the Ohio River in Newport, Kentucky, decided the powerful Cincinnati team could beat any other baseball team anywhere. To do so, they would have to travel, so Wright organized the Cincinnati Red Stockings, the first professional baseball team anywhere. Pay ranged from $600 to $1,400 a year.

In the next two years, the team proved to be as good as Wright

High-angle view of the Ohio River shows the Riverfront Stadium, Suspension Bridge, and the network of highways that bring visitors to the riverfront area. (Photo by George Laycock)

had predicted. Game after game went to the Red Stockings until they ran up a total of 130 consecutive victories before the Brooklyn Atlantics finally broke their magic spell. When the National League was organized in 1876, the Cincinnati team was a charter member.

Until 1935 all professional baseball games were played in daylight. That year, Cincinnati became the first team to play a home game under lights on May 24, 1935, after lights were installed at Crosley Field.

The 1970s were golden years for the Reds and their fans. In 1970 the team moved to the new Riverfront Stadium and into the decade of the "Big Red Machine," and a roster that included Rose, Bench, Morgan, Foster, Concepcion, and Perez. In one decade the "Big Red Machine" won 953 regular season games, 6 Western Division titles, 4 National League pennants, plus 2 world championships to become the most successful team in professional baseball. The Reds continue to bring fans to Riverfront Stadium from throughout the Ohio Valley.

The Bengals

Cincinnati's long-standing reputation as a sports city took a major leap forward in 1968 when Coach Paul Brown began building a new professional football team. The Cincinnati Bengals are members of the Central Division of the American Football Conference. Bengal games bring capacity crowds to Riverfront Stadium to see the team that by 1981 had become a Super Bowl contender.

The Zoo

For many Cincinnatians, and out-of-town visitors as well, the best show in town is out at the zoo at 3400 Vine St. The Cincinnati Zoo draws more than a million visitors a year.

This is the second-oldest zoo in the United States (Philadelphia was first) and is internationally known for its success in breeding rare and endangered animals. Cincinnati holds the world record for raising lowland gorillas in captivity. Says the zoo curator, Bob Lotshaw, "We're lucky enough to have gorillas that are very much in love." When we last talked with Lotshaw and zoo director, Ed Maruska, one pair of gorillas there had presented the zoo with a total of seven babies and another pair had produced four.

As the hour approaches for the birth of a new baby gorilla, special quarters are made ready. There is an around-the-clock watch mounted. Once the baby is born the mother is observed. If she takes good care of her new infant, she is permitted to keep and raise it. If she is not a good mother, the youngster is taken from her and reared by human volunteers who stay with it day and night, feeding and caring for it. In case of illness, the zoo veterinarian sometimes consults with specialists in human medicine at Cincinnati's medical research centers.

Visitors can see the new baby gorillas through a glass wall in the nursery. Or they can go outdoors and see adult gorillas in the new primate center where only a moat separates gorillas and people.

Nearby are the famed white tigers, and these cats have also brought attention to the zoo by successfully raising their rare kittens.

This is also the zoo where people stand in line to see bugs. Cincinnati has the only zoo in the United States with a special building for raising and displaying insects, and these smallest of its animals are among its most popular. Cages contain colonies of army ants, hives of bees, and giant 14-inch-long walking sticks that look like dead twigs. There is also a tropical room where visitors move among dozens of brilliantly colored free-flying butterflies.

The zoo has developed methods of raising the rare food plants needed by some of its insects. And, as with the gorillas and white tigers, the zoo has been successful in breeding and raising insects.

This lowland gorilla is one of the gorilla family that has brought the Cincinnati Zoo international acclaim. (Photo by George Laycock)

The Cincinnati Nature Center's trails are a sanctuary for people and wildlife alike. (Photo by George Laycock)

It may be the only institution in the world to win an award for raising insects. Its success in rearing the giant goliath beetles, which are baseball-sized insects from the jungles of Africa, was acclaimed by the International Association of Aquariums and Zoological Gardens.

There are sharks in the aquarium; hippopotami, elephants, and giraffes in the big animal house; and alligators, crocodiles, and turtles in the reptile house. There are cheetahs, lions, and bears. There is even a pair of American bald eagles, our national bird, that have a giant nest in a huge fenced area on a hillside. In all, 2,500 animals live in the zoo, the finest in the valley and one of the best anywhere.

The zoo is open every day but Christmas, and the admission charged supports its animals.

Kings Island

If you are in Cincinnati and want to ride an elephant, the genuine living breathing variety, drive out to Kings Island. The elephant, however, may provide the gentlest of all the rides in this giant theme park. If you really crave excitement, try the Beast, listed in the *Guinness Book of World Records* as the longest, fastest, and tallest roller coaster anywhere. The Beast climbs to the top of towering slopes, eases across the crest, and then swoops and clatters down into deep valleys and loops with speed that scares off the faint of heart.

As if the Beast were not frightening enough, Kings Island intro-

International Street at Kings Island is a favorite with thousands of visitors who flock to the theme park every summer. (Courtesy Kings Island)

duced the Bat in 1981, and this one is unlike any other ride in the world. The Bat (cost $3.8 million) is a suspended "coaster." Trains of steel cars dangle from overhead tracks and do all the scary things a roller coaster does, and more. As the Bat whips around corners its cars swing out to the side, sometimes at a 90-degree angle. At the same time the cars travel in spirals, climb to peaks, and hurtle into valleys.

Kings Island first opened its gates in 1972 and now welcomes more than two and a half million visitors a year from all parts of the Ohio Valley and beyond. Among the nation's theme parks, only Disneyland outranks Kings Island in size.

The park is divided into 6 areas. First there is International Street, a European-type boulevard lined with colorful shops and restaurants and made lively by music everywhere. There is the Eiffel Tower, high as a 33-story building with elevators that lift visitors to observation towers. The Royal Fountain on International Street is spectacular. It is big as a football field, and its jets shoot 10,000 gallons of water into the air to sparkle in the colored lights.

Oktoberfest is a section of the big park where there are more gentle rides plus a beer garden, German foods, and German-style music and dancing.

Kings Island also has the Wild Animal Safari, with 400 beasts including free-roaming (more or less) lions, giraffes, zebras, elephants, rhinos, deer, antelope, bison, tigers, and camels. Guests ride a monorail 2 miles through the animal park, snapping pictures as they go. It is here that arrangements can be made to ride an elephant.

Coney Island is the section depicting the old amusement park, on the banks of the Ohio east of Cincinnati, as it was at the turn of the century. There are restaurants, rides, thrills, and music.

Rivertown is Kings Island's effort to recapture riverboat days along the Ohio years ago. This is the home of the Beast, out of character in its Mike Fink surroundings. There are boats that shoot the rapids and trains that convey visitors, a thousand at a time, through a wooded area where cowboys and Indians pop out of the brush shooting and whooping at each other.

There is also a special section for the younger visitors who are entertained by Hanna-Barbera characters and their elaborate cos-

The Beast is a Kings Island thriller that drops 135 feet into an underground tunnel. (Courtesy Kings Island)

tumes, inside which young seasonal employees perspire in the summer heat. There are special rides for the small fry and shops offering good things to eat.

Live entertainment fills the Kings Island theater stages, and as you pass through the gates you are handed a schedule of these productions starring young performers from many states. Admission charge is high but includes all rides except Wild Animal Safari. Phone: (513) 241-5600. Open late May through Labor Day.

Kings Island is on the east side of I-71, 20 miles north of Cincinnati. Outside the Kings Island gates are motels and places to eat. Kings Island Inn is open the year around. Campers stay in the Kings Island Campground, 350 sites with electric and water hookups, general store, swimming pool, and bike rental agency.

National College Football Hall of Fame

Although Kings Island closes its gates for the winter, the adjacent National College Football Hall of Fame remains open. Once inside, visitors become caught up in the razzle-dazzle spirit of the place and stay an average three hours and forty-five minutes. They watch football film in 3 theaters. They also kick a field goal (get cheered if they make it and booed if they don't), play computerized football games, then pass through the mazelike Time Tunnel, which, in a distance equal to the length of two football fields, traces the history of the game all the way back to its origins in the glorious days of the Roman Empire.

The Hall of Fame idea was born in 1947 as Grantland Rice talked football with a group of other sportswriters. Three years later they began choosing college players whose names belonged in a Hall of Fame. But the hall itself did not materialize for another twenty-eight years.

Ohioans wanted the Hall of Fame, and when it was put up for bids by its New York sponsors, the Taft Broadcasting Corporation of Cincinnati, creators and owners of Kings Island, bid on it. Taft donated land for the Hall of Fame next to Kings Island. By its second year the new Hall of Fame was attracting more than 100,000 visitors a year.

The National College Football Hall of Fame charges admission, and is open every day but Christmas, from 9 A.M. to 6 P.M. in summer, 10 A.M. to 5 P.M. in winter.

Jack Nicklaus Sports Center

Across Interstate Highway 71 from Kings Island is the Jack Nicklaus Sports Center, known widely among tennis players and

The National College Football Hall of Fame is part of the Kings Island complex, 20 miles north of Cincinnati. (Courtesy National College Football Hall of Fame)

golfers. Each June 100,000 people come here to see the Ladies Professional Golf Association meet, and in August the Center hosts the Association of Tennis Professionals Championships.

Those who come here to play tennis and golf, however, are not all professionals. "The courses are open from March to Christmas," Dick Craig, general manager of the Sports Center, told us, "and we get people from all over. Many come from Michigan, especially in early spring when they're suffering from snowitis and want to get started on their golf game." There are two 18-hole courses here; the Grizzly Course and the Bruin Executive Course.

The tennis courts too are open on an hourly basis.

Last of the Steamboats

As you travel the Ohio Valley you see the hard-working towboats and their heavily loaded barges. But keep an eye open for the *Delta Queen,* the historic riverboat that keeps steamboating alive on the inland rivers. From Pittsburgh to New Orleans citizens come to the riverside to see her and listen to the notes of her calliope. When the boilers are fired up, the giant 18-foot-wide

Cincinnati is the home port for the giant river cruiser the Mississippi Queen. (Delta Queen Steamboat Co. Photo)

Best-known boat on the Ohio River is the famous Delta Queen *operating out of Cincinnati.* (Delta Queen Steamboat Co. Photo)

paddlewheel dips into the river faster and faster working up to her average speed of 7 miles an hour. Her passengers, there may be as many as 188 of them, line the decks watching America drift by on either side.

The *Delta Queen* has come a long way. After she was built in 1926, in a shipyard on the River Clyde in Glasgow, Scotland, her prefabricated parts were transported across the ocean to Stockton, California, for assembly. She is a floating museum with teakwood handrails on her outside decks, stained-glass windows, paneling of oak and mahogany, and fittings of brass; a river-going master-

The Delta Queen *at the Cincinnati waterfront. The famous Suspension Bridge is in the background.* (Photo by Ellen Laycock)

piece. Although she stays no place for long, the *Delta Queen* is listed on the National Register of Historic Places.

She was cruising California waters when World War II came, and the Navy pressed her into service transporting troops and casualties within San Francisco Bay. In 1946, now decommissioned, the *Delta Queen* went up for auction, and the successful bidder was Captain Tom Green, whose Cincinnati family had been leaders in the river steamboat business since shortly after the War of 1812. To move the *Delta Queen* to her new home port, she had to be towed 5,000 miles over open sea, down along the Pacific Coast, and through the Panama Canal. Then it was up the Gulf of Mexico to New Orleans, and from there upriver under her own steam to Pittsburgh where she was renovated. By the summer of 1948, the *Delta Queen,* all painted and outfitted, was ready for passenger cruises on the rivers.

She remains one of two steamboats still carrying overnight passengers on the inland rivers. The other is the *Mississippi Queen,* a much newer boat owned by the same Cincinnati company. One evening we saw them tied side by side at the riverfront in Cincinnati, preparing to take on passengers. They are rarely seen together on the Ohio River because the larger vessel is more often traveling the Mississippi.

The schedule for both steamboats varies each year, and trips aboard the *Delta Queen* range from 2 to 11 nights with a wide choice of places for boarding and debarking. Travel agents everywhere have the details because the *Delta Queen* draws her passengers from all over this country and from other countries as well.

Cincinnati Convention Center

Once a year, in the heart of winter, local entrepreneur Bob Hart transforms the Convention Center into a wonderland of all that is new for the coming vacation season. Over a 10-day period thousands of people troop through the turnstiles of the Bob Hart Sport, Vacation, and Travel Show to see the latest in boats, motors, fishing tackle, recreation vehicles, and tents. They stroll along the rows of booths to visit with representatives of the travel industry where they can make reservations for houseboat vacations or arrange family fishing trips to lakes in and beyond the Ohio Valley.

In May each year the Convention Center becomes a regional showcase for the Appalachian Folk Festival, with craftsmen who journey to Cincinnati to offer their handiwork or perform mountain songs and dances.

November brings the International Folk Festival to the Convention Center. In late winter this is the scene of the Home and Garden Show and the annual Custom Car Show.

There is also an annual Antique Show here, plus many more exhibitions and conventions, for the Convention Center has been a busy place since it was built as part of Cincinnati's plan to bring new life to the downtown area.

For those in Cincinnati at the right time there are special annual family events in the outdoors. Each year for two days on a May weekend Garfield Place, opposite the main library on Eighth

St. is blocked off for "A Taste of Cincinnati." Twenty-five of Cincinnati's top restaurants set up booths, decorate them, and offer their finest specialties in sample-sized portions for modest sums. Meanwhile, street vendors and sidewalk artists are at work. And all day long there is big-band dancing. Thousands of people come for the color and the food and the music.

Then for two days on a September weekend people come to Cincinnati, often from distant states, for Oktoberfest Zinzinnati when the downtown resembles, as much as possible, the Munich Oktoberfest. There are booths and tents, 60 of them, offering beer, bratwurst, and other goods of German flavor. Twelve German bands make oom-pah-pah music, while costumed groups present authentic dances on Fountain Square. This is a family affair that goes on from 10 A.M. to 11 P.M., and according to the city's Downtown Council, Oktoberfest Zinzinnati brings 400,000 people to the downtown area for the weekend.

Music and Theater

The Symphony Orchestra

There are frequent summer evenings when the Cincinnati Symphony Orchestra goes outdoors to play for thousands of people who gather to hear its free concerts in the park. People stream into Eden, Ault, or Stanbery parks, Sharon or Burnett woods, and Mt. Airy or Sweetwater forests, carrying their folding chairs, blankets, and picnic baskets, and leading dogs and children.

For the CSO these concerts in the park, sponsored for years by the First National Bank, offer one more opportunity to bring its music to Cincinnati and other communities throughout the Ohio Valley. Every year the orchestra's music is heard by 700,000 people in some 300 concerts ranging from a program of Beethoven in Cincinnati's famous old Music Hall to a pop concert in Batesville, Indiana. The Cincinnati Symphony Pops Orchestra, for more than a decade, has taken to the road for the summer season when 8 communities in Ohio and Indiana host their 2-day festivals in an atmosphere that draws large crowds.

The CSO became among the first symphony orchestra anywhere to present pop concerts, one of the earliest American symphony orchestras to broadcast on radio, and the first to circle the
world on tour.

The Cincinnati orchestra was organized in 1895, and only four
orchestras in the United States are older. CSO is the official orchestra for the May Festival and the Cincinnati Opera. It has also
made numerous records and broadcasts nationally over National
Public Service Radio.

Showboat *Majestic*

On summer evenings people go to the foot of Broadway on the
Cincinnati Public Landing to board the last of the true river
showboats still operating. Flags fly, lights sparkle, and the calliope plays "Showboat's a-Comin'."

The showboat *Majestic* is not some aging towboat rescued from
the grave and refashioned into a floating theater. Instead, she is
working today in exactly the role for which she was built more
than half a century ago by Captain Thomas Jefferson Reynolds.

He built the showboat and launched her in 1923, and he was

*Showboat productions are still staged during a regular season on
the showboat* Majestic *on the Cincinnati waterfront.* (Courtesy
showboat *Majestic*)

the captain, pilot, general manager, and director of drama. In the years that followed, the *Majestic* brought melodrama to almost every port from Pittsburgh to Cairo. Up and down the river, people watched for the showboat and listened for the notes of her calliope.

The *Majestic,* in more recent years, has been used by a succession of university drama departments. The city of Cincinnati purchased her in 1967 and leased her to the University of Cincinnati, whose Theater Department presents riverboat dramas on her stage through the summer season. Several University of Cincinnati's showboat alumni have gone on to Broadway and television stardom.

There have been changes that Captain Reynolds would probably approve. Instead of a fan blowing cool air off 220-pound blocks of ice into the theater during performances, there is now a modern air-conditioning system. There are also cushioned seats and carpeting. Even though she is secured to the shore today, Captain Reynolds' *Majestic* remains what she was built to be, a genuine river showboat bringing the magic of riverfront drama to all who come aboard.

Opera

In the summer of 1920 Opera came to Cincinnati in a strange setting. Seven operas were performed during an 8-week season in an outdoor pavilion at the Cincinnati Zoo. For many years Cincinnati Summer Opera at the zoo continued, sometimes to the accompaniment of lions roaring in the background.

After Cincinnati's beautiful Music Hall was renovated in 1972, the Opera moved there, and in 1975 changed its name to The Cincinnati Opera.

The Cincinnati Opera ranks among the most respected and successful opera companies in the United States. Phone: (513) 621-1919.

The May Festival

Singing was an excuse for social gathering in early Cincinnati. Ethnic groups, especially people of German heritage, assembled in the parks on Sunday after church when the weather was fair to sing and drink beer. Out of these early *sängerfests* grew the idea that all the singing groups in the city should come together for a giant music festival. The first of these festivals was held in May 1873, when 1,083 singers were accompanied by a 108-piece orchestra.

For many years the May Festival was conducted every second year, but in recent years it has become an annual affair, one of the major music events in the Ohio Valley.

Playhouse in the Park

Gerald Covell had an idea; the old Shelterhouse had stood for a hundred years on Mt. Adams at the edge of Eden Park, overlooking downtown Cincinnati. Covell was the leader of a little group of actors seeking a stage for dramatic productions, and the Shelterhouse, capacity 219, seemed an excellent choice.

The Playhouse in the Park became a popular Cincinnati attraction almost from the time it was first opened in 1959. Cincinnati outgrew the Shelterhouse Theater, and nine years after the old building was put to work, a new theater opened adjacent to it. This one, the Robert S. Marx Theater, seats 627 patrons. It has won acclaim from both dramatists and architects. Both theaters are now used. The Playhouse in the Park has become the professional theater for the heart of the Ohio Valley, and well-known actors from the Broadway stage come to star in productions here. Located at 962 Mt. Adams Dr. Phone: (513) 421-3888.

Canoeists' Favorite Stream

As far back as the 1950s Cincinnati newspapermen Dave Roberts and Glenn Thompson, both then with the Cincinnati *Enquirer*, talked of rescuing their favorite fishing and canoeing stream from the threats of pollution and construction. They agreed that the Little Miami River, emptying into the Ohio on the east side of Cincinnati, deserved to be saved for future generations.

The river was prominent in Thompson's thinking in 1965 when he traveled to Washington for Lady Bird Johnson's White House Conference on Natural Beauty. During that meeting Thompson first heard talk of a Congressional bill to bring Federal protection to the cleanest and most beautiful remaining streams in America.

The following autumn Thompson, while quail hunting in South Carolina with a group of friends, was eating breakfast and reading the morning paper. He learned from a news story that on that same afternoon the wild rivers legislation would go before the U. S. Senate.

Thompson immediately made a call to Senator Frank J. Lausche in Washington. Senator Lausche was convinced, and that day argued successfully that the original list of 28 streams to be studied under the new bill should include Ohio's Little Miami.

Others joined the fight to save the stream, and today the Little Miami, all 105 miles of it, is classified by the Federal Government as a recreational stream in the national system of protected rivers. No other stream on the official list runs through an area so heavily populated. The lower 5½ miles of the Little Miami lie within the Cincinnati corporation limits. A group of citizens, Little Miami, Inc., carries on the fight to keep the little river safe from threats.

The Little Miami has no wild, brawling white water, but it is highly popular with both canoeists and fishermen. Those who arrive without canoes can rent them at liveries at Milford and upstream at Ft. Ancient. Or there are launching areas where the canoeist can slip his own canoe into the Little Miami to float beneath giant sycamores that screen out the noise and the view of civilization.

In downtown Cincinnati there are two main locations where visitors can obtain current information. One is the Visitors' Information section of the Cincinnati Chamber of Commerce in the Fifth and Race Tower, 120 W. Fifth St. Phone: (513) 579-3100. The other is Greater Cincinnati Convention & Visitors' Bureau in the Convention Center, at 200 W. Fifth St. Phone: (513) 621-2142. Both have leaflets that answer many of the more frequently asked questions about Cincinnati features and attractions. Group tours can be arranged through Tourcrafters, Inc. Phone: (513) 721-8230.

Visitors can also follow self-guiding motor tours of the city. Leaflets describing this tour are available from the Chamber of Commerce or the Convention Bureau.

Presidents' Country

From this southwestern corner of Ohio came 10 percent of all the men ever to hold the office of President of the United States. All four were either born or resided within a few miles of the Ohio River, and three of them came from homes within sight of the river. Two of them came from the village of North Bend, downstream from Cincinnati, and only a few miles from the Ohio-Indiana border. William Henry Harrison, the ninth Presi-

In 1929, far above the Ohio River in Cincinnati, President Hoover dedicated the channelizing of the river. (Photo by George Laycock)

dent, established his home here, on a sweeping bend of the Ohio, after moving west from Virginia. His grandson, Benjamin, the twenty-third President, was born here. William Henry Harrison is buried in North Bend in the family tomb. Ohio erected an imposing monument 117 years after his burial to the first of its citizens to serve as President of the United States. The memorial is maintained, and kept open to the public, by the Ohio Historical Society.

The twenty-seventh President, William Howard Taft, was born in Cincinnati, in the same county (Hamilton) in which the Harrisons lived, and the eighteenth President, Ulysses S. Grant, was born on the banks of the Ohio, in the next county to the east.

Up the Road

Lebanon, Ohio

This small city, 25 miles north of Cincinnati by I-71 and Hwy. 48, is a gem for those who like to eat well and explore historic places. The most famous place in Lebanon is Ohio's oldest inn, The Golden Lamb, which started out as a tavern in 1815. It has undergone various remodelings and name changes over the years, and is today a favorite restaurant drawing its customers from a considerable distance. It is still an inn and you can stay in rooms used by earlier guests whose names are instantly familiar.

Among the famous who have stopped here were Presidents William Henry Harrison, Martin Van Buren, John Quincy Adams, Rutherford B. Hayes, James A. Garfield, William McKinley, William H. Taft, Warren G. Harding, U. S. Grant, and Benjamin Harrison, one fourth of all the Presidents to date. Other guests have included Charles Dickens, Mark Twain, James Whitcomb Riley, and Henry Clay, as well as the famous "Copperhead" Clement L. Vallandigham, who shot himself here. Vallandigham, while demonstrating that the man his client was accused of killing probably shot himself, picked up an "unloaded" revolver and killed himself by mistake.

Lebanon had its beginning in 1796 when Ichabod Corwin built a log cabin near Turtle Creek. Others followed him, and eventually the town flourished. One stimulus was the building of the canal system before the age of railroads.

Visitors stop at the Warren County Historical Society Museum on South Broadway. They also search out Glendower State Memorial, a classic example of Greek Revival architecture. Glendower is only one of the fine homes along Cincinnati Ave. It is furnished with impressive period furniture and is maintained as a museum by the Ohio Historical Society. Open May through October.

Indiana

Into Indiana

We left the freeway that encircles Cincinnati (I-275) at Lawrenceburg, Indiana, and from there drove beside the river all the
way to Madison, a distance of 60 miles or so, following highways
50 and 56, then Hwy. 156. The route is marked "scenic" on the
Indiana highway map, and scenic it is. This river drive takes on a
special beauty as spring turns the slopes to green, and again in
autumn when grain combines are on the move and warm, rich
colors spread over the wooded hills. This is a drive through
southern Indiana's fertile riverbottom lands, and the flood plains
are flanked by hills.

A sign on the edge of Lawrenceburg tells us this is the "Home
of the Tigers." But everyone around town knows it is also the
home of two giant distilleries that employ a large share of the
local labor force. The adjoining distilleries, one owned by Joseph
E. Seagram & Sons, Inc., the other by Schenley Distillers, Inc.,
were enticed here in the 1800s by the reservoir of limestone water
on which the area sits. The sweet water from the hidden aquifer
was credited with adding special quality to locally produced whiskey. The distillers have now, however, turned to well water which
they deionize and further treat. Visitors are welcome at both of
these plants.

At Seagram's the 2-hour tours include both the distillery and
bottling plants and can be arranged as you arrive. The best times
are 10 A.M. and 1:30 P.M. At the Schenley plant you will see
only a bottling operation because the whiskey is distilled in Ken-

tucky and brought to Lawrenceburg for bottling. Call in advance to schedule tours. Phone: (812) 537-0200.

Aurora, a few miles downriver, was once dominated by the steamboat industry, and the best place in town to capture the mood of those days along the inland waterways is at the top of Main Street. We drove up the hill out of the business district toward a magnificent old yellow mansion, which commands a view of the broad curves of the Ohio from its eminence on the hillside.

Here was the summer home of Thomas Gaff, who had his fingers in many pies—papermaking, distilling, building turnpikes, banking, farming, and mining. But his favorite enterprise was river commerce, and he owned all or a share of many important steamboats. There are features of Hillforest, the mansion he built in Aurora, that so reflect this love of riverboats that some call the house the best example of Steamboat Gothic along the Ohio.

The sign in the yard said the building was closed until April 1, but while we were making a picture Shirley Meyer, one of the local citizens organized to preserve the mansion and open it to the public, came to ask if we would like to see inside the house.

The interior design, the decorated walls and ceilings, the an-

On the hill overlooking the Ohio in Aurora, Indiana, stands Hillforest, once a famous home, now a museum. (Photo by George Laycock)

tique furniture, make this a valuable museum of Ohio River lore of the 1800s. We visited the wine cellar, wandered through the furnished living quarters, then climbed to the top level of the mansion by a narrow stairway. Here, from the windows of Gaff's pilothouse-like observatory, we looked out upon the Ohio as Gaff saw it in the age of steam. This was the room where women were forbidden, but from which Gaff, it is said, could eavesdrop on the ladies visiting in the room below.

Hillforest is among the most interesting old homes we found in the Ohio Valley. It is open from April 1 to January 1, and admission is charged. On the first two weekends in December Hillforest is open for the annual Victorian Christmas celebration.

Perhaps the best place to eat in Aurora is the Treehouse. It is two and a half miles west on Hwy. 50, an attractive restaurant built around a living tree.

The Sun Rises

Nobody knows how the next town downriver got its name. Perhaps, as one early writer said, one of the village founders, up and about at daybreak, witnessed the sun coming up over the Ohio. The view so inspired him that he named this corner of southern Indiana, Rising Sun. And so it remains. Rising Sun is the county seat of Ohio County, and here is found the oldest courthouse in continuous use in Indiana.

The Swiss Invasion

Switzerland County, the next county downriver, has no Alps, and yodeling is seldom heard from the surrounding hills, but it nurtures memories of the Swiss people who settled the county town, Vevay (pronounced "Veevee"). The founders were seventeen Swiss-French settlers who migrated from Vevay, Switzerland, on the north shore of Lake Geneva in 1802, and chose this place beside the Ohio River because it seemed promising for wine production. The wine industry eventually withered on the vine, and today Switzerland County produces corn, soybeans, tobacco, and livestock.

Old times, however, have not been forgotten. Vevay trades on its past. Renovated downtown shops preserve the Swiss look, while, once a year, usually on the second weekend in August, the annual Swiss Alpine Festival brings music and dancing to the streets. Singing groups and dancers, both local and professional, bring back the folk songs and dances of the Dufours and other early families who arrived here to "cultivate the vine."

This annual festival had its origin in the town's sesquicentennial celebration in 1963. Wine, which had been so important to Vevay in its early days, was prominent in the planning, and as the festival grew in size from year to year, wine assumed growing importance in the celebration. By the early 1970s Vevay could expect 100,000 people at its festival, and the combination of milling crowds and flowing wine brought rowdiness until, in 1974, town fathers brought the curtain down on Vevay's annual celebration of the vine.

In due time Vevay's festival was reborn, without wine, except what is sold in local lounges. During the Swiss Alpine Festival owners of several fine, old historic houses open their homes to the public for tours. One of the old buildings open all through the year is the LeClerc House, an inn built in 1850 by Robert LeClerc and his wife, Julia. This building, at the corner of Ferry and Main streets, is still operated as a restaurant and hotel and called The Swiss Inn. More than 300 structures in Vevay date back before 1883 and are included in the Vevay Historical District.

Jefferson County and Its Historic Town

Halfway between Cincinnati and Louisville lies the picturesque town of Madison, county seat of Jefferson County, Indiana.

Madison was founded in 1809 by John Paul, a veteran of George Rogers Clark's campaign to capture Vincennes. Paul, with Jonathan Lyon and Lewis Davis, laid out the town and named it Madison for James Madison, then President of the United States.

The location was good, and the town grew rapidly as settlers came from all parts of New England, the middle states, and the South, both overland and by flatboat. The arrival of river steamboats brought prosperity to many river towns, including Madison, which soon became Indiana's largest city.

After the state capital of Indiana was moved to the new town of Indianapolis, the state decided to build its first highway north from the Ohio River to the capital and on to Lake Michigan, and Madison's leaders had enough foresight and clout to have their town designated the southern terminus of the highway. In addition, when railroads began to dominate the Eastern Seaboard, progressive Madison saw to it that the first railroad west of the Alleghenies was built between here and North Vernon.

The first fire department in Indiana was Madison's own Fair Play Company No. 1, established in 1841. You can see Fair Play No. 1 today at the northeast corner of Main and Walnut streets. Built in the 1880s this building is a landmark in Madison. Look for "little Jimmy," the locally famous weathervane, on top of the firehouse bell tower.

Melanie Renschler, a knowledgeable employee of the Madison Chamber of Commerce, introduced us to "little Jimmy" and other attractions around town. The greatest of these is probably Clifty Falls State Park a short distance to the west. Visitors can stay there at Clifty Inn or in the adjoining motel wing, or camp in the large modern campground. For the more adventurous, there's a primitive campground.

Clifty Falls has a swimming pool plus tennis courts, 9 hiking trails, numerous picnic areas, nature center, gift shop, and a camp store. Visitors also use the archery range and playgrounds, go horseback riding, and ride the rental bicycles.

With Clifty Falls or one of the local motels as a base, you can take as much time as you want to explore Madison. The city boasts that nowhere else in the Midwest can comparable architecture be found. West Street marks the dividing point between the east and the west parts of town. We noticed that the houses on the east are generally older and of more simple design while those on the west are larger and more elaborate. Architectural styles range from Gothic, Georgian, and Regency to Classic Revival, Federal, and the Americanized Italian Villa so popular in the Victorian Era.

Madison was fortunate in 1837 when the fine architect Francis Costigan came here from Baltimore. Costigan had studied under Benjamin Henry Latrobe, then America's premier architect who was responsible for the establishment of Greek Revival in this country. The entire downtown area of Madison, some 133 blocks, has been listed on the National Register of Historic Places.

Park your car at the city lot at Main St. and Poplar Lane, and take a walking tour. Some historic houses are open to visitors for a small fee. Walk south on Poplar to the Jeremiah Sullivan House, 304 W. Second St. It was built in the Federal style in 1818 by Sullivan, who was a state legislator and Indiana Supreme Court Justice. Open May 1 to November 1.

Across the street at 301 W. Second St. is the Talbot-Hyatt House. The first owner, Richard C. Talbot, bought the land here in 1819 and built the house somewhat later, then died in the Mexican War. The house is being restored, and the Pioneer Garden, just to the west, is open to the public.

On the southeast corner of Second St. and Poplar Lane is the Schofield House, built about 1817. Federal in style. It was in this house in 1818 that the Grand Masonic Lodge of Indiana was organized, and The Masonic Heritage Foundation now owns the house and opens it daily to the public.

Farther south on Poplar Lane is the Shrewsbury House Museum at the corner of First St. and Poplar. This house, built by Francis Costigan, 1846–49, has outside doors 12 feet high, and the central hall contains a famous freestanding spiral staircase. Open to the public. This house is privately owned and used as an antique shop.

Turn west on First St. The Presbyterian Church, built in 1846, has a Christopher Wren-style bell tower.

The James F. D. Lanier State Memorial, 500 W. First St., is the best-known building in town. It is Indiana's finest antebellum mansion. Lanier was a prominent banker, financier, and statesman. Architect Francis Costigan designed and built the mansion

The Lanier Mansion overlooks the Ohio River in Madison, Indiana. (Photo by George Laycock)

for him, completing it in 1844. The fine wrought and cast iron was made in Madison foundries. The ironwork found in so many of the river towns was inspired by the architecture of New Orleans, but much of it, even that found in New Orleans, was manufactured in the Ohio Valley.

The Lanier Mansion is an excellent example of the Greek Revival style. One of the most interesting features of the interior is the three-story spiral staircase, "unsupported except by its own thrust." There are silver plates in the newel posts bearing Costigan's signature. The Lanier House is open all year.

Walk north on Elm St., cross Main St., and behind the Public

Library in a restored carriage house you will find the Jefferson County Historical Museum. Open summer months. Admission free.

At 323–27 W. Main St., notice the iron storefronts; examples of the Italianate style.

On the north side of W. Main there is an iron balcony, at number 306, with an unusual lyre pattern. It was made around 1850.

There is one other house open to the public, the Dr. W. D. Hutchings House at 120 W. Third St. The doctor's weatherbeaten "shingle" hangs outside, and the office and hospital stand just as he left them after practicing medicine here from 1882 to 1903. His black cape is thrown on the bed; his saddle bags over a chair. All furnishings, instruments, and medication are authentic pieces once owned by him. Open afternoons, May 1 to November 1.

Dr. Hutchings' office, the Sullivan House, and the Talbot-Hyatt House are owned by Historic Madison, Inc., a local group formed for the preservation and restoration of significant old buildings and historical monuments in Madison and Jefferson County.

But Madison does not spend all its time looking backward. The annual Madison Regatta is held during Fourth of July weekend and lasts for a week. A beauty pageant to choose Miss Madison Regatta is the first event, usually June 29 or 30. On the second evening comes the Firefighters Waterball Fight, involving "the five volunteer fire companies" in front of the courthouse. On other days there are hot-air-balloon races, music, a parade, the 10K Marathon Race, the Governor's Ball at the Moose Lodge, then the limited hydroplane and, finally, unlimited hydroplane races featuring the biggest and fastest racing boats in the country, in the Indiana Governor's Cup Race.

Jefferson County also looks forward to the Chautauqua of the Arts, a big show that comes the last weekend of September when three blocks of Vine Street are blocked off from Main Street to the river. Working artists and craftsmen give demonstrations and sell their artwork.

The Old Court Days' Festival is held twice a year, first on Memorial Day weekend in May and again in the fall during Chautauqua. There are booths and tables on Courthouse Square and along Jefferson Street where visitors gather to buy and trade craftwork, antiques, and collectibles.

Another event during Chautauqua, and only on the even years, is the Tour of Historic Homes. Admission is charged, with receipts going to a worthy cause, and eight to ten families open their private homes to visitors.

Dining Out

If all this exploring has made you hungry and thirsty, stop at the Broadway Hotel Tavern, 1313 Broadway. But hurry if it's Friday afternoon. A friend in Madison tells us the tavern is locally famous for ribs, a Friday special. "Why," he said, "you'll find people taking off work early on Fridays, because if you don't get there before five, you don't get ribs!"

Burgers of many kinds are the specialty of the 307 Saloon and Eating Establishment on West St. where we stopped one day for lunch.

If seafood is your choice, drive out to the Key West Shrimp House at 117 Ferry St. where the restaurant is located in an old button factory in the east end of town.

On the hill above Madison, at 1111 Clifty Dr., there is the Dark Horse Restaurant serving Chinese foods.

Then, too, there is the large dining room at Clifty Falls State Park with its view of the river.

Just west of Madison is the village of Hanover with Hanover College. The sweeping view from the campus features the Ohio River from an elevation of 500 feet. The college buildings were built in Georgian style. Visitors are welcomed.

Clark and Floyd:
The Sunny Side

Across from Louisville are three small cities clustered along the river—New Albany, Jeffersonville, and Clarksville—that live in the shadow of the big city on the Kentucky side. But local people like to call this community on the north bank of the Ohio "the sunny side" of Louisville.

This is steamboat country where the biggest of all inland boat-builders stretches along the riverbanks. Throughout the valley, where the steamboat rose to prominence, there is no place that can claim a closer bond with these powerful workboats and their modern diesel-driven descendants than Jeffersonville, Indiana.

The first steamboat built in Jeffersonville was the *United States,* and she slid down the ramp in 1819. Fifteen years passed, however, before Jeffersonville saw the arrival of the young man who would become the most successful of all builders of steamboats for the inland waters.

James Howard had apprenticed as a boatbuilder in Cincinnati and spent four years learning his trade. He was still a teenager when he moved downriver to Jeffersonville, at the head of the Falls of the Ohio. Howard's first boat was the *Hyperion,* built for a captain at Apalachicola, Florida, who for some unrecorded reason entrusted the costly job of creating his boat to a nineteen-year-old youth.

Other boats followed, and it was said that Howard-built packets became easily recognized by their graceful lines and the beauty of the workmanship that went into them. Boats built by Howard also gained a reputation for longer life and smoother running than other boats.

When the steamboat age was at its peak, 80 percent of the new boats sliding into the waters came from the Howard Shipyards. Among the famous boats built here were the *Glendy Burke,* in

The Howard Steamboat Museum, in Jeffersonville, Indiana, pre-
serves the colorful story of commerce on the inland rivers. (Courtesy Howard Steamboat Museum)

1851, on which Stephen Foster was inspired to write plantation
songs; the second *Robert E. Lee* in 1876; the *J. M. White,* which
when launched in 1878 was the most luxurious steamboat ever
built; the fastest steamboat ever built, the *City of Louisville,*
launched in 1894; and the *Cape Girardeau,* later renamed the
Gordon C. Greene, and then the *River Queen.* She was filmed in
Gone With the Wind.

James Howard met his death in the river which had shaped his
life. He was aboard a ferry with his horse and buggy, coming
back to the boatworks carrying a hoard of silver dollars with
which to meet his payroll. The whistle from a passing steamboat
caused his horse to rear and the buggy rolled off the ferry taking
horse, driver, and all into the water where Howard, weighted
down with silver dollars, sank swiftly to the bottom and drowned.
So respected was he by friends, clients, and employees, it is
recalled, that 50,000 mourners came to his funeral to pay their
respects.

His company was in the Howard family for 107 years until World War II, when it was purchased by the United States Government as a facility for building LSTs.

Today those who drive along the river in Jeffersonville find the boatworks still there. The American Commercial Barge Lines and Jeffboat, Inc., build barges for use on inland waterways throughout the country.

The heritage left by Howard is preserved in the Howard Steamboat Museum at 1101 E. Market St., Jeffersonville. This building was the home of Howard's son and successor, Edmunds J. Howard. It is a magnificent Victorian structure with 22 rooms. Fifteen different kinds of fine woods were used in finishing and paneling the rooms, and Howard imported a German woodcarver who worked for two years on the hand-carved decorations. Some of the rooms still have the original furniture.

Models of many of the famous Howard-built boats are displayed in the museum. There are also boatbuilders' tools once used in the shipyard, as well as rooms furnished to show what staterooms on the finest steamboats were like for the passengers in the 1800s.

The curator, guiding us through the museum, paused to ask mischievously, "Do you know why they always call ships 'she'? Because they're so hard to handle and expensive to maintain!"

The museum is owned and operated by a private foundation. A small admission charge.

Another famous home in the area is the Culbertson Mansion at 914 E. Main St. in New Albany. This one, owned by the state of Indiana, is open to the public the year around, with a small charge for admission.

William S. Culbertson, who came to southern Indiana from Pennsylvania in 1835 when he was twenty-one, found a job clerking in a dry goods store and eventually became one of the state's leading merchants. He made a fortune from shrewd investments. When he died at the age of seventy-eight in 1892, he was believed to be Indiana's wealthiest man.

The mansion he left behind in New Albany has 26 rooms and was built in the style of the French Second Empire. Woodwork and the three-story rosewood-and-mahogany staircase reflect the high degree of skill attained by the finest boatbuilders Culbertson employed to work on the interior. The mansion includes many elements of steamboat design. When the house was completed in 1869, it was said to be the grandest of all the large homes built on New Albany's Mansion Row. Other homes can be viewed from the outside as you walk along Main Street on brick-paved sidewalks.

The Floyd County Museum is in New Albany at Spring and Bank streets. The Greek Revival structure was originally the Carnegie Library. There are both permanent and changing exhibits for those interested in the history of southern Indiana.

The Culbertson Mansion at New Albany, Indiana, is open to the public the year around. (Photo by George Laycock)

A favorite place for outdoor activities in this region is Deam Lake State Recreation Area off Hwy. 60 near New Providence. The area is 15 miles or so north of the Ohio River.

This recreation area and the adjacent Clark State Forest have excellent camping facilities as well as hiking trails through cool, green forests, picnic areas, hunting in season, fishing, boat-launching ramp, and swimming. This is camp living where the traveler is surrounded by the beauties of natural scenery only minutes from the southern Indiana cities and the Greater Louisville area across the river.

Accommodations

The most posh and most unusual lodging facility here on the north side of the river is the Louisville/Clarksville Marriott Inn. This complex is reached by taking the Stansifer Avenue exit off I-65. Considerably more than a place to sleep, the Marriott is designed to be a destination—a complete family vacation center and often a honeymoon destination.

Swimmers use both the heated indoor pool and outdoor pool, but in the summer season there are other outdoor activities. Guests ride small boats on the 12-acre lake behind the hotel. And children catch bluegills there. The Cypress Gardens Water Skiers usually perform on the lake during Memorial Day weekend.

The Wave-Tek Ocean Pool is built to resemble an ocean beach where three-foot waves roll while vacationers ride them on special rafts. Energetic guests also find a Water Boggan Slide that is kept busy on hot days, a Water Trolley Jump, and the Rampage.

Across the street from the hotel is another part of the complex, the Kentuckiana Convention and Sports Center. This includes a complete health spa, tennis courts, game room, and small specialty shops. There's a flea market on Saturdays. The Marriott's phone number is (812) 283-4411. Camping families can share all the hotel privileges by checking in at the KOA Campground nearby.

There are many other good motels on "the sunny side" of Louisville, including a Hilton, two Holiday Inns, a Best Western, and the more moderately priced Days Inns, Thrifty Dutchman, Key Stop, Robert E. Lee, and Colonial.

Nothing could be more fitting in Jeffersonville than a festival called Steamboat Days. This event comes to the port of Jeffersonville in September. People congregate and start the festivities with a Steamboat Days dance. Then come parades, music, and drinking in the beer garden while the children frequent the midway. Within sight of the Ohio, along Riverside Drive, artists and craftsmen display their works. Meanwhile there are contests and races and numerous other activities including sternwheeler rides on the river.

Nearby, at Clarksville, there is, in July, a festival known as George Rogers Clark Days honoring the name of the famous soldier who settled this area and once lived on this side of the river. The typical festival events are staged during this week, but a touch of frontier history is tossed in as contestants take their places in tomahawk- and knife-throwing contests and black-powder shooting events.

Beginning the first Saturday in October the annual Harvest Home-coming Festival opens in New Albany. This is the second-largest festival in Indiana, and thousands of people turn out for the pumpkin shows, antique show, folk music, hymn singing, parade, and the midway attractions.

Factory Tours

There are at least two factories on this side of the river that open their gates for visitor tours. One is the Colgate-Palmolive

Fishing in the Ohio River has been improving in recent years.

Corporation in Clarksville. Atop the main building of the plant is the second-largest clock in the world, forty feet in diameter. Tours on Tuesday at 9 A.M. by appointment. Call Employee Relations. Phone: (812) 283-6611.

The other is Hillerich and Bradsby the world-famous manufacturers of baseball bats. The H&B offices are in Louisville, but the factory is in Jeffersonville, just east of I-65 at Hwy. 131. Here is the opportunity to see how big league bats are made, and to visit the company's baseball museum. Tours twice daily, Monday through Friday. Phone: (812) 288-6611.

Dining Out

For those who like a river view with dinner, there is Barbara's Rustic Frog Inn at 1720 Old River Rd., New Albany. Our conclusion was that the food was excellent and the servings larger than offered in most places. Good variety of seafoods.

Or there is Ray Parrella's Ristorante, 214 W. Court Ave., Jeffersonville, for Italian cuisine. Dinner only.

Rocky's Sub-Pub at 1207 Market St., Jeffersonville, is noted for its pizza.

There are two Tommy Lancaster Restaurants in New Albany, and they are especially popular with families. The larger more modern one is at 2813 Grant Line Rd. For old-world atmosphere try the one at 1629 Market St. They're known for a Sunday smorgasbord.

The Derby Dinner Playhouse offers a buffet dinner combined with theater in the round, featuring Broadway musicals or comedies with Equity actors. The playhouse is beside the Marriott Inn at 525 Marriott Dr. Phone: (812) 288-8281.

These, plus the excellent hotel restaurants.

On a midsummer afternoon we drove west on I-64 to the Paoli-Greenville exit and took Hwy. 150 to Navillton Rd., then followed the signs to the Huber Winery. The Huber family has been on this 450-acre rolling-hill farm for six generations. The farm is operated now by brothers Gerald and Carl and their families. Wine making here is a long-time tradition, but for decades the wine was made for home use only. The Hubers decided in the early 1970s to make wine commercially, and the business became a reality in 1978. There is a pleasant tasting room where wines and food are sold.

Even before the Hubers were growing grapes for their wines, they grew fruits and vegetables in wide variety and invited customers to come in and harvest their own. We saw families arriving from all over the Louisville area to go into the fields and pick their own produce. Peppers, squash, green beans, peas, apples, peaches, and especially strawberries are carried back to the big barn where they are weighed and paid for at bargain prices. All summer long there is some crop ripening out at Hubers, and trips there have become a tradition.

Saturday night is a good time at Hubers, not to pick fruit and vegetables, but to eat, drink, and listen to the country-music band on the top floor of the big barn.

The most select group of river captains on the Ohio are those who operate their own sternwheelers. For them, river life will always be exciting and challenging. We had met a few of these confirmed river people along the valley, and in Jeffersonville we added Captain Lloyd Poore to the list.

Boat sales, river construction work, and operating marinas were all jobs that kept Lloyd Poore on the river. Then in 1978 Lloyd and Bonnie Poore learned that the sternwheeler *Border Star*, an excursion boat in Chattanooga, Tennessee, was for sale. The Poores bought her and ran her upriver to Jeffersonville, her new home port. Captain Poore changed her name to the *Bonnie Belle* in honor of his wife, Bonnie, and his mother, Belle, and today the *Bonnie Belle* is the pride of Jeffersonville. She has a 160-person capacity and offers regular cruises including dinner cruises. Reservations are needed for dinner cruises. Captain Poore's phone number is (812) 282-9500.

Harrison County:
And an Early Capitol

Highway I-64 sweeps across the Ohio River from Louisville, through New Albany, Indiana, and on to Harrison County, a journey of some 25 miles. That is time enough to transport travelers into the quiet rural countryside—near the center of Harrison County, a mile or so from historic Corydon, the county seat. Traveling on westward from here you have your choice of roads. Interstate 64 is a fine modern highway, a fast and relatively scenic route across southern Indiana toward St. Louis. If you are in a hurry, this is the road to take. But our sympathies go with those who must pass through southern Indiana at top speed. If time permits, we suggest that you leave the Interstate highway at Corydon and follow instead Hwy. 62 westward because it is a scenic route through deep forests and past historic caves.

Take time first to explore Corydon and the surrounding countryside. Right in the heart of Corydon is the square stone building that once served as Indiana's first state Capitol. Here, on the first floor, the House of Representatives met, while the State Senate and Supreme Court held sessions upstairs.

In 1816 Indiana's founding fathers wrote the state's first constitution nearby in the shade of a giant elm tree whose limbs spread across 132 feet. The famous Constitution Elm lived until 1925, then its trunk was encased in a sandstone memorial. It stands on High Street.

In the heart of Corydon there are several structures of historic interest. One of these is the Governor Hendricks Home, built in 1817, where William Hendricks, first elected governor of the state, lived. His home is now open to visitors and maintained by the Indiana Department of Natural Resources.

Near the corner of High and Mulberry streets stands the first state office building, erected in 1817, complete with a cellar that once served as the vault for the State Treasury. The building is now a private home.

Cedar Glade, a private residence, was built between 1808 and 1810 by Jacob Kintner, Sr. Thomas McGrain acquired it in 1849, and it is still in the family.

In 1817 Colonel Thomas Posey built a massive brick house in a U-shape and lived here much of his life. What remains of the Posey House (one side of the U) is now a museum. It is located on Oak Street a block behind the county jail.

Guides provided by the state lead regular tours of the Governor's House and the Old State Capitol. There is a modest charge. The points of interest are grouped closely enough around the center of town to be seen in a short walking tour.

Few towns anywhere have more historic plaques per mile than does Corydon. Perhaps the plaque that stirs the imagination most tells of Corydon's capture by Confederate troops during the Civil War.

Up and down the Ohio Valley we have crossed the trail of General John Hunt Morgan, but we were always backtracking the general. He traveled upstream while our journey has led us

The historic town of Corydon, Indiana, the state's first capital, is a major tourist attraction. The first state legislature met in the Old Courthouse shown here. (Photo by George Laycock)

downriver. We had seen where he attempted to recross the river at Buffington Island and escape to the south, only to give up the attempt and later be captured near Lisbon. At Corydon we were near the place where he first crossed the Ohio from Kentucky.

General Morgan, commanding 2,500 cavalrymen in two brigades, started his historic journey at Sparta, Tennessee, in June 1863, and swept northward across Kentucky toward the Ohio. His forces captured two steamers and these were used to ferry his troops over the river to a landing near Mauckport, about 12 miles south of Corydon.

In a quiet secluded roadside park a mile south of Corydon we traced the series of events following Morgan's crossing of the Ohio. This memorial park is where Morgan's troops met a force of 400 home guards.

The battle lasted for half an hour. During that time the defending home guards suffered forty casualties including eight dead. The names of the dead on both sides are listed on a stone monument in the little park. The Battle of Corydon is an officially recognized Civil War battle; it was here that Morgan met the first organized resistance as he rode east through the Ohio Valley. He surrounded and captured Corydon and its greatly outnumbered home guards on July 9, 1863.

On the edge of Corydon we also discovered the most distinctive art glass factory we found anywhere. The factory occupies a green corrugated metal building measuring 24 × 48 feet. A sign supplied by Coca-Cola and erected outside the shop says that visitors are welcome.

Here partners Joe Zimmerman and Gene Baxley come every day to work at what they insist is not work at all, but pure pleasure. "I haven't really worked a day since I came here," says the jovial Baxley.

When Baxley came to Harrison County to escape the pressure of city life in Louisville, he met Joe Zimmerman and they began bass fishing together in the nearby creeks. As they fished, they talked. Zimmerman, who had learned the art of glassmaking from his father, was then working in a glass plant that has since vanished. He was considering starting his own business and needed a partner. In 1963 the two friends heated up their first batch of glass. They have been working at it ever since while re-

Corydon claims perhaps the smallest commercial glass factory in the Ohio Valley, shown here with its entire staff. (Photo by George Laycock)

sisting all temptation to grow big. "If I hired other people," says Zimmerman, "the work they'd have to do is what I want to do. So I don't hire other people."

Conversation in the Zimmerman Art Glass Company goes on while production continues at a steady but leisurely pace. Zimmerman picks up a long steel rod and crosses the shop to the furnace. He works the rod around inside the glowing furnace until he removes it with a red daub of fluid glass clinging to it like taffy. Sitting at his work bench, he rolls the rod while shaping the glass in a hand-held tool until it takes the form he wants, then cuts it off to cool.

Meanwhile, Baxley is working at a table inlaying decorative materials in layers of glass to form the sparkling old-fashioned paperweights which are a popular item in their line of glass products. They vary their work with other products, but never use molds. "Our success is measured in the pleasure we get from our work," explains Baxley.

As they finish the sparkling new glassware, they place it among others on a rough wooden shelf, which serves as the sales center for their factory. They don't take time to put prices on the pieces. A person wanting to know the price asks. Enough ask, and enough buy to keep the products moving and the Zimmerman Art Glass Company busy.

Baxley continues talking. "Visitors are welcome here," he says, "because we figure that if we are fortunate enough to earn our living doing what we like, we owe something." Visitors come from up and down the valley, as well as from distant parts of the world. Baxley recalls the lady who came from the Australian Outback to order a lamp which they made and shipped to her in Australia. Shipping charges were higher than the cost of the lamp. In spring, schoolchildren arrive by the busload. They gather around the furnace, in which there is a glowing 1,800° F. fire, and around the two working men, asking the questions which are patiently answered.

Sometimes things go wrong in spite of all that Zimmerman and Baxley can do. "One man came in here," says Baxley, "to order 1,000 paperweights for a convention his company was having. We didn't want to make a thousand of the things all at once. It gets too boring, so I figured I'd price them out of reach. But that man went right ahead and ordered the thousand; there wasn't anything we could do but make 'em for him."

Squire Boone Was Here (and Maybe Still Is)

On a pleasant summer evening we drove out of Corydon headed south on Hwy. 135 and, after 10 miles or so, came to a narrow side road leading off toward a famous cave and its owner. We were searching for Rick Conway.

Conway, still in his twenties, has a reputation as a hard worker and an imaginative businessman. "My father, Fred Conway, bought this place in 1970 sight unseen," Conway told us. "He was looking for land as an investment property, and because he had always been interested in caves, he especially wanted a property that might have a cavern under it."

The senior Conway especially liked the legends and history of this place on Buck Creek. Squire Boone was Daniel Boone's younger brother and, like Daniel, he was born in Pennsylvania. Although he never gained the fame of his elder brother, Squire was also a noted pioneer in Kentucky and southern Indiana. He was a frontier scout, Indian fighter, explorer, and mill owner as well as the minister who performed the first marriage ceremony in the Kentucky territory. Squire's son, Enoch, was the first white male child born in Kentucky. After being victimized in land frauds, Squire Boone with his family crossed over the river to Harrison County, Indiana, and found his way to Buck Creek. Here, he discovered a magnificent spring of cold water gushing from the earth. For the pioneer, the selection of a homesite often depended on where he could find a suitable spring.

He also found there on the slope above Buck Creek a cave with a vine-covered entrance. Later, when he was hunting several miles away, a band of Indians saw him and gave chase. Squire Boone sped through the forest, headed straight for Buck Creek. There he slid down through the vines into the cave and, although the Indians milled about overhead, they could not discover where the white hunter had gone. Eventually they departed, and Squire Boone emerged from his hiding place convinced that the Almighty had guided him to this refuge.

Here, near the big spring, Squire and his four strong sons built not only a new home, but also a fine mill with an 18-foot-high wheel that was powered by the water flowing from the cave. The Boone mill was a success from the beginning.

Squire Boone never forgot the cave that had delivered him from death at the hands of the Indians, and as he grew old he asked his sons to bury him, when the time came, in a walnut coffin deep inside the cave. This was done. In later years the story of Squire Boone's burial became widely known, and in more recent times souvenir hunters were believed to have invaded the underground sanctuary and carried away bits of the casket and perhaps Squire's bones, until nothing remained.

Then, on an August afternoon in 1974, Rick Conway and his brother, Allen, were exploring in the cave when they found a skull and 23 other bones. The Conways had authorities match injuries on the bones with injuries Squire was known to have suffered in frontier battles. As a result, these bones are believed to be the remains of Squire Boone, rediscovered after 159 years. The Conways fashioned a new walnut coffin and, as Squire had requested, once more returned his remains to the cave he had discovered.

Rick's father opened Squire Boone Caverns to the public for the first time in 1973, offering tours through parts of the cave that did not include the coffin. Business, however, did not grow as fast as it might, and Conway was about to give up the venture when Rick said that he wanted to take over the business.

Restored 1809 mill grinds grain for Squire Boone Cavern visitors. (Photo by George Laycock)

At that time Rick was, at the age of twenty, a year short of completing his undergraduate studies. He dropped out of college, and he and his wife moved to Buck Creek and went to work. Primarily, Rick was selling the beauties and mysteries of the cave. "This is a living cave," he told us. "The formations are still growing because there is water in the cave." There is so much water that few caves anywhere can match it for its rushing underground streams that tumble over rock formations into roaring waterfalls. Water from these hidden streams comes from a source unknown, then leaves the cave to form the giant spring that once drove the wheel of Squire Boone's mill. A trail one third of a mile long inside the caverns leads visitors past sparkling formations unlike anything they have seen before. There is life in this cave—blind crayfish, amphipods, isopods, cave crickets, and a few bats.

After moving to Buck Creek, Rick Conway never counted the hours he worked. One of his first ideas, and among the most successful, was to build a community of log houses near the entrance to the cave. He and his friends moved an ancient log house, log by log, to the site and reassembled it. Then Rick found and moved another, and another, until he now has 10 log structures dating far back into the 1800s.

One of these is a mill, rebuilt on the original foundation used by Squire Boone, and powered by water carried from the cave through a flume to move the stones and grind meal that modern tourists come to buy.

Other log buildings house craft shops operated by Rick Conway. There is an art gallery, leather shop, candy shop, rock shop, craft cabin, and restaurant. Conway's staff numbers 25 people, including the guides who lead 50,000 people a year through the famous caverns. Conway feels a responsibility to protect these underground treasures that have been forming for millions of years. "Our guides are given a very intensive course," says Conway, "because protection of the caves and the formations is especially important."

Opposite: *"Rock of Ages" is only one of the spectacular formations in Squire Boone Caverns.* (Courtesy Squire Boone Caverns)

Conway also maintains a campground nearby for those who want to stay.

Visitors arrive from every state during the year, and from foreign countries as well. Conway has his project moving. "I'm going back to school," he told us. "I can do that now."

Squire Boone's favorite cave has fallen into good hands.

Canoeing

This is also canoeing country, and the favorite stream for paddlers is the Blue River, Indiana's first wild and scenic river. The Blue winds down through the hills and hollows toward the Ohio, which it joins east of Leavenworth, and everywhere along its course the canoeist is shut away from the outside world by walls of towering green trees. Anglers find that the Blue is also an excellent fishing stream.

There are two canoe liveries on the Blue River next to the old mill dam in Milltown. They rent the essential canoes, paddles, and life jackets, and sell other supplies as well. On summer weekends they often have all their canoes booked in advance.

The canoe trips on the Blue River can be selected to match the time and energy available to the paddler. One of these runs is a trip of 7 miles, good for 2 to 4 hours depending on water conditions. Another trip covers 58 miles from Fredricksburg all the way to the Ohio River and can take up to 3 days. There are also trips of 14 miles and 20 miles available.

Harrison-Crawford State Forest

Along the Blue and Ohio rivers, where forests shade the hills and herds of deer roam, Indiana has established a 20,000-acre state forest with a complete recreation area. There is a Class-A campground with 281 sites, a network of trails, swimming pool, and picnic grounds. There are also a launching ramp and a floating dock for boaters. A good place for campers to stay while touring caves, historic sites, and backcountry roads.

Crawford County: Cave Country

Leavenworth, Indiana, is perched on a hilltop offering a spectacular view of the Ohio River far below. And the best place to enjoy it is from Leavenworth's favorite restaurant.

Until 1937 this town was down by the riverside, but that year the infamous "great flood" inundated Leavenworth, and local people, appalled by the destruction, took to the hills where floods could never touch them again. A little cafe was opened here in conjunction with a grocery store, and in due time the cafe expanded and became known as the Overlook Restaurant.

Buses stopped. Tourists found the place. The word spread. The Overlook, which has been enlarged and updated over the years, still features the same view—one of the finest found anywhere in the valley. The view changes with the seasons, but diners can always see 20 miles or so of the broad Ohio sweeping around a huge horseshoe bend and beyond that in the distance the peaceful farms and forests of Kentucky.

Southern Indiana is cave country, and two of Indiana's famous caves lie in Crawford County. Marengo Cave at Marengo, privately owned, has been open to the public since 1883, and hundreds of thousands of people have filed through its vast underground corridors on the Crystal Palace tour. The Dripstone Trail has recently been opened. Both are easily negotiated underground trips. The cave is open the year around, and in addition there is a park with campground, swimming pool, picnic areas, and nature trails. Phone: (812) 365-2705.

The other cave for which this county is noted is the famous Wyandotte Cave, the largest, and perhaps the most widely known, of southern Indiana's caves open to the public. The cave was known as Saltpeter Cave when saltpeter was mined here for the manufacture of gun powder in the War of 1812. The Rothrock

This river view is seen from bluffs on the north side of the Ohio near Leavenworth, Indiana. (Photo by George Laycock)

family bought the cave, and later it was opened to the public. The Rothrocks sold it to the state of Indiana in 1966 and the state established its own system of tours. The Indiana Department of Natural Resources operates Wyandotte Cave.

One room in Wyandotte Cave is 200 feet high and a quarter of a mile in circumference. Within this room is "Monument Mountain," billed as "the world's highest underground mountain." Its height is 140 feet. Rare and beautiful formations are seen along the underground trails.

On the surface, the green hills surrounding the cave lie within the Harrison-Crawford State Forest, a section of wild and wooded hill country where hiking trails take people through the homes of whitetail deer and wild turkeys. One section of this forest is set aside as the Wyandotte State Recreation Area with a large Class-A campground, open April through November. There is a primitive campground for canoeists beside the scenic Blue River, and this campground is open the year around. The recreation area has an Olympic-size swimming pool, picnic areas, and shelter houses as well as a horse camp.

A more water-oriented vacation land has opened up in recent years near Birdseye and northwest of English. Patoka Lake reaches into the hills and hollows of three counties, including the northern part of Crawford County, and encompasses 26,000 acres. The 8,880-acre flood-control reservoir is surrounded by 4 large state recreation areas operated by the Indiana Department of Natural Resources. One of these recreation areas is Lick Fork on the west side of Patoka Lake. Another is the Newton-Stewart area lying to the south of the lake and covering more than 4,500 acres. Tillery Hill off Hwy. 145 has nearly 1,800 acres, and the Jackson site on the north has nearly 1,300 acres.

Within these recreation areas, there are campgrounds, beaches, boathouses, picnic grounds, marinas, visitors' centers, and trails for hiking and bicycling. There are large boat-launching ramps for those who bring their own watercraft. These areas are large enough for people and wildlife too, and wildlife management methods are actively practiced. Hunting is legal during the regular hunting seasons.

Fishermen exploring the hidden coves of this major new lake in southern Indiana may catch largemouth bass, smallmouth bass, crappie, channel catfish, rockbass, northern pike, walleyes, and white bass, all of them stocked heavily by the state. For information call the Indiana Department of Natural Resources, (812) 685-2211, or write Rt. 1, Birdseye, IN 47513.

Up the Road

Spring Mill: Pioneers and Astronauts

Thirty-two miles north on Hwy. 37 out of Crawford's county seat, English, and east on Hwy. 60, is a gem in Indiana's famous state park system. More than half a million visitors a year flock to this park. Some of them come because Spring Mill Pioneer Village contains the finest collection of log buildings in Indiana. Others come to see the memorial to an outstanding pioneer astronaut who grew up nearby. Still more come because Spring Mill State Park contains outdoor attractions, including campground and hiking trails plus Donaldson Cave and a virgin forest of native Indiana hardwoods, standing as it did before the settlers came.

A major attraction is the old Spring Mill, a three-story stone structure built in 1817 and powered by a giant overshot wooden wheel measuring 24 feet in diameter. The water to power the mill flows from a cave through a flume resting on stone piers, and the mill, from which flour was once shipped down the Ohio River to New Orleans, still grinds grain into flour for sale to visitors.

Nearby is a rare water-powered sawmill that employed two water-driven wheels. One wheel slowly moved the log into the saw blade. The other wheel moved the vertical saw up and down, cutting the log into boards. In addition, the restored village includes homes, a general store, distillery, tavern, post office, and several shops. The log cabins show various kinds of construction employed by the early settlers.

As a boy, Virgil I. "Gus" Grissom, who was born in nearby Mitchell, frequently rode his bicycle out to Spring Mill. Grissom, the second man in space, died with two other astronauts in January 1967, when the space rocket he was to pilot to the moon burned on the launching pad at Cape Kennedy. The Indiana Legislature created in his memory, the Virgil I. Grissom State Memorial at Spring Mill State Park. Those who travel here may visit the memorial and study the space travel equipment, including the model of Titan III, also called *The Molly Brown,* in which Grissom and John Young made three successful orbits of the earth on March 23, 1965.

Perry County:
For Outdoor People

Across the scenic forested hills and quiet settlements of Perry County there lies a deceptive impression that there is little to do here. But take a closer look. This is quality country for the outdoor person interested in anything from wild turkey hunting to taking a Sunday afternoon drive through unforgettable hills.

The county seat is Cannelton, but the biggest town is Tell City. We came here on a fine afternoon in August to find Main Street blocked off and an entire block in front of City Hall filled with rows of tables and chairs. On the town square people were busy preparing for the evening's festivities, and out of curiosity we stopped to talk with a merchant, Renus Hess, across from the square. "This has been going on since Wednesday," he told us, "and will continue through the weekend. It's our annual Schweizer Fest, and frankly, what we do is drink beer. There are a lot of German communities around here, and this is a popular affair." During the Schweizer Fest, people come in from the surrounding hills and the hills beyond that. Old schoolmates choose this time for class reunions. We are willing to assume that all those tables would be filled. Having no Tell City classmates, we decided to slip out of town early and avoid the traffic.

But before leaving Tell City, we stopped at the District Office of the U. S. Forest Service to talk with Ted Senior about the attractions of the big Hoosier National Forest whose holdings spread out over the Indiana hills for miles. Senior is a youthful and enthusiastic professional forester who took a special interest in telling us about the woodlands he helps manage. "There are excellent hiking trails through the forest," he explains, "including trails that are used by backpackers who camp in the forest." He spread out a map of the hiking trails on which broken lines trace loops that intersect and connect in a pattern of trails that enable hikers to backpack for several days or walk only a short distance, depending on time and energy. "The Mogan Ridge Trail," said Senior, "is twenty-one miles long and at one point comes within half a mile of the Ohio River. There are scenic overlooks from the trail, and hikers are free to camp wherever they like in the forest, except that certain places near water reservoirs are non-camping areas."

The Mogan Ridge Trail leads into Indiana's special wild turkey management area. Here in the deep forests, the state began to re-establish the giant bird in 1963 by trading native ruffed grouse to Missouri for wild turkey breeding stock. Since then the turkeys of Indiana have prospered. Hikers who walk quietly may see the elusive and sharp-eyed turkeys as well as whitetail deer, squirrels, grouse, and other animals. Those who go exploring the back roads by car also see wildlife frequently, especially in the early morning or late evening.

The Two Lakes Loop Trail, which extends through the woods for 12.2 miles and goes around both Indian Lake and Lake Celina, is popular with hikers. This can be either a one- or two-day hike. The trail head is at the parking lot at Lake Celina, but the map available from the Forest Service office shows other access points on various forest roads.

The Forest Service is always concerned about the fire hazard, and everyone who uses the public woodlands should heed the Smokey Bear suggestions for dealing with fire. One-burner gasoline stoves are better than open cook fires. If you do build a fire, choose a place away from brush, dead grass, and overhanging limbs. Then clear the spot to the non-burnable mineral, build a small fire circle with rocks, keep the fire small, have water close by to control the fire, never leave the fire unattended, and before departing, soak the ashes and stir ashes and soil until you are certain all embers are cold and dead. Return the stones to where you found them.

Senior considers a hike in the Hoosier forest a challenging family adventure, and we agree. Those who go should remember a few important guidelines. Set a steady pace that is comfortable for the slowest hiker of the group. Take it easy and make frequent stops, especially early in the hike, for brief rests. Carry a map and stay on the trails. Drink only water you carried with you. Tell someone where you are going and when you expect to come out of the woods.

These national forest lands of southern Indiana include beautiful ridgetop drives that take on a special brilliance when autumn brings its colors to the hills. The German Ridge Auto Tour is a favorite one covering 11 miles of country roads and beginning at the German Ridge Recreation Area off Hwy. 66 east of Tell City. The Tell City Ranger District offers a free map of the drive.

Fortunate visitors to the Hoosier National Forest may encounter a wild turkey because the giant native birds have returned to these woodlands. (Photo by George Laycock)

U. S. Forest Service District Headquarters in Tell City is at the corner of Fifteenth and Washington streets. Phone: (812) 547-7051.

The Ohio River is a major attraction for anglers. Bass fishing is especially good around mouths of the creeks where the new high-level dam has backed the water up deeper than it was formerly. Best known of these creeks, in Perry County, is at Rocky Point, where Deer Creek empties into the river. This is one of the few places anywhere along the Ohio that canoes are rented specifically for use on the big river. Gary Dauby had the idea.

Dauby, who is in business with his father, Gervase, keeps a fleet of canoes at Rocky Point on Hwy. 66 two miles upriver from the Cannelton Locks and Dams. Those renting his canoes are hauled upstream by marina vehicles to the launching site. They take as much time as they like (some camp overnight on a sandbar) to paddle back to Rocky Point. Along the way they may explore the mouths of the creeks and cast for bass and the other fish for which the Ohio is becoming noted. Bass, crappie, bluegills, and channel catfish. There is a campground at Rocky Point. Ohio River boaters will find Rocky Point at Mile 719. Phone: (812) 547-7416.

A favorite scenic overlook along this section of the Ohio is Buzzards Roost, north of Magnet. Follow the signs from Hwy. 66 at Dexter.

The annual Dogwood Festival, the third weekend in April, also brings visitors to Perry County. Cannelton, Rome, Tell City, and Troy all participate and feature flea markets, antiques, sawmill demonstrations, and other events. Tell City and Troy have Dogwood Drives.

Spencer County: Santa Claus and Abe Lincoln

In all the Ohio Valley no other settlement has become as famous and prosperous for its name alone as a little town in the heart of Spencer County. According to legend, the idea was born in December 1852.

The settlement was a community of farmers and a few craftsmen. There were mud roads, and in town there was a store and a church. Occasionally, there was a town meeting with discussions about a fitting name for the village if it should be granted a post office of its own. On that Christmas Eve in 1852 there was a special program for the children, and as the church service ended, sleigh bells could be heard in the distance. Someone—the name was never recorded—said, "We should call this town Santa Claus."

The suggestion so pleased the assembled citizens that a meeting was called into session and the motion was made, seconded, and passed on the spot. Unanimously. Four years later, when the town was granted its post office, the name became official. There really is a Santa Claus in Indiana.

People from far away began sending their Christmas mail to Santa Claus to be postmarked. The mud roads were sometimes impassable in this season, and the post office became so overburdened with the thousands of letters that Santa Claus in desperation changed its name to Santa Fe.

This, however, did not last for long because residents of Santa Fe could not easily forget the name that gave the town a year-around holiday atmosphere. So, they changed it back to Santa Claus, and this time the name persisted.

The major business here is Santa Claus Land, a sparkling, clean, little well-run theme park older than Disneyland. The park had its beginning when Louis J. Koch, Sr., came out to Spencer

County, seeking a place where he and his family could escape to the country. Koch was an industrialist from Evansville. He found his place in the country and began installing exhibits and rides that he thought would amuse his nine children. The neighbors' children were welcome too, and the project grew until the inevitable happened. Koch's place was enlarged and opened as a commercial park where people could bring their children when the season permitted. Open daily Memorial Day through Labor Day. The name for the new park was obvious.

Santa Claus Land opened in 1946 with a toyland, restaurant, gift shop, museum, and a few rather gentle rides. The park prospered and today there are 20 rides, many of them designed especially for children, but including a white-knuckle roller coaster called "Blitzen." There is a petting zoo, House of Dolls, Hall of Famous Americans, game rooms, arcade, gift shops, souvenir shops, and restaurants. There are also 5 live shows, including puppet shows and musical productions. The single price of admission, modest by today's theme-park standards, covers all the attractions.

Adjacent to the park is Lake Rudolph, and on its shore is a Class-A campground with 220 campsites and a swimming beach. Santa Claus Land is near the junction of highways 245 and 162.

The most prominent staff person anywhere in Santa Claus Land is the old gent who wears a red suit and has long, flowing snow-white whiskers. No matter what month you visit this park, Santa Claus is there talking with the children who line up to see him.

One afternoon in midsummer we stopped at the pleasant home of Jim Yellig to visit with Santa Claus. We sat in his comfortable living room talking about the experiences of this short, stout man with the gray hair who has been Santa to millions, and who, in spite of his 88 years, was still working four days a week hoisting kiddies onto his knee and bellowing "Ho-ho-ho" from deep inside himself.

Yellig enlisted in the Navy in 1913 and spent sixteen years in the service. His friends in the Navy, after finding out the name of his hometown, stopped calling him Jim and called him Santa Claus. As time went on, Jim Yellig really began to think of himself as Santa Claus.

Later, after leaving the service, he helped organize his hometown American Legion Post and over the years represented the post as its official Santa. "I was in parades all over this country," he said. "Traveled to every big city to be in parades. I had a little sleigh I took along and a couple of little mechanical reindeer that jumped up and down. Cutest thing you ever saw."

When Santa Claus Land opened, Jim Yellig had the job he had wanted. He went to work in the theme park and every day, right through the heat of summer, Yellig sat inside a building while long lines of visiting children waited to sit on his knee and talk to him. "Oh, I have no idea how many there have been. Millions!" For years he was Santa Claus seven days a week. Nobody else in the world has played the role more than Jim Yellig.

As his fame spread, so did requests for public appearances, both on television and at public affairs. Miami, Florida, brought him down to kick off its Christmas shopping season one year. "I ate my Thanksgiving dinner on the airplane," he remembers, "in order to be there the next day for the parade.

"The joy the children get from my work is my reward," he says. "Little children keep me going. They don't change," he says. "They're always well behaved. They think I'm the real Santa Claus, so they don't pull my beard. You have to keep up with the new toys though so you can talk about them. I used to go to the International Toy Show in New York to see what new toys there were.

"You have to be careful how you answer questions. You never know whether they are really going to get the things they ask for, so if they ask, 'Santa, am I going to get a doll for Christmas?' I just say, 'You're going to be surprised.' And if they want to know if reindeers really can fly, I ask them, 'Have you read the story?' and they say, 'That's right, I remember,' and I don't tell them one way or the other."

This fielding of questions by the world's leading professional Santa has obviously given Jim Yellig a certain skill in carrying on a lively conversation without getting himself backed into a tight spot. We were ready to leave when we asked if he thinks parents should really tell their children there is a Santa Claus. Santa Claus went into a three-minute inconclusive soliloquy about child-parent relationships, character forming, and good moral up-bringing.

Although the red clothes and long white beard remain the same, Santa Claus revises his approach to stay abreast of the times. When he puts a little boy down off his knee these days he says, "Give me five," and the grinning child slaps his hand. "Never once did I find a boy who didn't know what I meant," he says, that broad Santa Claus smile spreading over his face. "The little girls give me a kiss," he adds. "We're getting more and more senior citizens," he laughs, "and they all want to kiss Santa too. The women that is."

Jim Yellig doesn't know how long he will go on making his happy public appearances. "I'd love to go on working seven days a week," he says, "but I've cut back to four. I began to notice there were two problems. One is it's harder lifting kids onto my knee than it used to be. The other is in the 'Ho-ho-ho.' It comes from way down here, and it isn't easy anymore. But they expect it, and you can't disappoint little children."

Later as we drove off down the highway and over the rooftops, we realized that we still did not have an answer to that question about telling the kids there is a Santa.

Give me five, Santa.

Lincoln City

Down the road, near Lincoln City on Hwy. 162, is the farm where Abraham Lincoln lived from the age of seven until he grew to manhood, laboring on his father's land. He stood 6'4" tall, could drive an ax deeper than any man around, and outwrestle all challengers. The Lincoln farm has become a favorite destination for travelers in southern Indiana since the National Park Service established the Lincoln Boyhood National Memorial.

Visitors arrive first at the impressive stone headquarters and museum building. The receptionist points out the trails and attractions and supplies a Park Service folder that includes a map.

The Lincoln story can be followed in the museum exhibits. When Thomas Lincoln, a muscular dark-haired pioneer, came from Kentucky to Indiana in 1816, it was to this place on the Little Pigeon River 12 miles from the Ohio that he led his little cara-

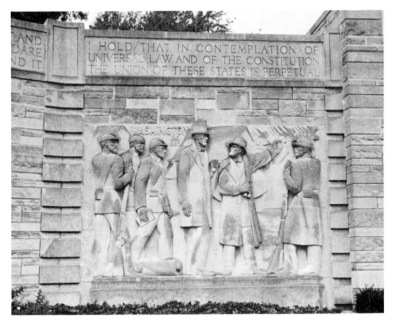

Lincoln's boyhood farm is maintained by the National Park Service in Spencer County, Indiana, scene of this monument and tableau. (Photo by George Laycock)

van with the creaking wagons and walking livestock. The quarter section (160 acres) of government land on which he had filed a claim was covered with towering trees that cast the land in deep shade.

By December when the Lincolns arrived, the trees were bare of leaves and winter was upon them. Thomas and Abraham, big for his seven years, built a shelter probably open on one side and faced with a fire that was kept burning day and night. Through that winter the family lived on wild game taken in the woods, plus food brought with them from Kentucky.

They cleared land and in the spring planted and grew the same crops everyone else in the neighborhood grew. Corn was the special favorite because of its many uses both for people and livestock. There was a vegetable garden. A wheat patch provided wheat enough to make flour for family use. The flax and cotton patches provided fibers for making cloth.

Here, in the fall of 1818, after spending only two years in Indiana, Abraham's mother, Nancy Lincoln, was stricken with "Milksick," supposedly after consuming the milk or butter of a family cow that had eaten the poisonous white snakeroot. Some recovered from this dreaded frontier disease, but Nancy Lincoln died as the first colors of October were coming to the woods around the little farm, and Thomas and the neighbors carried her coffin to a wooded knoll south of the cabin.

Thomas went to Kentucky the following year and brought back a new wife, Sarah Johnston, a widow, along with her three children. Sarah raised the two Lincoln children as if they were her own.

Abraham first attended school during the winter when he was eleven. He was in school on occasion when he was thirteen and again when he was fifteen. Schooling was not a necessity on the frontier, and boys growing up in a rural community where nearly everyone became a farmer saw little reason for working over a book. But Lincoln, when he attended school in his buckskins and

Lincoln's boyhood farm is operated by costumed Park Service employees working with tools used a hundred years ago. (Photo by George Laycock)

coonskin cap, was a serious student, who developed a love for reading.

Here Thomas Lincoln and his family scratched a living from the land. But there was not much else to show for the years of work so in 1830 he sold his land, packed up his family, and once more led them down the road, this time toward Illinois.

The grave of Nancy Lincoln remains where Thomas and Abraham dug it, and each year thousands of visitors walk the short trail from the headquarters building to the graveyard.

From there the trail leads to the place where the Lincoln home stood. Or those who prefer not to walk can drive to the farm, and this is a stop which no one who visits the area should miss. The Park Service could have stopped with plaques and engraved stones that tell only the bare facts of the story. Instead they skillfully re-created the farmstead much as it was when the Lincolns lived there. Furthermore, a staff of workers operate the farm, using the tools and methods the Lincolns once used. Costumed workers are busy at their work, but they encourage visitors to talk with them about the farm as it was more than a century and a half ago.

The log house, modeled after the original, has one large room and a loft. Over the open fire in the big fireplace, on the day we stopped there, the "pioneer" woman was preparing dinner for the staff people who work the farm. Two iron rods rested on logs above the fire to hold pots and skillets. Pieces of chicken stewed in one black pot while corn bread baked in a skillet that had an iron lid covered with hot coals. Vegetables were simmering, and dumplings were dropped into chicken broth to cook.

In the other end of the room stood the spinning wheel, which is still used, as well as pieces of rough furniture. Rows of herbs hung from the whitewashed wall and pegs in the wall led to a loft like the one where young Abe once slept.

Outside were other buildings, including a chicken pen, shed for the cattle and horses, and a shop where other costumed workers repaired harness and split red oak shakes for the roof, using the ancient froe and a wooden mallet.

In the little fields around the building, open-pollinated corn grew where Lincoln once planted and hoed it, as well as patches of the other crops the Lincoln family grew here. The fieldwork is done with horses and oxen. The hay is lifted with a wooden fork. Chickens from the pen are sometimes converted to human food in the pioneer kitchen. Young or old, a visit to the Lincoln Living Historical Farm makes the learning of history fun.

Across the highway from the Lincoln Boyhood National Memorial is the Lincoln State Park. Visitors often make this their headquarters. There is a modern campground with showers, as well as a primitive campground. One of the reasons for the popularity of this state park is the 85-acre lake which has a good reputation as a fishing lake. There is also a beach with lifeguards where swimming is free, plus a launching ramp for privately owned boats and boats that can be rented.

The park also has family housekeeping cabins that can be rented in advance for a week at a time. Write the Property Manager, Lincoln State Park, Box 216, Lincoln City, IN 47552.

Hiking trails wind through this park sometimes leading to points of historic interest. Within this state park stands the Little Pigeon Primitive Baptist Church, a restored version of the earlier building where the Lincoln family worshipped on the same spot. The graves of pioneers, including Sarah Lincoln Grigsby, Lincoln's only sister, are in this churchyard.

In the heart of this famous Lincoln country, visitors can plan

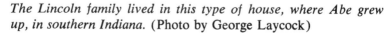

The Lincoln family lived in this type of house, where Abe grew up, in southern Indiana. (Photo by George Laycock)

an entire vacation around the travels of Abraham Lincoln. Along the highways are markers for the Lincoln Heritage Trail leading through Kentucky, southern Indiana, and into Illinois. The Lincoln Heritage Trail Foundation at Champaign, Illinois, is responsible for the trail. Phone: (217) 352-1968.

Along this route are numerous attractions, not all of them related to Lincoln. The markers lead to the Abraham Lincoln Birthplace, Lincoln's Boyhood Home, and the Lincoln Homestead State Park all in Kentucky. In Indiana, the Lincoln Boyhood National Memorial and Lincoln State Park as well as the Lincoln Pioneer Village at Rockport, are on the trail. In Illinois the trail leads to the Lincoln Trail Monument where the family crossed the Wabash, the Lincoln Trail State Park near Marshall, the Lincoln Log Cabin State Park near Charleston, Lincoln Trail Homestead State Park near Decatur, Lincoln's New Salem State Park near Petersburg, and then to Springfield with its concentration of Lincoln sites including Lincoln's home which is kept open by the National Park Service.

Those who like buildings of Medieval-style architecture should drive out to the famous St. Meinrad Archabbey, Order of St. Benedict, at St. Meinrad, near the junction of highways 62 and 545. Daily tours from 8 A.M. to 5 P.M. are self-guided and free.

Rockport to the south is another river town that was also prominent in the story of Lincoln's Indiana days. For the Lincolns, and other farmers, this was the port by which goods were shipped up or down the river to market. Lincoln Pioneer Village here is a collection of 16 log buildings owned by the city and kept open to the public from late March through November. Visitors, after paying a modest fee, wander through the buildings to witness the way of life of people in this region more than a century ago. There is a fully stocked store (that does not sell its goods), a complete school, church, homes, and a museum described to us in advance as "having a little bit of everything." It does.

Warrick County:
And an Old Town

Boonville is the busy seat of government for Warrick County, Indiana, a prosperous farming community lying just east of Evansville.

Campers and fishermen in the area find their way to Scales Lake Park a half mile or so out of Boonville. The central attraction is a 77-acre lake where the water is clear and green and the shores pleasantly wooded. The lake is stocked with bass, blue-gills, crappie, and channel catfish. Anglers who do not bring their own boats can rent them here. There is a public launching ramp.

Scales Lake has a campground with 165 campsites tucked away in the shade of tall trees. There are electrical hookups and a dumping station for trailers.

The most popular corner of the lake is the sandy beach, staffed with lifeguards and heavily used by swimmers from the Saturday before Memorial Day until Labor Day.

To the south on the Ohio River is Newburgh, Warrick County's most historic community. This was one of the earliest Indiana settlements along the Ohio. In 1803 young John Sprinkle, drifting down the Ohio on a log raft, guided his craft ashore at this spot. There was wilderness everywhere. Sprinkle hacked himself out a fragment of the wilderness and stayed. In this same spot he later established the first blacksmith shop in Warrick County. He obtained land grants signed by President James Monroe, and as other settlers joined him, the town took on his name. Although Sprinklesburg became Newburgh in 1837 by an act of the Indiana Legislature, the memory of John Sprinkle lives on. The site of his pioneering blacksmith shop just east of Sycamore Street is marked by a plaque.

Newburgh has the distinction of having been invaded during the Civil War. On July 17, 1862, a 32-man Confederate scouting party crossed the river and announced to residents of Newburgh that they were the advance party and that the major force awaited only their word before crossing the Ohio. The Newburghers had no way of knowing that the Confederate soldiers were lying. Neither did they realize that the two cannons mounted on a wagon were really pieces of stove pipe fitted over smooth logs. There seemed to be little resistance as the Confederates looted the local department store, perhaps because some Newburgh residents were southern sympathizers. This may also have had something to do with the ease with which the invaders escaped. But one messenger slipped out of Newburgh and raced off to Evansville, spreading word of the invasion. Within an hour, the story goes, 1,000 state militia were rushing overland toward Newburgh while two steamers churned upriver toward the town. Whether by land or by sea, however, the rescue parties arrived too late; they found that the invaders had already slipped back across the river into Kentucky. Newburgh would go down in history as the site where Confederate soldiers first crossed the Ohio River to stage an attack on the North.

The modern visitor to this little city can still recognize links with the past. There is the waterfront site where the Confederate raiding party landed, the department store that was used as a Union hospital in later years of the War, and numerous old prewar homes which give the town an antebellum atmosphere. The old Presbyterian Church, built in 1851, is restored now and serves as the Town Hall and Community Center.

Evansville

In the southernmost corner of Indiana is Evansville, a clean and attractive medium-sized city situated on a sweeping bend of the river. This city in the lower part of the Ohio Valley is a healthy mix of old river tradition, historic architecture, and modern progressive living. The visitor to Evansville gathers the impression that this is a good place to live, and local residents agree.

With a population of 140,000, Evansville is manageable; her promoters say "ideal," and they rattle off the reasons: a distinctive character and charm, the right amount of large and small industry, active service organizations, rich historic tradition, plus two universities, three hospitals, lower per capita crime rate than larger cities, an absence of slums, cleaner air than most large cities, good places to eat, and sports and cultural events.

From its earliest days as a frontier settlement the people behind this community wanted it to be big. Colonel Hugh McGary, Jr., bought the original 200 acres from the government in 1812, nourishing dreams of a giant city at this bend in the Ohio. Although McGary went bankrupt, the place grew and people and industries did settle here.

We went one day to tour the Old Vanderburgh County Courthouse. Throughout the land there must be no courthouse anywhere that is grander. Floors are marble, handrails solid brass, and exterior encrusted with sculpting. One writer called it, "the envy of many a banana republic," But the old Courthouse, built between 1881 and 1891, is an indication of the intense competition then between cities along the Ohio River. Cities wooed railroads, investors, and industries. Evansville, feeling that it must compete with larger cities upriver, decided to build the grandest edifice in the valley. And did. The resulting structure is regarded as one of the Midwest's outstanding examples of Neo-Baroque architecture. It now houses small shops, galleries, theater, and party rooms.

An area of Evansville that is an irresistible attraction for those who enjoy studying old buildings is the Riverside Historic District. The entire neighborhood of 17 blocks is on the National Register of Historic Places, and the variety of architectural styles found here seems endless. The massive homes express the taste and reflect the wealth of the owners who imported woodworkers and stonemasons from Europe in their efforts to build homes bigger and grander than others in the area.

In many places these old homes have fallen into disrepair as their wealthy builders died or moved from Evansville's Riverside

This ornate structure in Evansville, Indiana, is the most elaborate courthouse building in the Ohio Valley. It now houses shops, studios, and cultural events. (Photo by George Laycock)

District into the suburbs. Then, recently, people began buying up the historic old homes, renovating them, and returning to the city to live.

Most of these homes are occupied and not open to the public except on special occasions. But the most impressive of them all is open as a museum. John Augustus Reitz came to Evansville

Old homes in downtown Evansville are being renovated.

more than a century ago and became a pioneer lumber king. The three-story French Imperial-style home he built offered nineteenth-century river-city living at its finest. The interior is noted for fine-carved wood, parquet floors, stained glass, and massive chandeliers. The Reitz Home, 224 SE First St., showpiece of the neighborhood, is open on weekends.

The Evansville Museum of Arts and Science is located on the riverfront in Sunset Park. There are magnificent paintings and sculpture exhibited from the museum's collections of old masters. Other displays include Indian artifacts, early regional history, and ethnic materials. Outside the museum is a display of early railroad equipment with an antique steam locomotive.

Evansville keeps its riverfront pleasant and functional. The *Spirit of Evansville* is docked here at the foot of Main St. This diesel-powered sternwheeler, rated for 150 passengers, offers both public and private cruises. There are dinner cruises and moonlight river cruises as well. Kentuckiana Packet Line, Inc. Phone: (812) 422-1424.

Also near the river is the James C. Ellis Park where Thoroughbred races are held. Although this track is north of the river, it is, by a quirk of nature, part of Kentucky. After the original boundaries of Kentucky were set at the low-water mark on the north shore, the Ohio River changed its course to leave the land on which J. C. Ellis Park stands, north of the water's edge. As a consequence, Evansville people get the races, and Kentucky gets the taxes.

Annually, in the third week of June, the Ohio River at Evansville roars to life as the unlimited hydroplane races get underway for Thunder on the Ohio, the opening act of the annual Freedom Festival which goes on for 14 days. If you like watching hydroplanes speeding along a two-and-a-half-mile course at speeds approaching 200 miles an hour, filling the valley with their thunder, you will enjoy this event on the Evansville waterfront.

The boat races are only a fraction of the events that flower in Evansville during the Freedom Festival. There are balloon races, bike races, mock military battles, rugby, soccer, and a swim meet, biergarten, queen pageant, parades, marathons, fireworks, and a chili cook-off.

True festival goers will also want to know about the Ohio River Arts Festival which comes in mid-May and brings people downtown for art and crafts shows, concerts, and now and then a race of whatever can be assembled to race.

The annual Thunder on the Ohio celebration brings to Evansville, Indiana, the world's fastest speedboats. (Evansville *Courier* photo by Kevin Swank)

The Blue Grass Festival is held in conjunction with the Arts Festival, and the music goes on non-stop out at the Mesker Amphitheater.

Then in mid-August comes the Germania Maennerchor Volkfest, a re-creation of Munich's Oktoberfest where the main attractions include beer drinking, German music, German foods, and German dancing.

Another favorite among Evansville festival goers is the West Side Nut Club Fall Festival. Franklin Street is converted to a midway with rides, booths, and local entertainers, combining the best of a carnival, county fair, and a community social. Two hundred thousand may come out for this one.

The Annual Mid-States Art Exhibition in November is a "big art show," one of the finest and most competitive shows in the Midwest. It's held at the Museum of Arts and Science.

Angel Mounds

Angel Mounds State Memorial is a few miles east of the center of town. For two or three centuries, ending about the time Christopher Columbus arrived in the New World, Angel Mounds was the homesite of a community of two or three thousand people, the ancestors of various Indian tribes native to the Ohio Valley. Angel Mounds people were farmers as well as hunters and

Prehistoric earthworks can be explored in Angel Mounds State Memorial east of Evansville.

gatherers. They lived on the corn they grew, wild plants they gathered, deer and wild turkey taken from the surrounding forests, and fish caught from the river. Their ways of life have been studied by teams of archaeologists excavating here. As a result, this is one of the country's best-preserved and most understood prehistoric Indian sites.

The story can be traced most easily in the modern interpretive center maintained by the Indiana Division of Historic Preservation. After a visit to this museum, the visitor walks the trails that the ancient people followed to their village and the mounds. Along these trails are reproductions of their fortifications.

This place was well chosen as the site for a fortified city. Three Mile Island is a long ribbon of wooded land just offshore in the Ohio River. The island hid the village from the eyes of enemy war parties canoeing down the river. Around the other three sides of the village the people erected a fortification by digging a trench and setting logs upright in it. They filled the spaces between the logs with woven sticks plastered with a mixture of mud and grass. This waddle-and-daub stockade stood 15–18 feet high with stations every 125 feet or so, where archers could defend the community against attack.

Inside the 103-acre town site there were 11 mounds, the largest of them covering 4 acres and standing 44 feet high in terraced levels. Families lived here in square thatch-roofed homes made of waddle and daub similar to that used in constructing the fortress.

This state memorial park deserves an hour or two of the visitor's time, and those who are especially interested may want to allow more time than this.

Mesker Zoo

Visitors to Evansville, especially families with children, go to the zoo. The zoo is on St. Joseph Ave., which you can reach off the Division Expressway or Diamond Avenue Expressway. Many of the zoo animals live in big, open outdoor areas. Pathways lead through the animal areas past elephants, tigers, bears, monkeys, and hippos. This is a roomy pleasant zoo that includes a petting zoo where young visitors meet the more gentle barnyard animals at close range.

Dining Out

There are excellent restaurants in Evansville and a wide choice in the kinds of food available. Here are some of the more popular ones, listed in alphabetical order:

Andy's Steak and Barrel, 2207 S. Kentucky Ave., has a fine salad bar and makes a specialty of steaks. On the wine list here are some produced by the Golden Raintree Winery, one of southern Indiana's award-winning wineries.

Bockelman's, 4001 Big Cynthiana Rd., also makes a specialty of serving fine steaks. Chicken too. Plus fiddle music.

The Briarpatch, 4400 First Ave., a good bet for steaks, shrimp, and salads.

Butterfield's, 405 S. Greenriver Rd. This one rates very high with both local people and visitors, especially those seeking good prime rib or seafood in a pleasant atmosphere.

Executive Inn, Mayfair Room, 600 Walnut St. Menu offering a wide choice of excellent foods. One of the best.

F'S, 125 SE Fourth St. Widely known for its Cantonese cuisine plus excellent seafood, lobster, and steak.

Hilltop Inn, 1100 Harmony Way. This one has been in business since 1839; was once a stagecoach stop and has a bar more than a century old.

Kabuki Japanese Steak House, 960 S. Hebron Ave.

Mac's Famous Barbecue, 1409 E. Maryland St. Evansville calls itself "the barbecue capital of the world." Owensboro, Kentucky, disputes this, but at any rate, Mac's is an Evansville favorite.

Pop-O's Riverboat Restaurant, 1 SE First St. Riverboat-style dining.

Ramada Inn, LaChateau, 4101 Hwy. 41N. French atmosphere with entertainment nightly.

Robert F. Brandt, Waterworks Rd. The dining room has a view of the river.

Sheraton Inn, Potter's Restaurant, 5701 Hwy. 41N. Steaks, crab, lobster, and live entertainment.

Shing-Lee Chinese Restaurant, 215 Main St. Walkway. This downtown restaurant offers authentic Chinese dishes for lunch and dinner.

Western Rib-Eye, 1401 N. Boeke Rd. Steaks and seafood.

Wolf's Barbecue, 6601 First Ave. A good bet for those interested in hickory-smoked ribs, chicken, and pork. A family restaurant.

As we've said before, part of the fun is exploring on your own and discovering for yourself some restaurant not on the "lists." Evansville has many worthwhile restaurants to enjoy.

Accommodations

Evansville has a plethora of hotels and motels. Many of them are clustered along Hwy. 41. The chains are well represented, and Ramada Inn Spa rates high with gourmet restaurant, indoor heated pool, sauna, and whirlpool. The Drury Inn has Jo Jo's Restaurant, open 24 hours. There is a Holiday Inn, as well as a Sheraton and Regal 8 Inn. Also several other smaller locally run motels where rates may be lower.

In other areas of town: The largest of all the motor inns is Executive Inn, downtown, with indoor pool, waterbeds, sauna, tennis, racquetball, shops, and restaurants. Travelodge is downtown on First Ave., and the Jackson House, 20 Walnut St. Their Wheel House lounge has a river view. Out on the east side, Williamsburg Inn on Division St. is a pleasant stop. There's a Farmer's Daughter Restaurant across the parking lot.

There is a KOA Campground on Warrenton Rd. It has water and electrical hookups, also primitive camping, pool, showers, laundry, and playground. Phone: (812) 867-3401.

Scattered throughout the city are city parks where there are a wide range of activities. The parks have nature centers, miniature golf courses, hiking trails, and pedalboats to rent, plus swimming pools, playgrounds, skating rinks (both ice and roller), courts for tennis, handball, and basketball, as well as room for picnics. There are also golf courses in the city parks. For details, call (812) 426-5605.

Those who enjoy a quiet walk through natural areas drive out to the Wesselman Park Nature Center at 51 N. Boeke Rd., a sanctuary for wild creatures and a place for people to escape the pressures of crowds. The nature center covers 200 acres with marked trails through woodlands that help visitors visualize the virgin forests covering this region when the earliest settlers arrived.

Evansville is a good place for golfing. There are, at various locations in and around the city, 7 golf courses open to the public. For those who prefer tennis, there are courts in 22 locations.

The Evansville Convention and Visitors' Bureau can supply visitors with information on these activities or any other attractions in the city. Phone: (812) 425-5402. The Convention and Visitors' Bureau is located in the Vanderburgh Auditorium and Convention Center at 715 Locust St.

The Auditorium and Convention Center itself is worth a look. It's large, modern, and impressive. The Auditorium seats 2,000 people, and the Evansville Philharmonic Orchestra holds its concerts here.

Posey County: Harmony and an Unusual Lake

Twenty miles west of Evansville, on Hwy. 62, is Mt. Vernon, a pleasant rural town and the county seat of Posey County. The first log cabin here was built in 1805 by Andrew McFadden. The high ground above the river appealed to early settlers, so the village grew, and by 1820 there was need for a new hotel built at the corner of Main and Water streets. Here a man and his horse could be housed for twenty-five cents a night.

Mt. Vernon has several municipal parks with playgrounds. There is also the 56-acre Brittlebank Park maintained by the Indiana Department of Natural Resources. Brittlebank has a large swimming pool, wading pool for toddlers, picnic grounds, tennis courts, jogging trail, and small fishing lake that is kept stocked.

If you like a smorgasbord restaurant, try the Southwind on E. Fourth St. at the edge of town, a favorite with local residents.

The 4 Seasons Motel is about 2 miles west of the center of town on Hwy. 62. Small pool. Reasonable. Continental breakfast included.

A Lake with Cypress

One morning at dawn we drove down Hwy. 69S for 9 miles out of Mt. Vernon to Hovey Lake, which is widely known among hunters, fishermen, and naturalists. In the flat gray light of dawn the lake seemed part of a scene far to the south. Giant cypress trees grow in these waters, considerably north of their usual range, the only large stand of cypress in Indiana. Some of them are more than 200 years old.

Hovey Lake was once part of the nearby Ohio River, but about 500 years ago the river cut a new channel straight across the base of the big oxbow and left the old channel as an oxbow lake. At that time Hovey Lake was deep, but sediment filled it until it was shallow. Then the Army Corps of Engineers built new high-level dams and lifted the level of Hovey Lake.

Fishing then began to improve. Hovey Lake is especially known for crappie, bluegill, bass, and catfish. Fishing boats were already on the lake when the rising sun broke through the limbs of the cypress trees. We spoke with a fisherman as he launched his boat at the concrete ramp. "I'm no specialist," he said. "I fish for whatever is hitting, and I've done well here. I always catch fish. Got your fishin' pole with you? Come go along." Topnotch idea, partner, except for the early appointment back in town.

This is also one of Indiana's prize waterfowl areas. Through the fall and winter months, ducks and geese by the thousands funnel in to rest and feed on the quiet secluded waters of Hovey Lake. In midwinter, when more northern lakes are freezing over, the goose flock at Hovey builds up to 20,000 or more.

In addition to waterfowl, the birds here include ibis, bald eagles, osprey, various hawks and owls, double-crested cormorants, great blue herons, and American egrets. The nesting birds include prothonotary warblers and various woodpeckers, among them the giant pileated and the flashy redheaded woodpeckers. We spotted four redheaded woodpeckers on our morning visit. The annual Christmas bird count here usually gives a list of more than 70 species.

The lake, now covering 1,400 acres and standing 11 feet deep, is part of the 4,200-acre Hovey Lake Fish and Wildlife Area managed by the Indiana Department of Natural Resources. The Department's Fish and Wildlife Division conducts waterfowl hunts here in season, and hunters shoot from the blinds under carefully controlled conditions.

The area includes a campground plus a primitive camping area. The address is Hovey Lake State Fish and Wildlife Area, RR 5, Mt. Vernon, IN 47620. Phone: (812) 838-2927.

On the way north by Hwy. 69 toward New Harmony, Indiana, we came to Harmonie State Park where camping families vacation. Covering 3,465 acres on the banks of the Wabash River, this is an excellent park for wildlife watching. On a brief evening visit, we spotted a red fox, a whitetail deer fawn, and a respectable list of birds as we drove the winding roads.

Six miles of hiking trails are marked through the park, and there is also a bicycle trail in addition to the miles of surfaced roads. There are picnic areas with playgrounds, and there is also an Olympic-size swimming pool that is popular through the summer. The campground is modern and there are sites especially for recreational vehicles and a horsemen's campground.

The address is Harmonie State Park, New Harmony, IN 47631. Phone: (812) 682-4821.

One of the best-known wineries in the Ohio Valley is in this county near Wadesville, at St. Wendel. George Fox, an Evansville restaurant owner, believed the banks of the Ohio and Wabash rivers where there is nearly a 200-day frost-free growing season, with plenty of water and sunshine, would be ideal for growing the French hybrid grapes needed to produce fine wines.

He and his partners hired an expert winemaker and began planting grapes. Now, not too many years later, the Golden Raintree Winery is in full operation. Furthermore, there is a fine restaurant in a Swiss chalet set in the rolling hills. The menu offers anything from wine and cheese to steaks. Once a year there is a wine festival here.

Golden Raintree enters its finest wines in national competitions and has won numerous gold medals. To drive to this winery from Evansville, follow Hwy. 66 northwest to Blairsville, then turn northeast to St. Wendel.

New Harmony

To reach New Harmony, drive north on Hwy. 69 from Mt. Vernon and Harmonie State Park. Or take Hwy. 66 northwest from Evansville. If you are traveling I-64, exit at Poseyville and follow Hwy. 68 southwest to New Harmony.

This village is the other half of our story about the Rappites, those followers of George Rapp whose early settlement we encountered upriver at Ambridge, Pennsylvania. Rapp came here to Indiana and founded New Harmony, where his people lived for ten years before packing up and returning to Pennsylvania. George Rapp sold New Harmony to Robert Owen, a Welsh philanthropist, who wanted to establish a Utopian society of culture and science. Owen's experiment in communal living eventually failed also, but some of the buildings survive and are open to the public; others are still privately occupied.

Living in New Harmony is living in a museum, and although the population (about 1,000) is not much greater than it was in Rapp's day, the community is alive and vital. "Our young people stay here," we were told by a shop owner who was obviously proud of her town. "My husband drives ninety miles a day just because we prefer living in a small town and like it here." Many local people work as guides or shop operators catering to the visitors. This village is also an architectural display, ranging from log cabins like those the early Harmonists used, through the sturdy brick residences they later built, and on to the new futuristic Atheneum, a special interpretive center where tours of Historic New Harmony start. This white contemporary building contains four galleries and an auditorium where tourists view a short film.

The 15 buildings and sites on the walking tour are owned and maintained by Historic New Harmony, Inc. Phone: (812) 682-4474. Highlights of the walking tour include David Owen's geological collection in the George Keppler House, built in 1820, and the Panorama of New Harmony, an automated model presentation in the Solomon Wolf House.

The Roofless Church, an interdenominational church designed by award-winning architect Phillip Johnson and built in 1959, is not on the organized tour.

The New Harmony Inn, 508 North St., blends beautifully with its surroundings and successfully combines the past with the present. Rather expensive, but comfortable and conveniently located.

The best place to eat in New Harmony is the Red Geranium, 504 North St. Pleasant atmosphere, children's menu, homemade bread. Open for lunch and dinner.

Mid-August is Melon Festival time in New Harmony. The festival is noted for homemade foods, arts, and crafts, and contests including melon throwing.

Visitors also flock to New Harmony during the third week in June when the Golden Rain Trees, the town's locally famous exotic trees, are in bloom.

In New Harmony, Indiana, the historic buildings include the Opera House. (Photo by George Laycock)

Illinois

Gallatin: Into Illinois Country

As we approached the western edge of Indiana, the highway led to a bridge above the flood plains. We stopped at the toll booth, paid the lady forty cents, and crossed the Wabash River into a land different from any we had yet seen in all the Ohio Valley. This ancient lake bed is rich farmland now where giant machines move back and forth through the autumn afternoon, slicing off and digesting straight rows of tall corn. Each combine travels in its own dust cloud, but the dust does not reach the drivers sitting high in their glass-enclosed cabs as they move back and forth across the tabletop fields.

With some imagination the land is seen as it once was, tall grass prairies splashed with millions of yellow, white, and blue flowers. Instead of machines, there are herds of plodding buffalo, roaming packs of wolves, and hundreds of thousands of ducks passing back and forth between the potholes and sloughs. Through this scene move the early people, including the mighty Shawnees who gave their name to the county seat of this county in southeastern Illinois.

Shawneetown on Hwy. 13 is a center for oil, coal, and farm operations and not a noted tourist destination. Next door to the motel, Jim Fox, a tall busy man with a shock of silver hair, operates the Silver Fox, a combination lounge and restaurant.

After checking the menu, we ordered chicken, but the waitress suggested the catfish. Here in the lower Ohio Valley, we are in catfish country. Catfish with hush puppies is a regional dish of renown, and if you're ever going to eat catfish, this is the place. The deep-fried "fiddle" catfish were served piping hot and crispy brown, surrounded by slices of onion and pickle, with hush puppies made by the Silver Fox himself.

Hush puppies? The most frequently told story about the origin of this southern form of corn bread tells of slaves holding forbidden feasts in the dead of night, and dropping spoonfuls of cornmeal batter into boiling grease then tossing an occasional one to their master's restless dogs to keep them quiet. "Hush puppy." But hush puppies survived, not as a hound dog treat, but a regional food.

One soon discovers here that there are two Shawneetowns—the new and the old. In the early morning we drove 3 miles to the edge of a big bend in the Ohio River to see Old Shawneetown, which, except for periodic natural disasters, might still serve as the county seat of Gallatin County, Illinois.

In the mid-1700s this was the site of a Shawnee village—and by the early 1800s, this flat land where the Wabash flows into the broad Ohio, became the site of the first English-speaking settle-

The first bank in Illinois, established in this building, is now a museum. (Photo by George Laycock)

ment in Illinois. Here also was the first industry in the state, the saltworks at nearby Saline Springs. This southeastern corner of Illinois touching the Ohio River became the banking center for the Illinois country. John Marshall, a leading pioneer citizen, built his two-story brick residence in 1812, and four years later was given a charter for the first bank in the Illinois Territory. The vault was a barrel in the basement. Legend tells us that a village called Chicago was once turned down for a loan here on the grounds that it was too far from Shawneetown ever to amount to anything.

If you drive out to Old Shawneetown, you can see the old bank building all spruced up and reconstructed by the Gallatin County Historical Society which opens it on weekends. When John Marshall lived there, he could look out his door and watch the Ohio River flow past. The river is still there, but the view has changed because a high levee now stands between the house and the river.

Standing in the yard of the John Marshall building is a log house that looks as if it has recently been moved here and reconstructed. There is activity behind the log house on the morning we visit. Richard Walker, 83, and Harvey Bradley, 81, are attacking a towering patch of giant horseweeds that stand twice as tall as either of them. Bradley, leaning on his scythe, says, "We ain't like them Texans, always got to have the biggest of everything, but if these ain't the biggest damn horseweeds of all, I wouldn't know where to look."

"Big enough to save for seed," says Walker.

We asked about the log house and learned that Bradley was on the crew that moved it here so people, especially schoolchildren, could see what a log house looks like. There are still large black numbers painted on the ends of the logs. "We marked every log so we would know how they should go back together."

Bradley and Walker worked at their own pace, stopping to talk when asked a question. Walker spoke of the floods that always plagued this low land. "The big flood of 'eighty-nine came, and after that they built a levee and said, 'Now the river will never get up here again.'

"Then came the flood of 1913, and after that they built the levee higher and said, 'The river won't get into town now.' Then came the big flood of 1937 [covering much of Gallatin County and devastating Old Shawneetown], so they built the levee even higher and now they're saying, 'It won't come over this one.'

"There'll be a higher one," says Walker.

"Sure to be," says Bradley, and they go back to work, swinging their scythes, bringing down giant horseweeds, while we climbed the steps to the top of the levee to look out over the Ohio River from this historic spot.

Traveling through this southeastern corner of Illinois we soon learned that much of the land lies within the boundaries of the Shawnee National Forest. This forest stretches across the southern tip of the state touching both the Ohio River on the east and south, the Mississippi on the west. Within these sprawling boundaries, about one third of the land, a quarter of a million acres, belongs to the Federal Government, which is to say, all of us. And

This reconstructed iron furnace is in Shawnee National Forest. (Photo by George Laycock)

within this publicly owned forest lie countless opportunities for recreation.

Half a century ago these lands were showing the results of erosion, following unwise timbering of forests and overworking the soil. Then the Shawnee National Forest was established, and in the decades since, trees have returned and so has much of the forest wildlife dependent on them. People can once more hike, camp by a forest trail, and explore attractive wooded coves and ridges.

At the forest headquarters in Harrisburg, forester Robert H. Mason gave us a briefing on the forest and its attractions. Another staff person sent us off with a handful of helpful information leaflets and maps which are available to anyone who asks for them. They are before us as this is written, and here are a few examples.

For any of the following, write Forest Supervisor, Shawnee National Forest, Harrisburg, IL 62946 or call (618) 253-7114.

Sportsmen Maps. These black-and-white contour maps are printed by township and range. They list access trails and other information.

The Shawnee Is Camping. Gives details, with maps, of various forest recreation areas and includes information on trails, lakes, fishing, camping, boating, swimming, wildlife.

Shawnee National Forest map.

Checklist of Birds, Shawnee National Forest. There are 237 species listed here.

Little Grand Canyon Hiking Trail.

Canoeing.

Heritage Hiking Trail. (Nine-mile-long trail from Murray Bluff to Bell Smith Springs.)

The Shawnee National Forest offers a rare opportunity for campers to stay in places of their own choosing and not have their camping limited to established campgrounds. This freedom places certain citizenship responsibilities on the camper. Care with fire is essential. So is keeping the woods clean and clear of cast-off bottles, cans, and paper.

South of Harrisburg we left Hwy. 34 and traveled along Karbers Ridge, following the signs to the Garden of the Gods. We wanted to see the rock formations in this famous National Forest recreation area. We hiked the trail over and around spec-

Like a section of the Rocky Mountains transplanted to the Midwest, Garden of the Gods, in Shawnee National Forest, offers visitors scenic vistas. (Photo by George Laycock)

tacular rock outcroppings and stopped on scenic high points to photograph the forested hills, with a view for miles around. Geologists explain that the Garden of the Gods had its beginning 200 million years ago, as the earth shifted and layers of rock were upthrust, where they stood exposed to the forces of erosion. Wind and water carved away at them, leaving myriads of strange shapes found today. In addition to the much traveled foot trail here to Garden of the Gods, the Forest Service maintains several miles of trails into the surrounding hills. A good area in which to spend a day, or several days.

Hardin County:
An Outlaw Cave

Elizabethtown, population 400, sits on the edge of the Ohio River in Hardin County and is the smallest county seat town of all those visited up and down the valley. In the center of town the old red-brick courthouse sits on a rise at the bend of the road. But the oldest building is said to be the Rose Hotel built in 1812 by Captain James McFarland and known in early times as McFarland's Tavern. The hotel, in continuous operation for more than 165 years, is no longer open.

To the northeast and upstream from Elizabethtown, off Hwy. 1, there is an unusual park known as Cave-in-Rock State Park. The central feature is a cave with a name that brought terror to the hearts of early settlers traveling the river. The cave extends back into the solid limestone for 160 feet from the face of the riverside cliff. The arched entrance to the cave is 55 feet wide, and the cavern, dark and forbidding, looks out upon the river.

Such a natural shelter was certain to attract attention from early people. Prehistoric tribes used it before the first white explorers arrived. The earliest record of discovery was written by M. deLery, a French explorer, who came here in 1729 and called the place *Caverne dans Le Roc* (Cave in the Rock).

Following the Revolutionary War, the cave became a hideout for gangs of river pirates who lured travelers to their deaths. Some were lured by promises that the cave was a tavern with drink and entertainment. Other travelers were met upstream by pirates pretending to be guides, who then wrecked the boats near the cave where other gang members could rob and murder the newcomers. Worst of the outlaws were the Harpe brothers, Big Harpe and Little Harpe, who traveled with three women. They left behind them a trail of robbery and murder until outraged relatives of victims eventually ran the Harpes down and rid the world of them. Although the Harpe brothers used the cave as a hideout, they did much of their lawbreaking across the river in Kentucky, and there remains, even today, a public thoroughfare called Harpe's Head Road because it was beside this road that the head of Big Harpe was impaled on a sharpened stake.

Today, however, Cave-in-Rock is all peace and beauty (except

This was Cave-in-Rock as the flatboaters saw it. (Photo by George Laycock)

for the artwork of the occasional vandal who paints his name on the walls). Illinois turned the area, just upriver from the village of Cave-in-Rock, into a state park in 1929. The narrow 150-acre park stretches along the Ohio River bluffs for nearly a mile. Attractions include fishing and boating in the river, a trail system, picnic area, playground, and campground. The Cave-in-Rock State Park superintendent's phone number is (618) 289-4325.

Boaters will find Ohio River launching ramps at Rosiclare, Elizabethtown, Tower Rock, and Cave-in-Rock.

Camping families may camp not only at Cave-in-Rock, but also at Tower Rock, Dogwood Hollow Campground east of Karbers Ridge, and at Pounds Hollow Recreational Area.

Fluorspar, the state mineral of Illinois, is a glasslike substance that comes in beautiful hues of blue-green, purple, yellow, pink, and white—all prized by rockhounds. Most of the fluorspar samples found in either private or museum collections come from Hardin County, which is believed to be the country's principal reserve fluorspar region.

What's it good for? Fluorspar is basic in the manufacture of hydrofluoric acid, the basic chemical used in the manufacture of a wide variety of products. This mineral of volcanic origin is found on both sides of the river, with Hardin County being the center of known deposits.

In the village of Rosiclare, downriver from Elizabethtown, there is a red two-story brick building that houses the Hardin County Fluorspar and General Museum.

Pope County: And the World's Largest Locks

When Sarah Lusk came here in 1803 she set herself up in business, operating the first local ferry to transport people and belongings across the Ohio. Helping her in this task was her young son and a black woman who came with her. Sarah kept her long gun close at hand because rough characters, Indian or white, might be lurking nearby. A small settlement grew up around the ferry landing on the Illinois shore, and it was called Sarahville.

Although the town's name has changed, its residents still keep alive the name of this pioneer woman who founded Golconda, Illinois, county seat of Pope County.

Where the Ohio River flows past Golconda, it is wider than it was in the days of Sarah Lusk. Nearby is Smithland Locks and Dam, which ranks as the world's largest system of twin navigational locks. Each lock is 1,200 feet long, and the lock walls extend for three quarters of a mile along the river's Illinois shore. The dam is three quarters of a mile across. This massive structure cost an estimated $188 million.

Visitors can reach the locks and the visitors' center from Golconda by way of the New Liberty Road, and once there can trace the story of the river and its management by the Corps of Engineers.

While in Golconda, you may stop in the River View Mansion Hotel, built in 1836. It still offers food and lodging. Nearby, across from Courthouse Square in the center of town, the Pope County Museum occupies a neat, white building where it is maintained by the County Historical Society.

Ten miles west of Golconda on Hwy. 146, near its junction with Hwy. 145, is Dixon Springs, another of Illinois' popular state parks. This park, covering 496 acres of rugged hill country, with cliffs, boulders, strange rock formations, and intermittent waterfalls, is a photographer's delight, where wildlife and seasonal wild flowers add color to the scene.

Early settlers placed great importance on natural springs that could supply water to their homesteads, and this was among the reasons William Dixon settled here and built one of the earliest log homes in the county. Before his time, the seven mineral-rich springs bubbling from the rocky slopes were favored by the Algonquin Indians. During the 1800s, when it was the fashion for wealthy people to flock to such springs to "take the waters," Dixon Springs became a renowned health spa. Visitors traveled the Ohio by steamboat then went on by train to reach the springs.

Although the health spa is gone, Dixon Springs State Park remains popular for its natural beauty as well as its springs.

Campers set up their temporary homes in both trailer and primitive tent-camping areas. For trailers there is electricity and a sanitary dumping station provided. There are also self-guiding nature trails, picnic areas, playgrounds, swimming pool, and ball fields. Phone: (618) 949-3394.

Massac County: Anybody Seen Superman?

Standing above the river on the edge of Metropolis, Illinois, is a statue of George Rogers Clark who, in 1778, masterminded the frontier campaign that captured the interior of the continent for the United States of America. Clark brought his little military force down the Ohio, and they hid their boats in the mouth of a nearby creek while they marched overland toward Kaskaskia, which they captured from the English without firing a shot.

This statue of Clark is on the site of old Fort Massac, which the visitor passes when entering Metropolis on Hwy. 45. We recommend a stop at Fort Massac State Park, not for the statue alone, or because this park, begun in 1903, is the oldest state park in Illinois, but because the fort and the museum beside it tell the story of the lower Ohio Valley. The museum exhibits tell of the various forces that established forts on this location where they could look out for a considerable distance both up and down the river. The French were the first European arrivals. Then came the British, followed by the Americans. In 1794 General Anthony Wayne sent Major Thomas Doyle here with a force of only sixty-nine men, under orders to reconstruct the fort that had been abandoned by the British and then burned by Indians. Major Doyle's troops completed the task in three months. More recently, the state of Illinois had a replica of the fort built; it took two years to complete the task. Bad weather slowed the heavy machinery utilized by modern builders.

Beside the fort and the adjacent museum, the park stretches upstream along the river for perhaps half a mile, covering 1,400 acres. Within this area there are places to picnic and camp beneath large trees that shade the area overlooking the river. Eventually, Illinois hopes to provide better camping and sanitary facilities; at this time the camping area is very scenic but lacks modern plumbing.

Metropolis, seat of government for Massac County, is an attractive and thriving small city of about 8,000 people, many of them employed in the several large industries situated along the Ohio River nearby. Near the center of town is a large boat-launching area for fishermen and boaters using the Ohio. Adjacent to it is the Dorothy Miller Park where local office workers sometimes take their brown bag lunches to eat and river watch.

If you inquire of local people about good dining places in town, you will be directed to Farley's Cafeteria across the street from the Chamber of Commerce. Try the homemade pies.

The best-known historic home in town is a block south of the

From his stone pedestal in Massac State Park, George Rogers Clark silently watches a modern giant river towboat. (Photo by George Laycock)

Courthouse at the corner of Fourth and Market streets. Here Major Elijah P. Curtis lived following the Civil War. Today, the home, surrounded by mimosa trees and towering magnolias, is the Massac County Historical Society Museum usually open on Sunday afternoons.

Biggest special event of the year in Metropolis is the Fort Massac Encampment or Fort Massac Days on an October weekend; it re-creates frontier atmosphere with costumed frontier soldiers, traders and settlers busy at their daily chores. The high point comes with a mock battle at the fort.

Fishermen in this area, in addition to fishing the Ohio River, concentrate on Mermet Lake, a state-managed 425-acre lake off Hwy. 45 northeast of Metropolis. Here they cast for bass, or fish for crappie, bluegill, and catfish. There is a launching ramp.

Outboard motors are limited to 10 horsepower or less.

As Superman fans well know, Clark Kent's home is Metropolis, a fact that has not eluded the Metropolis, Illinois, Chamber of Commerce. There is a giant picture of Superman, typically airborne, on the front of the Chamber of Commerce in the center of town, and Superman Celebration is held the second weekend in June. But Metropolis and Massac County, with or without Superman, is a good place to stop.

Where the River Ends

West of Mermet Lake Conservation Area, visitors traveling the scenic Hwy. 37 cross into Pulaski County which was named to honor Count Pulaski, a Polish nobleman who came to America to fight in the Revolutionary War. Mound City, the county seat, is a small river town today, but during the Civil War it was the site of the Naval Depot of the Western Fleet where the keels of four ironclad ships were laid. Mound City National Cemetery, where thousands of Civil War soldiers were buried, is at the junction of highways 37 and 51.

The Cache River flows down into Pulaski County and then across it and south again to form the boundary between Pulaski and Alexander counties.

In Alexander County, both Hwy. 127 and Hwy. 3 run north-ward, on either side of Shawnee National Forest, and both are considered scenic drives. Hwy. 127 leads to Tamms and Elco, which are famous for silica mining. In the town of Thebes off Hwy. 3, once the seat of Alexander County government, stands the historic Thebes Courthouse, built between 1846 and 1848 on the edge of a bluff overlooking the Mississippi, where it became a navigation landmark for boat captains on the river.

The location of the county government at Thebes proved un-fortunate since the jail and most legal offices were already in Cairo. When court was in session, the prisoners, judges, attor-neys, and witnesses boarded a steamboat and traveled thirty miles up the Mississippi to the courthouse at Thebes. If convicted, the prisoners were confined in the "dungeon" beneath the Thebes Courthouse, but everyone else trudged back down the bluff and departed once again for Cairo. The seat of county government was moved to Cairo in 1860. The historic Thebes Courthouse was declared a National Landmark in 1973.

This southwestern corner of Illinois is a land of big rivers, and at Cairo two long bridges over these rivers link three states: Illi-nois, Kentucky, and Missouri. The town was incorporated in 1818, the same year Illinois became a state, through the influence of John Comegys, a wealthy merchant from Baltimore who bought 1,800 acres and divided it for a settlement. As he looked at the flat fertile lands, he believed the setting similar to that of an ancient city on the Nile and named the new town Cairo (pro-nounced Kayro). Comegys soon ran into financial difficulties and his plans failed. After going bankrupt in 1840, the town was still floundering in 1855, when the Illinois Central Railroad reached it. The steel rails linked southern markets with the rich agricul-tural and industrial North, and Cairo flourished.

When the Civil War began, Cairo became strategically impor-tant, and within eleven days after Fort Sumter was fired upon, President Lincoln sent troops to the city where the Ohio meets the Mississippi. General Ulysses S. Grant, who was stationed here as commander of the western forces, cemented friendships with local leaders. The sudden influx of military personnel brought un-precedented demands for housing, food, equipment, and services. During this period General Grant met Charles A. Galigher, a prosperous merchant whose mills began supplying flour for the Federal troops.

Galigher's home, Magnolia Manor at 2700 Washington Ave., remains the best-known historic building in Cairo. This 14-room mansion was built in 1869. It had one of the earliest "air-conditioning" systems—double-brick walls that have a 10-inch space between them for insulation.

The furniture in the mansion is Victorian, and most of it is the original Galigher furniture. One of the bedrooms has the actual bed and other furniture used by former President Grant when he visited the Galighers after retiring from the presidency.

Of special interest is the 1870 kitchen, now restored and complete with its original brick-and-iron cooking stove, shipped downriver from Cincinnati.

Magnolia Manor, a National Landmark, is now owned by the Cairo Historical Association which charges visitors a small admission fee. Its most festive season starts on Thanksgiving Day and continues for ten days, during Holiday House celebration when the mansion is decorated for Christmas. Call the curator: (618) 734-9869, or Mrs. Ralph Gibson: (618) 734-1988.

Across Washington Ave. from Magnolia Manor stands a stately white-painted brick mansion with a mansard slate roof. This is

Magnolia Manor is an old home converted to a museum in Cairo, Illinois, where the Ohio River ends. (Photo by George Laycock)

Riverlore, built in 1865 by Captain William Parker Halliday. It is privately owned.

Other interesting buildings in Cairo are the old Custom House and also the Cairo Public Library given by Anna Safford in honor of her husband, A. B. Safford. This library is a treasure trove for Civil War historians.

For decades the area around Cairo has been one of America's prime goose-shooting areas. The impressive big Canada geese travel on down the Mississippi Valley for the winter. Then in 1927 the Illinois Conservation Department began purchasing riverbottom land along the Mississippi, seven miles northwest of Cairo where nature cut off an ancient oxbow lake from the main channel of the Mississippi. Conservation workers built a dam across one end of the oxbow to turn it into a permanent lake. On the island in the middle of the lake they planted corn, wheat, and grass, choice winter foods for geese, and the next winter a flock of 1,000 geese used the lake. In the following few years the geese began, not only staying longer but also arriving in larger numbers until the goose population at Horseshoe climbed to 100,000 birds.

The Horseshoe Lake area near Cairo is one of the nation's most famous wild goose wintering areas. (Photo by George Laycock)

Towboat, coming down the Mississippi, pushes its barges toward the bend where the Ohio joins the Mississippi. (Photo by George Laycock)

The Horseshoe Lake Conservation Area now covers 7,901 acres, including a shallow lake of 2,400 acres. In the lake grow large stands of beautiful cypress trees that give it a southern look.

Surrounding the lake are public hunting lands used by water-fowlers in season, and beyond the state area every farm appears to be a hunting club, catering to visiting goose shooters. Local people say this is the "goose capital of the world."

Meanwhile, Horseshoe Lake is also visited by fishermen who practice a special technique for shallow-water fishing. Using a fly rod equipped with monofilament line, the angler maneuvers a lead-head bucktail up and down a foot or so below the surface to catch bluegills, crappie, catfish, and largemouth bass.

Those who come to bird watch, or simply to get outdoors with their families, can bring a picnic. The Horseshoe Lake area has four picnic grounds with shade trees and playgrounds.

Horseshoe Lake Conservation Area is on Hwy. 3 northwest of Cairo. The telephone number is (618) 776-5281.

We drove south out of Cairo on Hwy. 51 a couple of miles and turned left into Fort Defiance Park. During the Civil War a formidable fortress stood here with a huge 64-pound cannon pointing downriver, defending the North against the Rebels. A strange concrete structure, vaguely resembling a ship's prow, now stands facing the point. We climbed to the third deck and looked out over the water across the point of land that marks the end of our journey.

From our right comes the mighty muddy Mississippi to meet the Ohio, flowing wide and clear from the left. This is the confluence finally, the coming together.

The valley of the Ohio, the beautiful river, lies behind us. And behind us too, the sparkling cities, quiet villages with their friendly smiles, the farms, the parks and open spaces, the wooded hills—and always the river.

Appendix

OHIO RIVER HIGHWAY BRIDGES

Name	Ohio River Miles
West End–North Side	0.8
Pittsburgh–McKees Rocks	3.3
I-79	8.7
I-79 (Main Channel)	8.8
Sewickley	11.8
Ambridge	16.8
Monaca–East Rochester	24.3
Vanport Hwy. 60	28.0
Midland–Shipping Port	34.5
Jennings Randolph Hwy. 30	42.7
Newell	44.5
National Steel Corp.	61.9
Steubenville–Weirton Hwy. 22	66.4
Steubenville	68.0
I-470	91.8
New Martinsville	126.9
St. Mary's–Newport	155.4
I-77	170.8
Marietta	171.9
New Parkersburg	183.4
Parkersburg–Belpre	184.3
Ravenswood	221.3
Pomeroy–Mason	251.2
Silver Memorial Hwy. 35	266.0
East Huntington	305.1
Huntington	308.8
Ashland–Coal Grove	322.8
Ironton–Russell	327.0
General U. S. Grant (Portsmouth)	355.5

Name	Ohio River Miles
Maysville—Aberdeen	408.5
I-275	461.9
I-471 Dan Beard	469.5
L & N Bridge	469.3
Central Bridge (Newport—Cincinnati)	469.9
Suspension Bridge	470.5
Clay Wade Bailey	471.0
Brent Spence Bridge	471.2
I-275 Carroll Cropper Bridge	491.8
Markland Dam	531.5
Madison Hwy. 421	557.2
J. F. K. Memorial I-65	603.1
Clark Memorial Hwy. 31E	603.5
K & I	607.4
Sherman Minton I-64	608.7
Brandenburg—Mauckport	647.8
Lincoln Trails (Hawesville)	723.8
Owensboro Hwy. 231	756.3
Hwy. 41 (Evansville)	786.9
Shawneetown	858.1
Irvin Cobb (Paducah)	937.2
I-24 (Paducah—Metropolis)	940.9
Cairo Hwy. 51	980.5

LONGEST DISTANCES WITHOUT BRIDGES

82.8 miles between I-24 bridge at Paducah, KY, and Shawneetown, IL.
76.0 miles between Hawesville and Brandenburg, KY.
71.2 miles between Shawneetown, IL, and U.S. 41 near Evansville, IN.
53.4 miles between I-275 near Cincinnati and Maysville, KY.

Source: U. S. Army Corps of Engineers

Index

Thomas, Jean, 104–5
Thompson, Glenn, 297–98
Three Rivers Stadium, 19
Tollesboro, Ky., 110
Tomlinson Run State Park, 54–55
TVA, 202, 204
Twain, Mark, 147–48
Tygart River, 3

Underwood, Gov. Cecil, 71
Union County, Ky., 194
U. S. Army Corps of Engineers, 45,
    99, 100, 183, 357, 370
U. S. Forest Service, 333–36, 367
University of Louisville, 160
University of Pittsburgh, 25, 27–28,
    30
Upper Ohio Valley Travel Council,
    56

Vallandigham, Rev. Clement, 215
Vallandigham, Clement L., 215,
    300–1
Vanceburg, Ky., 110
Vanderburgh Auditorium and
    Convention Center, 356
Vesuvius Recreation Area, 238
Vevay, Ind., 304–5
Vienna, W. Va., 80
Viking Glass Co., 65, 97
Virgil I. Grissom State Memorial,
    332–33

Wabash River, 361
Wadesville, Ind., 358

Warren County Historical Society
    Museum, 301
Warsaw, Ky., 133
Washington, George, 3, 6, 83, 218,
    232
Wayne, W. Va., 99
Wayne National Forest, 238–39
Weirton, W. Va., 54
Wellsburg, W. Va., 55–56
Wells Inn, 69–70
Wellston, Ohio, 239
Wesselman Park Nature Center,
    356
W. Pennsylvania Conservancy, 39
West Union, Ohio, 250–51
W. Va. Dept. of Natural Resources
    72
West Virginia Independence Hall,
    56
Wheelersburg, Ohio, 240
Wheeling Downs, 56–57
Wickliffe, Ky., 209
Williams, Dewitt, 83
Williamstown, W. Va., 80
Wilsey, Jack, 278–80
Woodsfield, Ohio, 220–21
Wright, Frank Lloyd, 7, 38–39
Wyandotte Cave, 329–30
Wyandotte State Recreation Area,
    330–31

Yellig, Jim, 338–40

Zimmerman, Joe, 321–23
Zimmerman Art Glass Co., 321–23